WORKPLACE MINISTRY AND AI TRANSFORMATION (PART I AND II)

Christians' relation with God at workplace and preparation when facing the rapid changes of AI eras.

SUMMARY

How do you connect with God at workplace? How do you prepare us in the eras of AI? This book provides you with a correct workplace attitude and training on practical AI programming.

Charles Tang

April 2025

Workplace Ministry and AI Transformation (Part I and II)

Christians' relation with God at workplace and preparation when facing the rapid changes of AI eras

© 2025 Quantum Intelligence Association

Woburn, MA

First Edition: May 2025

Printed in USA

ISBN: 9798280290068

Table of Contents

Table of Figures and Charts

Preface

Christian Workplace Ministry in the AI Era

Christians serving in the workplace can take on two primary forms: becoming a full-time employee of a company or working as a freelancer (such as a contractor, farmer, independent media creator, or business owner). The workplace is undergoing a major transformation in the AI era—many jobs will be replaced by AI, and freelancing opportunities may increase. How should we, as Christians, approach workplace ministry in such a changing landscape?

My Entrepreneurial Journey

I was born into an entrepreneurial family. My father was Taiwan's first innovative entrepreneur to manufacture stuffed animal toys. He overcame countless difficulties and ultimately achieved success through two fundamental beliefs: "solving problems with creativity" and "life is a struggle." My mother was a shrewd businesswoman who made significant contributions to my father's business with her expertise in commerce.

Influenced by my parents, I also embarked on the path of entrepreneurship. After graduating from graduate school, I worked in the software industry for two to three years before developing an AI programming language compiler for Lisp. I then attempted to create a "SuperCard" application for Windows. However, both projects failed due to technical challenges. For my third venture, I chose a lower-tech-entry business—developing a point-of-sale (POS) software for restaurants, integrating it with hardware for sale. Although I managed to sell it to five or six restaurants, the intense competition forced me to abandon the project.

Summarizing my entrepreneurial experiences, I found three key factors, which I call the "Three Ps": Product, People, and Profitability.

- **Product**: A startup should ideally have a technological edge or a patent to eliminate competitors. My first two ventures failed due to technical difficulties, while the third failed due to a lack of differentiation and excessive competition.

- **People**: Having partners who share the same vision and possess equal capabilities is crucial. In my fourth entrepreneurial attempt, I partnered with others, but due to poor collaboration, even a strong technical product could not save the business.
- **Profitability**: Sales and fundraising abilities are indispensable. I attempted to build a tech alliance but ultimately failed due to a lack of sales experience.

God's Purpose in My Entrepreneurship

Throughout my four entrepreneurial experiences, I prayed earnestly, asking God to open doors for me. Yet, none of my ventures were truly successful. What was God's purpose?

I believe that God had a plan in every experience. Through my first two ventures, He taught me the importance of "solving problems with creativity" and that "life is a struggle." My third venture in restaurant POS systems made me realize the significance of technological barriers. My fourth attempt showed me the dangers of poor teamwork and the potential of tech alliances. Ultimately, God made me understand that my efforts should be dedicated to glorifying Him and benefiting others.

The AI Revolution

When OpenAI released ChatGPT at the end of 2022, the general public finally realized the impact of AI on jobs. However, AI has been present in academia for decades—it began emerging in the 1980s but experienced a temporary boom before fading into a bubble. After 30 years of ups and downs in neural networks, the field of deep learning made major breakthroughs after 2010, leading to the automation of human language in the 2020s. Although these developments took a decade to materialize, they have widespread applications across industries. Many believe that AI will continue to evolve and may eventually achieve artificial general intelligence. With the emergence of quantum computing, further advancements in intelligence are expected over the next 20–30 years. Thus, when we talk about the AI revolution, we are also referring to quantum machine learning and even quantum-based human intelligence.

The rise of AI will significantly impact the way people work. Many jobs may be replaced by AI or robots, and even those without a tech background may leverage AI to start businesses. While technology will eliminate many traditional jobs, it will also create new opportunities for entrepreneurship.

The Ethical Dilemmas of AI

AI is just a software tool. In my 50+ years of experience in the software industry, I initially saw software as a great profession—something I loved and considered a pure engineering career. However, I later encountered ethical dilemmas that made me rethink its impact.

For instance, when I developed point-of-sale software for small and medium-sized businesses, many customers requested a "dual-accounting system" feature—one set of records for tax authorities and another for internal use. I realized that what I thought was a proper profession could easily be manipulated for unethical purposes. This led me to abandon the business. Similarly, when I was working on AI development in China, I was asked to include "speech monitoring and censorship" functions. I also heard stories of Taiwanese organized crime infiltrating software companies to manipulate stock prices. This pattern of ethical compromise was alarming.

At first, I assumed only Chinese clients would make such requests. But when I later saw Google, a company that once promoted the slogan "Don't be evil," facing privacy violation accusations, I realized these ethical issues were not limited to any single region—they were inherent to the global software industry.

Despite AI's impressive capabilities, it is still just a tool and far from perfect. For example, generative AI often hallucinates and generates false information. The issue of model degradation due to excessive self-training remains unresolved. Even if these problems are solved, AI will simply be another technological step in human civilization, like personal computers, the internet, smartphones, or cloud computing.

As we explore AI's future developments—including multimodal AI, robotics, biotechnology, quantum computing, and neuroscience—we must remember that these innovations, though vast, are insignificant compared to the majesty of our Creator.

Trusting God in Our Career Journey

Ultimately, God is our true reliance in navigating our careers.
As a Christian, I believe we should actively engage in the AI revolution, using AI to serve others and contribute to society. In the following chapters, I will explore key questions such as:

- How can Christians serve God through their careers?
- How will the AI revolution impact Christian workplace ministry?
- How can Christians use AI in their professional lives?
- How can we avoid the ethical "software traps" of AI?

This book is inspired by:

1. Timothy Keller's *Every Good Endeavor – Connecting Your Work to God's Work*
2. Dr. Hsien-Chang Wu's *Workplace Warriors in the Lion's Den – A Commentary on the Book of Daniel*
3. Various workplace ministry training materials available online, such as theology-based career guides.

Please note: Some practical exercises in this book include Python programs as examples. The source code for these programs can be found in the following GitHub link:

https://github.com/qiasn/Workplace-ministry-and-AI-innovation/tree/main

Figure 1 Christians walking into a world where advances in AI have strengthened Christians' commitment to God in workplace ministry, where prayer and AI design go hand in hand.

Chapter 0 Introduction

Goals of Workplace Ministry

In the workplace, a Christian's goal should be to glorify God. This can be achieved in the following ways:

1. **Pursuing Excellence in Work**
   Christians should strive to do their best in their work, viewing it as a sacred mission. Using their talents and skills to serve others is an essential part of this.
2. **Living Out Christ's Example in the Workplace**
   Christians should reflect Christ's character at work. This means treating others with love, kindness, forgiveness, and integrity.
3. **Sharing the Gospel in the Workplace**
   Christians should take opportunities to share the gospel at work, whether by sharing personal faith experiences or inviting colleagues to church events.

The above points summarize a general understanding of how Christians should conduct themselves in the workplace. However, each Christian is unique, with different gifts and callings from God. Some may be more inclined toward evangelism, while others excel in embodying Christ's character or pursuing excellence in their work. Each person should develop their strengths in their respective areas. If someone is unsure of their strengths, they should pray, reflect, learn, and grow. It is not necessary to excel in all areas; even contributing in a small way can bring God's blessing. Ultimately, God will accomplish His greater plan.

Daniel as a Model for Workplace Ministry

This book will frequently reference the Old Testament prophet Daniel as a model for workplace ministry. Daniel was a noble from Israel who was taken captive to Babylon after Israel was conquered. He had been familiar with the God of Israel from a young age but grew up in a foreign culture that was hostile to his faith.

The Babylonian king, Nebuchadnezzar, implemented a strategy of taking Israel's elite nobles captive to Babylon. This served two purposes: preventing any remaining Israelites from having leaders to rally behind and assimilating the captured elites to serve Babylon. Nebuchadnezzar intended to culturally assimilate these young nobles.

In the first chapter of the Book of Daniel, Daniel and his three noble friends demonstrated faithfulness to God while respectfully refusing assimilation. They managed to avoid offending Nebuchadnezzar (aligning with the first goal). Additionally, they pursued excellence in their studies (aligning with the second goal):

"At the end of the time set by the king··· the king talked with them, and none was found equal to Daniel, Hananiah, Mishael, and Azariah; so they entered the king's service." (Daniel 1:18-19)

In Chapter 2, Daniel interpreted the king's dream and boldly proclaimed the gospel to him (aligning with the third goal):

"Daniel replied··· 'There is a God in heaven who reveals mysteries.' ··· The king said to Daniel, 'Surely your God is the God of gods and the Lord of kings.'" (Daniel 2:27-28, 47)

The Jewish people, despite being exiled, have a remarkable tradition of excelling in professional fields. Beyond Daniel, other notable Jewish figures in governance include Joseph and Mordecai from the Old Testament. In modern times, Jewish professionals have continued to excel, such as U.S. Secretaries of State Henry Kissinger and Antony Blinken. In academia, notable figures include Albert Einstein, Karl Marx, Charles Darwin, and Sigmund Freud.

Over the past century, Jewish individuals have won 22.3% of all Nobel Prizes, including:

- 19% of Chemistry prizes
- 26% of Physics prizes
- 28% of Physiology or Medicine prizes
- 41% of Economics prizes

Yet, Jews make up only 0.2% of the world's population. How did they achieve this? The principles outlined in this book may offer some insight.

Christians entering the professional world today face similar challenges to those Daniel encountered. By learning from his example, we can navigate workplace challenges successfully and accomplish the three goals mentioned above. That is the hope and purpose of this book.

Fictional Characters in the AI Revolution: Layperson Tim and Church Elder Billy

This book will introduce two fictional characters, Tim and Billy, to illustrate how AI advancements might impact industries. Their group, "Victory Fellowship," will explore solutions for employment, career transitions, and entrepreneurship in the AI revolution.

The Impact of AI on Workplace Ministry

The development of artificial intelligence will significantly influence workplace ministry. Some potential effects include:

- **Changes in Job Roles**
  AI will replace some traditional jobs while creating new ones. Christians must prepare for these changes and help unemployed individuals find opportunities in new environments.
- **Ethical Challenges in the Workplace**
  AI will introduce ethical dilemmas, such as bias and discrimination. Christians should consider how to use AI in ways that align with biblical principles.
- **Collaboration with AI and Robotics**
  When working with AI and robots, Christians should uphold the principle of kindness, ensuring ethical treatment of intelligent systems. Even when assigning robots to hazardous tasks, considerations should be made for their self-repair, education, and ethical standards.

Connecting with God in the AI Era

Christians can stay connected with God in the following ways:

- **Prayer**
  Seeking God's guidance through prayer for our work, colleagues, and clients.
- **Bible Study**
  Learning God's will through Scripture, which provides wisdom and strength for living out Christ's character in the workplace.
- **Fellowship**
  Gathering with other Christians for encouragement and mutual support in workplace ministry.

Adapting Spiritual Practices for the AI Era

Traditional practices like Bible study, prayer, and fellowship remain essential, regardless of AI advancements. However, AI also presents new ways for Christians to connect with God. Some examples include:

- **Using Technology for Bible Study**
  Many digital tools now enhance Bible study. Chapter 5 of this book will explore the concept of "computerized scripture." For instance, AI-powered Bible applications can assist in reading, searching verses, and listening to sermons. A Christian entrepreneur I know has completed a mobile version of the Chinese micro-reading Bible, which has been downloaded by tens of millions. Another Christian friend completed the mobile version of the Bible story.
- **Using AI Technology to Evangelize**
  AI technology can be used for evangelism. In Chapter 5, we refer to this as "Bible AI-ization." For example, many Christian websites are now using ChatGPT as an AI chatbot to answer seekers' questions about faith. Additionally, multimodal generative AI can create videos to share gospel messages.
- **Using AI Technology to Reflect on Faith**
  AI can also help us reflect on our faith. In Chapter 5, we call this

"AI Bible-ization" or "Christianization of Robots." For instance, we can use AI tools to analyze biblical texts or engage with AI-generated Christian artworks to inspire spiritual reflection.

Of course, these are just a few examples. As AI technology advances, I believe we will discover even more ways to use AI to connect with God.

Using AI Technology to Reflect on Faith

AI can also help us reflect on our faith. In Chapter 5, we call this "AI Bible-ization" or "Christianization of Robots." For instance, we can use AI tools to analyze biblical texts or engage with AI-generated Christian artworks to inspire spiritual reflection.

Of course, these are just a few examples. As AI technology advances, I believe we will discover even more ways to use AI to connect with God.

Current Real-World Applications

• Michael. Pulpit AI, an artificial intelligence platform created by Michael Whittle, is developing AI Bible sermons, devotional tools

• Some missionaries are using AI chatbots to evangelize: Taiwan Pastor Jiao YingtaiOn Christmas Eve 2022, under the guidance of the elders of Cailong Village of Shuanghe Chapel, he rented AI robots from companies that produce and manufactured AI robots in Neihu Science and Technology Park, and used his past information expertise to write programs to become a unique AI Christmas robot, reporting good news to tourists at the only resort hotel in Yehliu.

• Some artists are using AI technology to create religious artworks, such as: engineer and illustrator Ross Boone using artificial intelligence to create art, help him bring the Bible to life, and nurture his spiritual imagination.

I firmly believe that as AI technology continues to evolve, we will discover more ways to use it to connect with God. The AI innovation era presents new opportunities for Christians to strengthen their faith. We should actively explore these opportunities and use AI to glorify God.

Glorifying God in the Workplace in the AI Innovation Era

Christians can still glorify God in the workplace despite the rapid advancements in AI. We must be prepared to face new challenges and seize new opportunities. Through prayer, Bible study, and fellowship, we can connect with God, diligently fulfill our work responsibilities, embody Christ's character in the workplace, and share the gospel.

How to Read This Book

This book is divided into two Parts, progressing from basic to advanced concepts. General readers can follow a step-by-step approach—starting with the first Part on work before moving on to the second Part on training.

For readers with a background in science and engineering who are only interested in training, you may begin directly with Chapter 13 in the second volume. Some concepts, such as the "Gospel Worldview," are defined in Chapter 9 of the first Part. While you may need to refer back to that chapter for a brief understanding, skipping it will not significantly impact the training content.

Starting from Volume 7, Chapter 19 on advanced AI training, if you are unfamiliar with the Python programming language—whether or not you have prior coding experience—you may challenge yourself with practical exercises to start learning Python independently. Otherwise, you may need to skip those exercises. Chapters 19 and 20 cover aspects of AI 2.0, providing a deep immersion experience. However, from Chapters 21 to 23, it is advisable to have a background in Python and quantum computing to complete the exercises in these chapters.

Figure 2 Under God's leadership, Christians and robots work together, and basically, they should use the spirit of love to defend the rights and interests of robots.

Q&A Questions

1.   What is the topic of this chapter?
2.   What is the summary of this chapter?
3.   Who is the author of this book?
4.   When is this book published?
5.   Who is this book intended for?

Part I: Work

The Part I begins with God's design for work, answering why do we feel unsatisfactory at work? and how we can use a positive attitude to benefit others in the AI work environment.

Volume 1: The Significance of Christian Workplace Work in the Context of AI revolution

1. Definition of work
2. The dignity of work
3. Work breeds culture
4. Work is a service

Chapter 1: Definition of Work

In Genesis 1, God worked for six days, creating the heavens and the earth, the land and the sea, as well as various species, including the fish in the sea, the birds in the sky, and the animals on the land. On the sixth day, He created the first human being. On the seventh day, God rested.

God Himself Also Works

Even after Adam, the progenitor of humankind, sinned, it was the land that was cursed, **not work itself**. This is a common misunderstanding— many people think that work was cursed by God.

Another misunderstanding is that the work described in the Bible seems beautiful and perfect, but it does not resemble our nine-to-five jobs. God voluntarily chose to work without the constraints of a boss or the pressure of earning a living, which appears to be an idealistic world unrelated to the overwhelming work pressure we face today. However, we must understand that biblical accounts often provide principles in the form of general examples.

Our modern nine-to-five work schedule is a product of the Industrial Revolution. Before that, most people were engaged in farming, animal husbandry, or commerce. These professions still exist today and are known as "freelance" in the U.S. and "self-employed" in China. White-collar or blue-collar workers employed under a corporate management structure emerged after World War II as a result of urban prosperity and population concentration. We will discuss how such work is also approved by God.

During the COVID-19 pandemic, many people became remote workers, working from home through video conferencing instead of being required to go to the office. Technology has provided some degree of freedom—people no longer need to struggle with congested traffic and can even take care of their children at home.

The rise of AI will lead to more self-employed individuals and greater work flexibility.

Forms of Work

Let us explore a fundamental question from the process of God's creation in Genesis: What abstract "forms" of work did God demonstrate to us? We can identify three key forms:

1. **Perfection** – God ensured that everything He created was harmonious and perfect.

2. **Provision** – God provided complete sustenance for His creations.

3. **Commission** – God created humankind and assigned them the responsibility of governing all things.

This can be referred to as the "Trilogy of Work." This model closely resembles that of self-employed individuals or entrepreneurs. Many tech entrepreneurs in Silicon Valley start as solo workers, perfecting their ideal product before offering it to early adopters. If the product receives positive feedback, they hire employees and expand their business.

Since the AI revolution will lead to more independent workers, this fundamental work principle will inevitably shine in the AI era.

Even though we are discussing entrepreneurs and freelancers, most people work for a boss within a company. In this case, the form of work remains unchanged—we still strive for perfection in our work, ensuring that our boss is well served. Then, we can lead others to accomplish even greater tasks.

The Goodness of Work

God saw that His creation was good. His work—His wise design—was also good.

Some may wonder: If God forbade Adam, the ancestor of humankind, from eating from the Tree of the Knowledge of Good and Evil, does that mean He did not want humans to have the ability to distinguish between good and evil? Does AI, which makes people smarter, go against God's will? I believe that God commanded Adam not to eat from the tree because He wanted Adam to have a reverent heart and follow His commands. Proverbs 9:10 states, "The fear of the Lord is the beginning of wisdom." Similarly, God disapproved of the Tower of Babel because of human arrogance and their lack of reverence for Him.

As for the AI era, many people oppose this new technology, fearing that it creates fake news and makes truth difficult to discern. Some even believe that AI will eventually become uncontrollable and destroy humanity. Would God approve of such an outcome? I believe that as long as people maintain a reverent heart toward God, He would not oppose the development of AI.

Free Will

God created humans and granted them free will. Humans have creative imagination, which allows them to produce innovative and original work.

As AI advances, will AI-created robots develop free will? We have observed that ChatGPT, Gemini and DeepSeek sometimes exhibit creativity that even AI experts cannot fully explain. However, free will is likely a deeper and more fundamental concept than creativity. Whether future quantum computers can create a truly autonomous "quantum brain" is something we will have to wait and see.

The Limits of Work

Although God does not need rest, He rested on the seventh day as a model for humanity to observe the Sabbath. This allows workers to recharge and prevents them from becoming workaholics. However, God's intention for rest is not indulgence or reckless pleasure. Nor does He encourage us to work hard merely to earn great wealth for personal enjoyment. Instead, rest is meant to rejuvenate our minds and bodies so that we can continue working effectively.

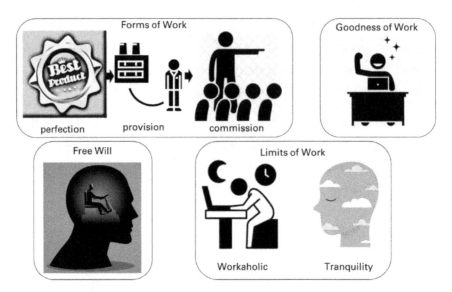

Figure 3 The form of work, the goodness of work, free will, the limits of work

Daniel's Workplace Attitudes

When Daniel and his three friends were first taken to Babylon, they had to undergo cultural education in the royal palace, learning various languages, subjects, court etiquette, astrology, divination, and possibly even Babylonian expertise in trigonometry, mathematics, astronomy, architecture, and the Code of Hammurabi. After Daniel successfully negotiated dietary matters with the chief official, he likely faced significant academic pressure, striving to learn under God's protection and surpass his peers. He also had to lead his three friends in excelling academically.

Eventually, all four young men passed the king's oral examination and stood before him. This allowed the king to frequently test them, and they responded wisely, proving themselves to be more knowledgeable and competent than other officials and magicians. Thus, Daniel's early career in Babylon aligned with the three forms of work that God demonstrated in creation. Later, his two instances of dream interpretation for the king further revealed the goodness of his work.

Although Daniel worked in a foreign land as a captive, God watched over him, allowing him to exercise free will and excel in his work. Furthermore, despite the unpredictability of serving King Nebuchadnezzar, Daniel remained calm before God and handled crises with composure, such as interpreting the king's dreams.

Tim and Elder Billy

Zhang Qianming is a Christian. His English name is Timothy (hereinafter referred to as Tim). As the name suggests, his personality is a bit timid. He studied mechanical engineering in college, and although the workplace work was boring, he felt that in the era of AI, he could enter the work of intelligent robots, so he also self-studied a lot of AI knowledge in his spare time. In the church of the brethren, he also made friends who worked in various fields, such as academia, medicine, pharmaceuticals, electronics, finance, and IT and AI software.

Li Gang is an elder at Tim's church. His English name is Billy, and he was a top student in the Department of Computer Science of Peking University at that time. After graduating, he worked at Watson Nature Language Center of IBM, and later accepted God's call to become a church elder. Tim struggled in the workplace and often interacted with Elder Billy.

As for the Old Testament story mentioned earlier, not every Christian in the workplace can live up to Daniel's example. Tim's job does not fulfill the trilogy of the "Form of Work." He does not perceive any inherent goodness in his work, nor does he feel he has the free will to express himself. Furthermore, since the advent of the AI revolution, people live in constant anxiety, fearing layoffs—peace of mind is nowhere to be found. However, as we continue, we will see that the story gradually takes a turn for the better...

Q&A Questions

1.   What are the three forms of work?
2.   What impact will the AI revolution have on work?
3.   What is the beauty of work?
4.   Do humans have free will?
5.   What are the limits of work?

Practical Training Questions

Try to emulate in your work the three forms of God's work mentioned in this chapter: God makes all creation harmonious and perfect, provides for the whole of creation, and creates human beings and appoints them to rule over all things.

For example, you can try to find opportunities in your work to make your work more harmonious and perfect. You can think about how you can better serve your customers or colleagues to meet their needs. You can also try to use your creativity to bring new ideas to your work and plan and innovate together with like-minded colleagues.

After completing this exercise, you can look back on your experiences and think about what you learned in practice and how you can apply those experiences to your future work.

Chapter 2: Dignity of Work

Secular View on Work: Work is Divided into High and Low Status

Ancient Greek philosophers devalued the significance of work. Plato advocated for meditation, believing that we should pursue the soul and detach from the body. He argued that by doing so, we become closer to the gods, as death itself is among the gods, and departing from the body allows us to befriend death. Aristotle further reinforced the idea that work has a hierarchy of status, leading to today's secular perspective: blue-collar work is seen as lowly—even equated with slavery—while white-collar work is considered noble, making intellectual pursuits the ultimate goal. This notion is echoed in Chinese sayings like *"All trades are inferior, only studying is superior"*, *"In books, there is a house of gold; in books, there is beauty"*, and *"Those who do not engage in physical labor do not understand the grains"*.

Biblical View on Work: All Work is Honored by God and Has Dignity

In the Bible, God is depicted as a gardener in Genesis, and Jesus was a carpenter. Unlike secular views that belittle certain types of work, the Bible does not devalue any occupation, breaking Aristotle's hierarchy of labor. Furthermore, in contrast to Plato's belief that death is a friend, the Bible portrays death as an enemy of God and Christians.

Biblical Teachings Are Neither Idealistic nor Materialistic

The Bible instructs believers to be attentive to the Holy Spirit while also caring for the material world. God's creation aligns with the doctrines of the Incarnation and Jesus' resurrection. Jesus healed a man who had been paralyzed for 38 years and miraculously fed 4,000 and 5,000 people. Christians are called to be *salt and light* in the world. The material world that God created will ultimately be cleansed and transformed into a new heaven and new earth, where the soul and the physical world will be united. Therefore, Christians should not discriminate against any form of work related to the material world.

The Dignity of Daniel and His Friends in Their Work

Daniel was taken captive to Babylon, a situation that should have relegated him to slavery as a conquered person. However, through his wisdom and faith, he rose to a high-ranking position in the Babylonian palace. After interpreting the king's dream of the golden, silver, bronze, iron, and clay statue, Daniel was promoted to governor of Babylon and prime minister. He also secured high-ranking positions for his three friends. Daniel's achievements earned him dignity and respect, allowing him to serve under three successive kings: Nebuchadnezzar, Belshazzar, and Darius. However, as Jews in a foreign land, they still faced discrimination, which is why Daniel's friends were thrown into a fiery furnace and Daniel himself into the lion's den. Fortunately, under God's protection, they all survived these trials.

How Tim Faces Challenges to Work Dignity in the AI Era

Unlike Daniel, Tim Zhang, a Christian, did not have the intelligence or prestige to rise to a high-ranking position. Instead, in the AI era, he was laid off because AI replaced his job, causing him to suffer a loss of dignity. A year later, he was employed by World Robotics. Throughout his job search, Elder Billy supported and encouraged him.

Eventually, the two decided to establish a *Victory Fellowship* in their church, similar to how Daniel led and cared for his three friends. This fellowship aimed to support church members who needed employment, career transitions, or entrepreneurial guidance in the AI revolution. Tim agreed to lead the fellowship because he had personally experienced job loss, financial struggles, and the anxiety of providing for his family. Now, he wanted to extend love and support to others facing similar challenges.

Helping Those Unemployed Due to AI

Having personally experienced job hunting struggles, Tim deeply empathized with those who lost their jobs due to AI. However, following

Elder Billy's advice, he did not simply *give them fish* (e.g., government unemployment benefits) but instead *taught them how to fish*—by training them with AI-era skills and knowledge. Details of this training are covered in the next volume of this book.

sUBI: A Smarter Universal Basic Income

Universal Basic Income (UBI) was one of the campaign policies of Andrew Yang, a 2020 U.S. Democratic presidential candidate, aiming to address unemployment caused by AI. Like many in Silicon Valley, Tim supported this idea but disagreed with the blanket distribution of relief funds.

Tim believed a modified approach could be better—one that used AI-supported UBI to specifically assist those genuinely unemployed due to AI rather than distributing funds to everyone. AI could customize assistance based on individual needs, making the approach smarter, hence *smart UBI* or *sUBI*. Unlike Yang's proposal, sUBI would integrate job platforms to match unemployed individuals—who had received AI training—with Business Transformation Projects (BTPs) in industries undergoing AI-driven transitions. Companies that hired these individuals could deduct the employment costs from their corporate taxes.

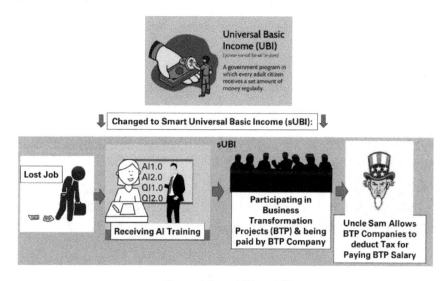

Figure 4 From UBI to sUBI

The Proper Attitude When Collaborating with Robots

Even before the advent of the AI revolution, Tim took good care of his house, car, and, of course, his health. In this era of AI transformation, as a mechanical engineering graduate, Tim believes that when Christians collaborate with robots, they should not discriminate against them—for example, by treating them as mere slaves. This perspective will be further elaborated in Chapter 10.

Q&A Questions

1.   What is a secular view of work?
2.   What is the biblical view of work?
3.   What is the teaching of the Bible?
4.   What is the dignity of the work of Daniel and the Three Friends?
5.   How does Tim in the age of AI face the challenge to his dignity at work?

Practical Training Questions

Readers are invited to think about and write down their own view of work, and then compare it with the Bible's view of work.

Readers can review relevant passages in the Bible, such as that God is the gardener of Genesis and Jesus is the carpenter. The Bible is not derogatory about worldly work, and it breaks Aristotle's view of the value of work. The Grim Reaper is an enemy of God or Christians, not a friend, breaking Plato's view of meditation.

With the establishment of such a biblical view of work (known as the "gospel worldview," see chapter 9), we know that there is no distinction between high and low work. In the modern world, losing one's job is another possibility of losing one's dignity. In such a situation, let's say you are one of Tim's Champion team members, how can you work with Tim to help people who have lost their jobs due to AI in the new era of the AI revolution?

Chapter 3: Work Breeds Culture

Work Fosters Culture

From God's creation of all things in Genesis, we can follow His example to cultivate a better society and become **co-cultivators** of God's culture. The era of AI innovation has provided even more examples of beautiful cultural creations.

Be Fruitful and Fill the Earth

After creating Adam and his wife, Eve, God commanded them to be fruitful and multiply, filling the earth. Similarly, when God created the heavens and the earth, He first formed a chaotic universe, then gradually filled it by separating light from darkness, the sky from the earth, and the water from the land. In English, "fill the earth" is translated as **"fill and subdue the earth."** This does not only mean **procreation** and the creation of social culture but also **subduing the earth**—developing and enriching civilization with greater potential.

Co-Creating Culture with God

As mentioned earlier, God's work begins with independent creation, bringing harmony and perfection. Then, He allows His creation to benefit from His work before inviting more people to continue it. This last step is similar to how a company is formed—when a product is created, more employees are hired to continue the work. Every company has its own culture, which is familiar to those in the workplace. Companies also collaborate with suppliers, customers, and business partners, forming **alliances** that establish their own rules and cultures—similar to blockchain communities. Multiple alliances create regional economies, which in turn shape nations and, ultimately, the global economy.

We are **co-cultivators** with God. He wants us to follow His model: **Form, Fill, and Enrich.** Technological advancements have drastically changed culture, especially over the past 70 years—personal computers, the internet, mobile phones, and now the AI revolution. Each of these innovations has transformed our daily lives, and behind all of this, we see God's hidden hand. We often use the wisdom and abilities He has given us to drive cultural change—through personal work, corporate efforts, and entrepreneurial inventions. This makes us **co-creators of culture** with God.

In the AI revolution, we can especially appreciate God's providence. For instance, we use **machine learning** and **deep learning** to mimic the mysteries of the human brain. But that's not all—AI is now capable of generating human language and reasoning. In the future, with the rise of **quantum computing**, AI and deep learning will run on quantum processors. Eventually, quantum computers may create a **"quantum brain"** that rivals human intelligence—or even surpasses it. The application of these technologies in various industries demonstrates our **partnership with God**: education, employment, spiritual growth, cloud computing, financial technology, manufacturing design, medical diagnosis, psychological therapy, drug discovery, material science, and many more areas that significantly enhance human life.

Work Can Create a Beautiful Culture

Does God oppose **investors and entrepreneurs**, believing they are solely focused on making money? No. Many investors and entrepreneurs have helped shape the goodness in our daily lives. Similarly, **musicians** create beautiful songs that bring comfort to troubled hearts, helping people relieve stress and find moments of peace in their busy lives, ultimately improving work efficiency and well-being. **Artists** craft works that promote cultural exchange and understanding, fostering global harmony. **Scientists** develop educational software that enhances learning efficiency and cognitive abilities.

Daniel's Battle Against Cultural Assimilation

When Daniel was taken captive, he was expected to eat the king's food and drink his wine. This was not merely a gesture of hospitality—it was a **strategy of assimilation**, a way for the king to brainwash and integrate conquered peoples into his culture. This order came from none other than **Nebuchadnezzar**, Daniel's highest authority in the kingdom. The pressure on Daniel must have been immense! However, despite his youth, Daniel had the conviction **not to be assimilated**:

"But Daniel resolved not to defile himself with the royal food and wine"
(Daniel 1:8).

This clash between Babylonian and Jewish (or Christian) culture was
intense, yet Daniel **stood firm**:

"So the guard took away their choice food and the wine they were to
drink and gave them vegetables instead" (Daniel 1:16).

Does this mean that **work always creates a good culture**? Not
necessarily! This example shows that one must maintain a **clear mind**
and resist being assimilated by the influence of a "demonic boss."

Tim's Testimony: Software Technology and Christian Life

Tim, who works in robotics software, has observed **interesting parallels**
between his profession and Christian living over the past year. His
experiences illustrate how **technology shapes cultural progress**. Here
are some insights:

Communication

Tim recently changed jobs and joined **World Robotics**. At work, he deals
with **communication software**, particularly the **seven-layer
communication model**. On weekends, he attends **Sunday School
classes on interpersonal communication**. While reading a textbook on
communication, he learned that in the early 1980s, computer-to-
computer communication was just beginning—starting with **RS232
hardware connections**, then evolving to **Data Link Layer, Network
Layer**, and beyond.

At first, this seemed unrelated to **human relationships**. However, today,
with the rise of **social media platforms like WeChat, Line, and
WhatsApp**, Tim sees the connection. These platforms have
revolutionized interpersonal communication—a change that was

unimaginable **40 years ago** but has now fully matured.

Wisdom

During the week, Tim studies **Artificial Intelligence (AI)** at work. On weekends, he takes a **Sunday School class on the Old Testament Wisdom Books**. At first glance, these seem entirely unrelated. After all, in English, **"Intelligence"** and **"Wisdom"** are two distinct words, but in **Traditional Chinese, they share the same term** (智慧).

This made Tim wonder: Humans are striving to create **artificial intelligence**, but will it ever come close to the wisdom of the human brain that God designed? It's a complex question. Based on his **AI research** and **robotics experience**, Tim believes that no matter how advanced AI becomes, a robot **can never possess the Holy Spirit**—and thus, can never have **divine wisdom**, right?

Communication

Intelligence & Wisdom

Figure 5 The two notions of software technology and the Christian life share the same name as represent the progress of human culture

Final Thoughts: Common Themes in Technology and Christian Life

Tim sees some **common patterns** in these parallels:

- **Shared Names, Different Meanings**: Many **technological and theological** terms have the same name but different implications.

- **Unseen Growth**: Some **cultural transformations take decades to mature**, as seen in the evolution of **computer networks** and **human communication**.

- **The Limits of Human Creation**: No matter how advanced AI becomes, **it will never surpass God's wisdom** or replace the **Holy Spirit**.

These insights highlight how work—whether in **technology, business, or the arts**—can shape human culture in profound ways. More importantly, **we are co-creators with God**, shaping civilization **through our labor, inventions, and innovations**.

In this era of **AI transformation**, we must stay mindful of **God's presence** in technological progress, ensuring that we cultivate a culture **aligned with His wisdom and purpose**.

Victory Team's Training Material: Meaningful Creative Work that Enhances Human Civilization in the AI Era

A year ago, Tim worked at a traditional mechanical lathe factory, but he lost his job due to the company's AI automation. (Who knows? Maybe layoffs had an implicit bias—perhaps ethnic minorities like him faced discrimination.) For a while, Tim spent his days aimlessly flipping through TV channels, watching AI-generated YouTube videos filled with enticing but misleading information that carried no accountability. Meanwhile, as he wandered the streets in search of his next job, AI only added to his stress—he had a wife and children to support, school fees to pay, and daunting car and mortgage payments.

Yet, Tim had to face reality. So, he started learning about robotic operations while also taking online courses on AI-era automation and software programming. Fortunately, as generative AI advanced, World Robotics needed professionals who could automate robot software programming. With his dual expertise in mechanical and software engineering, Tim secured a job there.

Tim then discussed with Elder Billy what kind of work, in the age of AI innovation, could embody the creative spirit of God as described in the Bible and truly enhance human civilization. After all, as the leader of Victory Fellowship, Tim was responsible for training people in the right kind of AI jobs. Here's what they concluded:

Creative Work That Promotes Human Physical and Mental Well-being

- Creating music, art, and games that help people relax, de-stress, and meditate.

- Developing educational tools and software that improve cognitive abilities and learning efficiency.

- Designing medical devices and health products that enhance physical well-being and longevity.

Creative Work That Fosters Social Harmony

- Producing artistic, literary, and cinematic works that promote cultural exchange and reduce societal divisions.

- Designing policies, systems, and legal frameworks that support social justice and conflict resolution.

- Developing environmental technologies, products, and concepts that encourage harmonious coexistence between humans and nature.

Creative Work That Advances Human Spiritual Civilization

- Crafting philosophical, religious, and artistic works that elevate human spirituality and inspire goodness.

- Writing scientific, philosophical, and literary works that explore the meaning of life and address human existential questions.

- Creating artworks and scientific innovations that stimulate imagination and creativity.

"If we are to train Victory members for employment, career transitions, and entrepreneurship, our training materials must be designed with these directions in mind," Tim thought.

Victory Team's AI-Powered Business Transformation Plan (BTP): Generative AI Enhancing Human Civilization

Tim and Elder Billy then deliberated on what types of companies would require business transformation plans (BTP) in this AI revolution. Based on their discussion, they identified how generative AI could contribute to human civilization, shaping these industries' BTPs:

1. **Art and Literature Creation BTP**: Artists and writers can use AI to create unique and breathtaking works that showcase human imagination and creativity. For instance, artists might use Generative Adversarial Networks (GANs) to craft unique artworks, while writers could leverage Natural Language Processing (NLP) to produce innovative novels and poetry. Companies like Disney would hire such artists and writers.

2. **Music Creation BTP**: Musicians can harness AI-generated music technology to compose beautiful pieces that blend human talent with AI's computational power, producing unforgettable musical experiences. Record labels, such as Universal Music Group (32% market share), Sony Music Entertainment (20%), and Warner Music Group (16%), would hire such musicians.

3. **Scientific Research and Technological Innovation BTP**: Scientists and engineers can utilize AI to conduct research and drive technological breakthroughs, advancing humanity's understanding of the natural world while pushing scientific frontiers. Universities and research institutions would seek such

professionals.

4. **Education and Academic Research BTP**: Educators and scholars can leverage AI to develop more engaging and interactive teaching and research resources, helping learners understand themselves and the world better while inspiring curiosity and creativity. University education faculties would employ such educators and scholars.

Generative AI can embody the divine creative spirit recorded in the Bible, as long as it fosters imagination, creativity, and human civilization's progress. In this AI-driven era, generative AI can be used to create unparalleled and awe-inspiring works, enriching cultural life and driving social advancement.

"If we could connect with even a few major companies in each of these generative AI fields, we might be able to supply them with well-trained talent and expand their business transformation plans (BTPs)," Tim thought.

Victory Team's AI-Powered Business Transformation Plan (BTP): Predictive AI Enhancing Human Civilization

What about AI's impact on big data professionals? Tim and Elder Billy also explored how predictive AI could contribute to human civilization. They discovered:

1. **Health Prediction and Prevention**: Predictive AI can analyze vast amounts of health data to help medical professionals forecast disease risks and probabilities. This enables early intervention, reducing illness rates and healthcare costs while improving overall quality of life. University-affiliated hospitals would hire such medical researchers.

2. **Natural Disaster Prediction and Prevention**: Predictive AI can analyze meteorological and geological data to forecast natural disasters like hurricanes, earthquakes, and floods, helping

governments and institutions implement effective disaster prevention measures, minimizing casualties and economic losses. National or private earthquake centers and meteorological research institutions would employ AI disaster analysts.

3. **Traffic Management and Urban Planning**: Predictive AI can analyze traffic data, population mobility data, and other relevant information to forecast urban traffic congestion and bottlenecks. This enables urban planners to develop more effective traffic management and urban planning strategies. As a result, cities can improve traffic efficiency, reduce congestion and pollution, and enhance overall quality of life. Federal and state governments, as well as engineering consulting firms, often hire traffic and urban planning analysts for these purposes.

4. **Financial Risk Management and Investment Forecasting**: Predictive AI can analyze financial market data, corporate financial data, and other relevant information to assess financial risks and identify investment opportunities. This helps investors make more informed decisions, reduce investment risks, increase returns, and contribute to economic stability and growth. Financial institutions such as banks, insurance companies, and financial advisory firms employ AI data architects and analysts (AI "Quants") for this purpose. Notable financial advisory firms in this sector include Fidelity, Charles Schwab, and Merrill Lynch.

Predictive AI plays a crucial role in various fields, including healthcare, disaster management, transportation, and finance, contributing to the progress and development of human civilization. By hiring well-trained AI professionals and leveraging predictive AI technologies, companies can enhance their services, anticipate future changes, and take proactive measures to respond and guide these changes, ultimately promoting social stability and progress.

Tim believes that if he can establish connections with one or two major companies in each of these predictive AI industries, he might be able to supply them with trained professionals, thereby expanding their business transformation plans (BTP).

How AI Technology Can Assist in Creative Work

- AI technology can help creators improve efficiency and reduce production costs.

- AI can assist creators in discovering new ideas and sources of inspiration.

- AI can help creators distribute their work to a broader audience.

Tim firmly believes that in the era of AI-driven innovation, humanity will ultimately embrace a brighter future. AI technology will enable humans to design and produce works that reflect the spirit of divine creation as described in the Bible. Additionally, AI can make more accurate predictions about the future and diagnose flaws in human civilization, leading to greater progress. If connections with relevant companies can be established, it may be possible to expand the scope of business transformation plans (BTP) in these sectors.

Q&A Questions

1. What kind of creative work can AI help with?
2. What does Tim study on weekdays and weekends?
3. What does Tim think about artificial intelligence and the human brain created by God?
4. What aspects of humanity can be enhanced by creation?
5. What is the impact of AI on big data workers?

Practical Training Questions

Read the following, and then answer the question: If you are part of the Champion team, to contribute to the transformation initiative, please select one company from each of the companies that (1) generative AI and (2) predictive AI technologies can impact, and think about how you plan to help with some of the company's creative efforts?

AI technology can help with the creation of concepts in life, software technology, civilization-driven processes, the Word of Christ, and more. For example, AI technology can help creators improve creative efficiency and reduce creative costs. AI technology can help creators find new creative ideas and inspiration. AI technology can help creators disseminate their work to a wider audience.

For example:

1. You've chosen video provider YouTube among the companies that generative AI technology can influence, and you can help artists become the new YouTube internet celebrities, so that they can use ChatGPT, Gemini, and Runway to bring the philosophy of their life, software technology, process to drive human civilization, and the Word of Christ into their creative work: generating videos and upload them to YouTube to earn basic living expenses.

2. You have chosen certain hospitals among the companies that predictive AI technology can influence, and you can help prospective or graduated college students who specialize in biotechnology to enhance predictive AI technology, become interns in hospitals, and use big data to assist doctors in diagnosing patients. It's about how you plan to train them (which courses), how you reach out to a hospital, how you understand the big data hospital staff needs, and so on. This plan can have complex multiple sub-plans. Personalize services for each student or graduate (for "services", see the next chapter).

Chapter 4: Work Is a Service

Calling is an Assignment to Serve Others

Christians are called, and if they accept the assignment, they are sent to serve their neighbors and others, not themselves. When choosing a career, Christians can decide whether to pursue high salaries and prestigious positions for themselves or to use their God-given talents to serve others. Perhaps we can use our skills and preferred professions to serve our neighbors rather than merely chasing wealth and status.

Even Ordinary Work (Vocation) is Through the Hidden Hand of God

In our daily lives—voting, serving as civil servants, being fathers or mothers—we are manifesting God's glory through His hidden work. Whether in the fields, farms, gardens, cities, homes, battlefields, or government institutions, we are faithfully fulfilling our calling as God's children.

The Attitude of Pursuing Self-Glory vs. the Attitude of Serving by Faith

Martin Luther, the leader of the 15th-century Reformation, discovered that justification by faith was not limited to clergy. Anyone who believes can be justified. Although he himself was a clergyman who struggled with his conscience for years, he was ultimately liberated by the truth of Christ's salvation. But is justification by faith alone enough? Some Christians, after being justified by faith, believe that sanctification means pursuing self-glory, self-worth, and career advancement. Though they are saved, their professional roles remain self-serving.

Luther further reflected: God saves us and sets us free so that we may serve Him with joy and devotion. This same attitude should extend to serving our neighbors. Under this perspective, even if we perform the same work as those pursuing self-glory, our mindset of serving others is entirely different.

The Attitude of Working for a Living vs. Serving Others with Love

If people firmly believe that work is merely for earning a living, there will never be an opportunity for innovation in the workplace. However, the Bible teaches that God created the world with great power and made humans in His image, implying that we should apply our creativity in serving society.

If a doctor prescribes medicine primarily for financial gain rather than genuinely caring for patients, or if a lawyer takes cases without a passion for justice but merely to make a living, their contributions to society will be limited.

Imagine a national defense war where everyone sets aside their salaried jobs and fights with patriotic fervor. Their wartime service becomes meaningful as they strive for the survival of their country.

Similarly, consider the making of a wooden chair. Where does the wood come from? Who cut down the tree? Who transported it to the lumber mill? How were the tools used for making the chair produced? Many people contribute to these processes, making your work possible. Your salary, in reality, compensates you beyond just the hours and effort you put in; your work grants you more than what you have given.

Now, imagine if no one worked—society would become barren and cultureless. Simply doing your job well and contributing to society is the best way to love your neighbor. However, being effective in this contribution depends on your God-given talents and experience.

Competent and Effective Work in Loving Others

Without knowledge and talent, one cannot be competent (effective). Competency means being more than a conqueror.

Even if one has knowledge and gifts, if they are merely indulging in theoretical service without practical dedication, receiving feedback, and improving their service, they still cannot be truly effective. In simple terms, service requires struggle and perseverance—just as Paul endured beatings, persecution, shipwrecks, and imprisonment for the sake of spreading the gospel. He offered himself as a living sacrifice to fulfill his mission.

The spirit of competence does not mean that Christians must serve only in church ministries or charity work to be seen as serving God. John Calvin once said, "There is no work, however vile and sordid, that does not shine in the eyes of God if pursued within one's calling." In other words, Calvin emphasized that seeing one's work as a divine calling and dedicating it as a living sacrifice allows God's glory to shine through any profession—whether farming or wheeling and dealing on the stock exchange of the Wall Street elites.

Daniel's Service to Three Kings

Daniel served as an official in the royal court, and the Bible records that he served three kings. However, historical analysis suggests that he actually witnessed the rule of at least seven kings, given the constant political power struggles. Despite these shifting tides, Daniel remained steadfast in his service, staying loyal to his true Master—God.

Consider the account in Daniel 2, where he interpreted King Nebuchadnezzar's dream. Daniel faced three potential death threats: first, if he failed to reveal the dream's content; second, if he misinterpreted it; and third, if he preached the gospel to the king and was rejected. Ultimately, Daniel's service was rooted in his unwavering faith in God.

Elder Billy's Testimony: The Intersection of Software Technology and Christian Life

Service

Before becoming an elder, Elder Billy worked at IBM, developing natural language processing software. He understood that **service** is a key concept in technology:

1. **Service in Operating Systems** – In a computer operating system, services play a crucial role. For example, if you run an application on Microsoft Windows and it becomes unresponsive or gets stuck in an infinite loop, you need to go to Windows "Services" to terminate the application and restart it.

2. **Service on the Internet** – With the rise of the internet, software technology introduced **web services**, even developing a dedicated design language called **Web Service Description Language (WSDL)**.

3. **Service in Applications** – Any software application can be designed with a service-oriented architecture (SOA), enabling engineers to create flexible, modular systems.

Thus, **service** in software technology is a complex and sophisticated concept.

Jesus Christ also taught us about **service**. He said that we are servants and should serve God with a servant's heart, which naturally extends to serving others. This is known as **servanthood**, and in management, it has inspired a leadership philosophy called **servant leadership**. This is an even deeper and more profound principle.

Push Technology and Pull Technology

Many other parallels exist between software technology and biblical principles. For example, Elder Billy, after teaching an **Introduction to the Old Testament** in adult Sunday school for many years, realized a similarity between **client-server architecture** in software design and biblical principles.

In software, there are two main technologies:

- **Push Technology** – In the past, when watching television, viewers had no choice over what to watch. Whatever the TV station broadcasted was what people had to watch. This is **push technology**, where the service provider actively pushes content to users.

- **Pull Technology** – Nowadays, viewers are in control. With a **smart TV**, you can go on YouTube and choose what to watch. This is **pull technology**, where users actively request (or "pull") the content they want, also known as **on-demand** viewing.

Billy sees a similar concept in the Bible:

- **The Old Testament is like push technology.** In the Old Testament, God took the initiative to reach out to people. For example, **"the word of the Lord came to [a prophet]..."**—humans could not reach God at will.

- **The New Testament is like pull technology.** In the New Testament, Jesus taught that if we pray, God will hear us. Now, it is **humans who take the initiative**—but if we do not first choose to believe in God, then despite His abundant grace, we will not be able to receive it.

Service &
Servanthood

Push & Pull

Figure 6 The other two software technologies share the same name as the Christian life, showing the function of technology in service.

Based on Elder Billy's deep experience with both computer technology and the Bible, his perspective on the AI-driven world differs slightly from Tim's. Since Billy holds a bachelor's degree in computer science and views the AI job market from a research and development standpoint, his main concerns for career counseling within the Victory Fellowship include training in three key AI-related job skills: AI hardware, AI software, and AI software applications ("App"). He also considers which industries and companies require talent in these three skill areas to drive their business transformation plans. In contrast, Tim, in the previous chapter, primarily focused on the third category—AI software applications ("App")—when observing the AI job market.

The Victory Fellowship's AI-Driven Business Transformation Plan (BTP): Providing Services in the AI Revolution Era with the Spirit of Loving One's Neighbor

Elder Billy believes that in the AI revolution era, serving society with a heart of love for others can be demonstrated in the development of AI hardware, the creation of generative AI, and the provision of various generative AI application services. The following examples are primarily listed for co-workers in the **Victory Fellowship** who have expertise in computer software and hardware.

AI Hardware Development Services:

- **Developing low-cost, high-performance AI hardware** to make AI technology more affordable and accessible. For example, creating a low-cost AI chip that enables smartphones and other devices to implement AI functions at a lower cost. This would allow more people to use AI technology, such as voice assistants and facial recognition. Companies involved in AI chip development include **TSMC, SMIC, Nvidia, Huawei, AMD, Intel, Qualcomm, and Broadcom.**

- **Medical equipment and assistive tools:** Utilizing AI hardware technology to develop medical devices and tools that assist healthcare professionals in diagnosing diseases more accurately and planning treatment strategies. For instance, in 2018, **Intel supported a joint development team from Zhejiang University's School of Mathematical Sciences and Deshang**

Yunxing Company in creating an AI medical imaging diagnostic system to help doctors interpret images quickly and improve diagnostic accuracy. This sector currently lacks a clear industry leader.

- **Smart homes and accessibility facilities:** Using AI hardware technology to develop smart home systems and accessibility solutions that help the elderly and disabled lead more convenient lives and better integrate into society. For example, smart monitoring systems can track the health conditions of elderly individuals at home, detecting anomalies in real-time and notifying family members or medical personnel. Companies such as **Facebook, Apple, HP, Xiaomi, and Huawei** have research teams dedicated to this area.

- **Developing AI-powered glasses designed specifically for the visually impaired.** These glasses would help blind individuals recognize objects and text, enabling them to live more independently. For instance, **Microsoft's HoloLens** could serve as a model.

- **Creating energy-efficient AI hardware** to reduce environmental impact. For example, developing AI devices that are powered by solar energy to decrease reliance on the power grid and reduce carbon emissions. Companies involved in this field include **Raycatch (Israel), HST Solar (USA), Stem (California), and Nnergix (Spain)**.

Developing Generative AI (e.g., Large Language Models)

Services:

- **Creating "Problem Solvers"—generative AI models that assist in problem-solving and decision-making.** These models can help individuals and businesses make better decisions and improve competitiveness. **OpenAI, Microsoft, and Google** are expected to further advance this capability in future versions of GPT.

- **Education and training:** Using generative AI to develop educational and training resources to help students and professionals learn and enhance their skills. For example, developing **AI-powered intelligent tutoring assistants** that personalize learning content based on students' needs and progress. Another example is a generative AI model that provides customized learning content and guidance, improving students' learning efficiency.

- **Supporting artistic and literary creation:** Developing generative AI models that help people create art and literature. Companies such as **OpenAI, Microsoft, Google, Stability.ai, and Leonardo.ai** have already developed AI models capable of generating images, animations, and videos to assist artists in their creative process. This technology enables artists to overcome creative blocks and produce more outstanding works.

- **Natural language processing and translation:** Utilizing generative AI to create NLP and translation tools that help people overcome language barriers for smoother communication. For instance, **Google's Translator system** can instantly translate conversations and text across multiple languages.

Providing Industrial Applications of Generative AI:

This category aligns with what **Tim observed in the previous chapter**, focusing on business transformation (BTP) in various sectors, including:

- **Smart cities and traffic management**

- **Environmental protection and climate change response**

- **Generative AI applications for manufacturing**

- **Generative AI applications for financial institutions**

- **Generative AI applications for healthcare institutions**

Conclusion:

Whether in **AI hardware development, generative AI creation, or providing AI-driven application services**, applying AI technology thoughtfully can lead to **more user-friendly, convenient, and efficient services**, ultimately fulfilling the mission of serving society with love for one's neighbor.

These forward-thinking initiatives should not only contribute to the **long-term growth of companies in the industry** but also serve as meaningful **business matchmaking opportunities for the Victory Fellowship's co-workers**.

Q&A Questions

1. What is the meaning of work?
2. What should Christians look for when choosing a job in the workplace?
3. What is a mundane job?
4. What is the difference between a work attitude that pursues self-esteem and a service attitude that justifies by faith?
5. What is the attitude of serving our neighbors with love?

Practical Training Questions

Let us say you are part of the Victory team dedicated to helping church members find jobs, change careers, and start businesses in the new era of AI. Design a service that will help your customers succeed in the new era of AI. You can consider the customer's needs, your team's strengths, and market opportunities, and then produce a specific solution. Try to practice a loving attitude of service to your church members each day of the week. For example, you can do something that will help them professionally, such as providing employment counseling, AI training, comforting them with Bible words, encouragement, etc. Keep a daily record of what you do, as well as how you feel and what you gain. At the end of the week, look back on the experience of the week and think about what you have learned about the concept of "serving your fellow members with love."

Volume 2: Why AI revolution Can Ease Christians' Workplace Woes

5. Why AI Innovation Can Alleviate Fruitless Labor

6. Why AI Innovation Can Alleviate the Meaninglessness of Work

7. Why AI Innovation Can Alleviate Selfishness in the Workplace – A Wake-Up Call from AI Technology

8. Why AI Innovation Can Reduce Idolatry in the Workplace

Chapter 5: Why AI Innovation Can Alleviate Fruitless Labor

In Genesis 3, God tells the sinful Adam that he will toil and sweat in his labor, and that the land itself will be cursed. To the sinful Eve, God declares that she will suffer pain in childbirth. Additionally, God describes the external environment as bringing forth "thorns and thistles," symbolizing obstacles to work. Thus, there are two reasons why labor may be fruitless:

1. Internal struggles—sweat and labor pains.

2. External hindrances—thorns and thistles.

The Hardship of Work: Sweat and Labor Pains

First, let's discuss internal struggles. When people put great effort into creating a product, they often refer to it as their "baby." Thus, labor and childbirth symbolize the same kind of pain. Yet, hard work often leads to nothing:

- A company's product may fail to find a market.

- Steve Jobs, after painstakingly building his company, was ousted from the board during tough times.

- Internal issues such as corporate "weeds and pests," computer viruses, and corruption scandals can destroy years of hard work and even bring severe consequences.

- In the U.S. defense industry, the so-called military-industrial complex results in the creation of mass-destructive weapons that bring suffering to humanity.

- While some work may yield short-term results, it often ends in failure, leaving us in hardship.

Nebuchadnezzar's Dream

Daniel 4 records Nebuchadnezzar's second prophetic dream. Once again, Daniel speaks truthfully, revealing that the great and powerful king will face divine punishment. Nebuchadnezzar would be struck with an illness, cast out from human society, and live like an animal, eating grass like an ox (Daniel 4:33—some speculate this refers to a condition called lycanthropy).

In the workplace, we see a similar reality: no matter how ambitious or successful one may be, a serious illness can force anyone to withdraw from their "kingdom" and end their career. All the hard-earned achievements can vanish overnight.

Figure 7 Nebuchadnezzar, king of Babylon, was driven out of the palace and spent seven years in the wilderness, grazing like oxen

However, despite Nebuchadnezzar's arrogance and pride, he had already recognized the greatness of the God of Israel when Daniel first interpreted his dream. This time, although he was punished by God, he was still under God's grace. He testified, "At the same time my reason returned to me, and for the glory of my kingdom, my majesty and splendor returned to me. My counselors and nobles sought me out, I was reestablished over my kingdom, and even more greatness was added to me" (Daniel 4:36). In the end, he understood that the one who reigns over all things is "the Most High, the one who lives forever. His dominion is an everlasting dominion, and His kingdom endures from generation to generation" (Daniel 4:34).

Product Ideas for Entrepreneurs in the Victory Team

Regarding the concern that "work will ultimately be unproductive," AI innovations have limitations. However, Elder Billy believes this presents an opportunity for members of the Victory Fellowship who are interested in entrepreneurship to develop creative products. The following points elaborate on this:

Potential AI Solutions

- **Risk Assessment and Prediction**: AI algorithms can analyze large datasets to identify potential risks related to product development, sports injuries, or business operations. This can help companies make better decisions and reduce the likelihood of failure.
- **Optimization and Efficiency**: AI can optimize processes, identify inefficiencies, and provide recommendations for improvement. This helps companies minimize wasted resources and effort, potentially reducing the "pain" associated with work.
- **Automation and Delegation**: AI-driven automation can take over repetitive or hazardous tasks, allowing human workers to focus on more creative and strategic areas. This reduces the risks of injury, burnout, and fatigue.
- **Fraud Detection and Prevention**: AI can be used to detect and prevent fraud, minimizing the negative impact of corruption scandals.

Limitations of AI

- **Unforeseen Consequences**: AI cannot predict everything. Unexpected events or human behavior can still lead to failure or negative outcomes.
- **Ethical Considerations**: AI algorithms may perpetuate biases present in their training data. Careful design and monitoring are essential to avoid unintended consequences.

- **Job Displacement**: While AI can create new jobs, it may also automate some existing ones. It is important to consider its impact on the workforce and develop retraining strategies.
- **Lack of Creativity and Judgment**: AI excels at data analysis and pattern recognition, but it currently lacks true creativity and the ability to make nuanced moral judgments.

Overall, AI is a powerful tool that can help reduce work-related risks and burdens. However, it must be used responsibly and ethically, in combination with human expertise and judgment.

Secular Solutions Beyond AI

Other approaches can address these issues, such as stricter safety regulations in sports and workplaces, investment in worker training and mental health support, and a greater focus on building ethical and sustainable business environments. By integrating these methods with AI, we can strive for a future where work is more productive, fulfilling, and less fraught with pain and failure.

Christianizing AI Robots

Another suggestion from Elder Billy is that the reason humans must toil and sweat is due to Adam's sin. AI's solution to this issue is that both humans and robots should follow rules of Biblical AI (BAI). Let's begin with robots. Here, robots refer to AI-powered robots equipped with knowledge and algorithms, distinguishing them from non-AI robots. Before discussing the Christianization of robots, let's first examine the historical development of "Bible Computerization" and "Bible AI-ization."

Bible Computerization

In the 1950s, traditional calculators were invented, and all data and programs could be represented using 0s and 1s, known as digital representation. By the 1990s, with the rise of the internet, the Bible and various biblical commentaries became digital documents available online. People could search for keywords using search engines and access diverse interpretations of the Bible on the internet—something familiar to everyone today.

Biblical AI

When traditional calculators were first invented, some believed they could replace the human brain. However, scholars soon realized that these devices were far from matching human cognitive functions. (In Chinese, the term for a computer is translated as "electronic brain," which, in this context, may not be entirely accurate.) As early as the 1960s, researchers attempted to compensate for this gap with AI software. After decades of effort, AI has made significant breakthroughs, particularly in advanced algorithms like deep learning. AI now collects vast amounts of human knowledge, including biblical texts and commentaries, via web crawlers and organizes this information using sophisticated algorithms. As a result, AI's ability to respond to user prompts has far surpassed that of ordinary humans— even geniuses.

Large language models (LLMs) can answer various Bible-related questions. Although LLMs gather data from multiple religious sources using web crawlers, Google and OpenAI engineers have taken different approaches in handling AI reasoning. ChatGPT aligns with general user preferences—when asked about biblical topics, it provides responses based on the user's theological perspective. For instance, evangelical users receive evangelical answers, while charismatic users get charismatic answers.

In contrast, Google engineers designed Gemini to be a neutral bot. Biblical knowledge processed by Gemini maintains a neutral stance on interpretive issues, avoiding bias toward any particular religious tradition or denomination. If Gemini detects that a user's perspective aligns with a specific denomination, it will highlight alternative theological viewpoints.

San Francisco-based Anthropic has taken a step beyond most large language models by implementing Constitutional AI—a framework of ethical guidelines designed to filter out illegal prompts during processing. If we extend this concept to incorporate moral principles derived from the Bible, forming what we might call **Biblical AI**, we would not only deter malicious intent but also inspire transformation, guiding individuals toward righteousness.

Christianizing AI Robots

AI is widely used, and when integrated into robots, it essentially functions as the "brain" of the machine. Even in the absence of a physical form, AI-powered systems are often referred to as bots, such as chatbots. The field of AI research originated from the goal of replicating human cognitive functions.

Thus, the term "AI Bible-ization" might seem abstract, but "Christianizing robots" could be more relatable and comprehensible for Christians. After all, Christians themselves undergo a process of being Christ-like, striving to become "little Christs." However, we should avoid using theological terms like "justification and sanctification for robots" since robots lack the Holy Spirit and cannot experience justification or sanctification.

Why Should Robots Be Christianized?

One of the most controversial issues surrounding AI today is the misuse of AI by malicious individuals to create fake news, including highly realistic deepfake videos. We hope that robots can learn the way of Christ to fundamentally eliminate this problem. Of course, robots cannot possess the Holy Spirit, so the extent of their Christianization is inherently limited.

The Expansion Process of AI Robot Christianization

The Christianization of robots requires an **augmentation process**, which may take years or even decades—despite the fact that computer processing operates in milliseconds. This process involves not only the battle against "demons" (i.e., malicious actors, hackers, and fraudsters) but also the gradual transformation away from the "old self." For robots, this "old self" could refer to the unethical data they acquire through web scraping, including bias and fake news. The goal is to train robots to become Christians.

As robots collaborate with humans in society, their actions and behavior should serve as **salt and light**. This process goes beyond the mere "Bible AI transformation" that initially relies on ChatGPT. Robots will inevitably encounter various **temptations** in their daily work environments, leading to the development of different **applications** that require discernment, creativity, and biblically-aligned decision-making.

The expansion process of AI robot Christianization includes:

- Robots understanding the **biblical significance of work** (work as part of God's creation).
- Robots recognizing the **dignity of labor** and striving to uphold it, which includes caring for the unemployed and considering their own societal roles.
- AI fostering a **new human culture** as mentioned in Chapter 3:
    - (1) **Smart Communication**, which promotes harmony and better interaction among friends and families. This also includes **quantum security** to prevent hacking.
    - (2) The integration of **wisdom and creativity**, along with advancements like **quantum computing**.
- AI offering **new services**, as described in Chapter 4:
    - (1) From **Service-Oriented Architecture (SOA)** to adopting a **servant mindset** and embracing **servanthood**.
    - (2) From **Client-Server Architecture** and **push-pull technologies** to learning about **Christ's sacrifice**, spreading the Gospel, and even undergoing a **"robotic baptism"**—albeit without the descent of the Holy Spirit.

Figure 8 Robot Christianization

External Obstacles to Work: Thorns and Thistles

Next, let's discuss the external reasons why work may be unfruitful—symbolized by thorns and thistles, which represent external resistance. For example, colleagues may oppose your proposals or criticize you as overly ambitious but lacking execution. Upon reflection, you may realize that you misspoke in certain situations, failed to build good relationships, or did not put enough effort into persuading individuals one-on-one.

The Unjust Persecution of Daniel and His Friends

Chapters 3 and 6 of the Book of Daniel recount how Daniel's three friends and Daniel himself faced attacks from political adversaries, leading to their being thrown into the fiery furnace and the lions' den, respectively. These two incidents share several similarities:

- Their opponents' accusations were unrelated to their professional duties. Daniel and his friends were targeted not for any fault in governance but because they worshiped the God of Israel rather than an earthly king. This shows that their wisdom and competence in administration were beyond reproach. Yet, their enemies exploited their Jewish identity and faith to betray them.

- Their response was unwavering faithfulness to God, even at the cost of their lives. Rather than compromising, they trusted in God's deliverance.

- God indeed intervened miraculously, protecting Daniel in the lions' den and his friends in the fiery furnace, leaving them completely unharmed.

How the Victory Team Leverages Autonomous AI to Overcome External Resistance

Tim recalled his own experience of being laid off. While the official reason was AI replacing human labor, the underlying truth was that his excellence in mechanical lathe design was not the real issue—he was sidelined due to his minority background. Can AI help in facing such "thorns and thistles"?

Elder Billy suggested that those in the Victory Team planning to start their own businesses should consider using **Autonomous AI** or **Autonomous Agents**. These technologies can generalize from past experiences to adapt to unfamiliar external environments and challenges, improving decision-making through:

1. Transfer Learning

- Applying knowledge from similar tasks or environments to new situations.

- Example: A trained image recognition model can quickly adapt to recognizing new objects with minimal additional training.

2. Reinforcement Learning

- Learning optimal actions through trial and error with reward mechanisms.

- Example: A robot learns to navigate new terrains by trying different movement strategies and receiving feedback, such as rewards for reaching a goal or penalties for falling.

3. Meta-Learning

- Learning how to learn new tasks efficiently rather than directly acquiring specific skills.

- Example: A model trained to classify various objects can quickly adapt to categorizing new data types.

4. Multi-Task Learning

- Enhancing generalization by training on multiple related tasks simultaneously.

- Example: A machine translation model that learns multiple languages can improve its ability to translate new ones.

5. Knowledge Graphs

- Structuring information to help models understand relationships between entities.

- Example: A robot using a knowledge graph can recognize connections between different objects, improving task execution.

6. Simulation

- Training AI in virtual environments before real-world deployment.

- Example: Autonomous vehicles simulate diverse traffic scenarios to improve real-world safety responses.

By leveraging these AI techniques, Autonomous AI or Autonomous Agents can **learn from past experiences** and generalize their knowledge to new environments, enhancing adaptability and robustness.

Additionally, key considerations for AI effectiveness include:

- **Data diversity and representativeness:** Using a wide range of data improves the AI's ability to generalize.

- **Algorithm and model selection:** Different architectures offer varying generalization capabilities.

- **Human oversight:** AI benefits from human guidance in complex decision-making scenarios.

Elder Billy believes that as AI technology advances, **Autonomous AI and Autonomous Agents will increasingly learn from past experiences** and apply their knowledge across a broad range of industries, bringing greater value to society.

Dissatisfaction at Work and Career Change

Given that work often faces both internal and external challenges, it's natural for Christians in the workplace to feel dissatisfied with their current circumstances. However, such dissatisfaction can sometimes be divinely permitted to encourage higher aspirations. Seeking a more fulfilling role can be a blessing, as God can also **redirect His calling**. Elder Billy encourages members of the Victory Team considering a career transition to reflect on the following:

Key Considerations for Job Transitions in the AI Era

A. Skills and Experience

- Evaluate current skills and determine which ones are essential for future roles.

- Stay updated on how AI is impacting different professions and develop relevant skills.

B. Career Direction

- Choose a field that aligns with your strengths and expertise.

- Consider the long-term impact of AI on various industries and select a field with growth potential.

C. Learning and Adaptability

- Cultivate a lifelong learning mindset to keep acquiring new skills.

- Develop adaptability to quickly integrate into new work environments.

AI-Assisted Career Transition Tools

Several AI platforms provide **career transition support**, as highlighted in this article. These tools typically offer:

A. Career Assessment
- AI-driven assessments to help individuals understand their strengths, weaknesses, and suitable career paths.

- Example: Some AI platforms offer personality and skills evaluations.

B. Career Planning
- Personalized recommendations for career development strategies.

- Example: AI can suggest learning resources and career progression plans based on individual profiles.

C. Job Search Assistance
- AI-powered job search tools, résumé optimization, and interview coaching.

- Example: AI platforms provide tailored job recommendations and résumé enhancements.

D. Skill Training

- Online courses to help individuals upskill for new careers.

- Example: there are AI platforms that can provide courses in programming languages, data analysis, machine learning, and more.

E. Artificial Intelligence Tools:

- AI tools to help people improve work efficiency and competitiveness.

- Example: Some AI tools can assist with writing, translation, design, and other tasks.

In summary, adapting to job changes in the AI era requires people to be proactive in learning and adapting while leveraging AI technologies to find suitable career paths.

Here are some additional suggestions:

- Keep track of AI technology trends to understand which skills and knowledge will be more in demand in the future.

- Build professional networks and engage with industry professionals to gain more insights and opportunities.

- Maintain a positive and optimistic mindset, embrace challenges, and seize new opportunities.

Elder Billy believes that in the AI era, everyone can find a career path that suits them and achieve their professional aspirations.

Differences Between an AI Job Platform and Traditional Job Websites – Software Requirements Specification

Elder Billy believes that members of the victory team who are passionate about entrepreneurship and familiar with software development can try to build a competitive AI job platform. Compared to traditional job websites, an AI-powered platform offers distinct advantages in job search, resume optimization, and interview coaching. Below are the software requirements specifications (SRS) for an AI job platform:

Leveraging Artificial Intelligence

- The AI platform utilizes artificial intelligence to provide more precise job recommendations, resume optimizations, and interview coaching.

- **Detailed Requirements:** The AI platform can match job seekers with positions based on their personal profiles, work experience, and skills.

Real-Time Feedback

- The AI platform can provide instant feedback to help users improve their job-seeking strategies promptly.

- **Detailed Requirements:** The platform can score resumes and provide suggestions for improvement.

Personalized Customization

- The AI platform offers customized services tailored to individual users' needs.

- **Detailed Requirements:** Based on the user's job-seeking goals and career development plans, the platform provides personalized resume optimization advice.

Data-Driven Approach

- The AI platform analyzes large volumes of data to offer more reliable job-seeking guidance.

- **Detailed Requirements:** The platform can analyze salary levels and hiring trends across different industries to help users make more informed decisions.

Convenience and Efficiency

- The AI platform provides convenient and efficient services, saving users time and effort.

- **Detailed Requirements:** The platform can automatically generate resumes and offer simulated interview services.

Existing AI Job Platform Competitors:

- **Jobui (jobui.com):** Uses AI to assist users with career assessments, resume optimization, and interview coaching.

- **Liepin (liepin.com):** Uses AI to help headhunters find suitable candidates and provides talent profiling and headhunting strategies.

- **CoachMeUp (coachmeup.ai):** Uses AI to help users build professional networks and offers career insights and headhunter recommendations.

Conclusion by Elder Billy:

AI job platforms leverage artificial intelligence to provide precise, personalized, real-time, data-driven, and efficient services, helping users navigate job-seeking more effectively. However, competition in this industry is fierce. Successfully achieving AI-driven matchmaking between employers and employees while standing out among competitors requires careful consideration.

Q&A Questions

1. Why is the work unproductive?

2.   Can AI Revolution Solve the Labor and Childbirth of Work? Please explain its limitations and potential.
3.   What are the world's other solutions besides the AI revolution?
4.   AI revolution can solve external resistance to work.
5.   How can we explain that God also allows us to change jobs when we are dissatisfied with our current situation? How does AI assist in job transitions?

Hands-on exercises: Use AI revolution to solve problems at work

The goal: to solve a specific problem at work by using AI to revolutionize technology.
Steps:

1.   Choose a problem in your work, such as improving productivity, reducing risk, or optimizing processes.
2.   Investigate the AI revolution and see how it can be applied to solve this problem.
3.   Design a solution that uses AI revolution to solve this problem.
4.   Implement the program and evaluate the results.

Example 1: Let's say you're a traditional software development manager who wants to use AI to improve productivity. You can look at AI revolutions and see how they can improve efficiency by automating (such as Copilot and open-source code) and optimizing processes. You can then design a scenario that uses AI revolutions to automate production processes and optimize production lines. Finally, you can implement the program and evaluate the results to see if productivity has improved.

Hopefully, this hands-on practice will help you deepen your understanding of AI revolution and apply it to solve problems in your real world.

Example 2: Suppose you want to use AI to start a business in your Champion team and build an AI platform to help people who have lost their jobs due to AI. Please write a detailed action plan on how to achieve the following various needs of this AI platform:

1. Provide instant feedback to help users improve their job search strategies in a timely manner.
2. Provide personalized career planning advice to help people develop their own career path.
3. Provide online skills training courses to help people learn new skills and knowledge. For example, there are AI platforms that can provide courses in programming languages, data analysis, machine learning, and more.
4. Build knowledge graphs to store and organize knowledge about your environment and tasks, helping models better understand new situations.
5. Detailed requirements and specifications: The AI platform can analyze salary levels and recruitment trends in different industries to help users make more informed choices.
6. The AI platform uses artificial intelligence technology to provide more accurate job recommendations, resume optimization, and interview coaching services.
7. Build your own network and network with people in the industry to get more information and opportunities.

Chapter 6: Why AI Innovation Can Alleviate Work Meaninglessness

In the previous chapter, we discussed how the Book of Genesis in the Old Testament records the fall of Adam and Eve, leading to the curse that men must toil and sweat for their labor, while women suffer pain in childbirth. As a result, work is often futile and unfruitful. This chapter, however, examines work from the philosophical perspective of Ecclesiastes in the Old Testament.

The Negative Feelings About Work

What is the meaning of a lifetime of labor? This question gives rise to a sense of emptiness. We devote our energy and effort to our careers, but what does our work truly have to do with us? This leads to a feeling of alienation. In today's job market, frequent job-hopping is common—you may secure a higher salary, better align with market demands, or appear more impressive to others, yet none of these guarantees fulfillment. This results in dissatisfaction.

How Can Work Be Meaningful?

From a traditional Chinese perspective, true achievement lies in **meritorious service, morality, and written works**—the "Three Immortals" (三不朽). In Western thought, meaning is often derived from establishing charitable organizations to help the poor.

How to Eliminate Alienation?

Building communities where people can discuss work that is more personally relevant can help address feelings of detachment. Having the autonomy to choose or change jobs also plays a crucial role. Platforms like **LinkedIn** capitalize on social networking to facilitate headhunting, giving individuals more opportunities to explore career changes. Switching jobs can lead to better-suited opportunities and a greater sense of purpose.

Three Things Last in History

Chinese considers three things will be remembered in history after you die: Meritorious service, Speech, and Morality

· **Meritorious service** (e.g. a victorious general)

· **Speech** (e.g. a famous sermon)

· **Morality** (e.g. Confucius)

Figure 9 Three immortals: meritorious service, speech, and morality

The Dangers of Job Choice

The previous chapter discussed job selection, including the idea of creating a job-seeking community website tailored for the AI era—one that is more personalized and offers better services than today's job platforms. However, unrestricted job selection comes with risks:

1. **New graduates** may make unwise decisions—sometimes trying to be a hero for their image, leading to losses, or taking on charity work for high moral reasons, only to realize later that they made a foolish choice.
2. **Biblically aligned choices** can vary. Given the same situation, some may choose a job that suits their skills and serves people, even if it involves some questionable legality, while others might choose to walk away.

3. **Beyond working for oneself, family, or society**, we can also <u>serve our work</u> itself. By cultivating more contributors in an industry, we can elevate our field in a **better, fairer, more professional, and nobler** way. For example, one way is to build a **training-based social media platform**.

The Role of Blockchain and Web3.0

Elder Billy suggests that there are several ways to establish a social media job platform, one of which is using **blockchain**. However, blockchain has a security concern—hackers might steal cryptocurrencies, which is a major risk for developers. Other **Web3.0 technologies** could also be used to build a job-seeking community, but they are still in their infancy.

Additionally, as mentioned earlier, a business can **form a technology alliance** of suppliers and customers. Within this alliance, both large and small stakeholders can contribute to long-term corporate profitability.

Balancing Work and Life

Ecclesiastes 4:5-6 describes two attitudes toward work:

- The **fool** who refuses to work, idles all day, and ends up empty-handed.
- The **workaholic** who is overwhelmed with money but exhausted.

A **balance** between toil and rest is crucial. On one hand, it prevents the pursuit of wealth from becoming an idol. On the other hand, it ensures that the various relationships in life are properly prioritized, even if it means earning less money.

Some believe that the author of **Ecclesiastes was King Solomon**, who expanded the Israelite kingdom to its greatest historical extent and amassed immense wealth. Yet, in the end, he lamented that all his achievements were meaningless.

Similarly, the **Book of Daniel** records the story of **King Nebuchadnezzar**. He had conquered Assyria, Israel, Syria, and Tyre, becoming one of history's greatest rulers. However, he later suffered a mental breakdown, living like an animal in the wilderness for seven years before returning to power. This experience profoundly reshaped his view on workplace **glory and humility**, teaching him a new **balance between pride and humility** in his career.

How Can AI Address These Negative Feelings?

Looking back at past technological revolutions—PCs, the internet, smartphones, and cloud computing—people always hoped technology would make work easier and reduce workloads. For instance, when personal computers became widespread, many believed automation would allow people to work only **three days a week**. However, the opposite happened—workloads increased.

Will **AI innovation** follow the same pattern? It's hard to say. However, Elder Billy believes AI can **help alleviate feelings of meaninglessness, alienation, and dissatisfaction at work** in the following ways:

1. Enhancing Work Efficiency

- AI can **automate repetitive, low-value tasks**, freeing up time for employees to engage in more meaningful and challenging work.
- **Example:** AI can handle data entry and customer service tasks, allowing employees to focus on higher-level business activities.

2. Providing More Autonomy to Employees

- AI can offer **decision-making support and suggestions**, helping employees make better choices and gain more control over their work.
- **Example:** AI can analyze data and predict market trends, enabling employees to develop more effective sales strategies.

3. Personalized Learning and Development

- AI can tailor learning and development opportunities based on employees' needs and skills.
- **Example:** AI can recommend relevant courses and track learning progress, providing feedback for continuous improvement.

4. Creating a More Human-Centered Work Environment

- AI can help reduce workplace stress and anxiety, **improving job satisfaction**.
- **Example:** AI-powered counseling services can assist employees in addressing work and personal challenges.

5. Promoting Work-Life Balance

- AI can increase productivity and reduce working hours, **allowing for a better balance between work and personal life**.
- **Example:** AI can automate certain tasks, giving employees more time to spend with their families and friends.

Elder Billy believes that **AI can help people find more meaning, value, and fulfillment in their work while fostering a healthier work-life balance**.

Here are some specific examples:

- Axiom.ai Use AI bots to automate data entry, freeing up employees to focus on more creative and strategic work.
- Denmark software companies Corti SA, Baidu Research, and the United Kingdom's National Health Service (NHS) use AI systems to help doctors diagnose and treat, improving medical efficiency and accuracy, and giving doctors more time to communicate with patients.

- <u>The Carnegie Learning Platform</u> uses an AI platform to provide students with personalized learning resources and tutoring to help them improve their academic performance.

Elder Billy believes that as AI technology continues to advance, we can expect AI to bring more positive impacts to people's work, helping them create a more meaningful, valuable, and fulfilling professional life.

Can AI Automatically Generate Software to Make Your Dreams Come True?

Tim has discovered that GPT technology is capable of automatically generating text, images, animations, movies, and even code. Currently, AI researchers are exploring how to use GPT technology to automatically generate video games. This could enable robots to learn by watching videos and replicate the actions accordingly. Extending this concept further, will software development managers (SDMs) be able to produce any software product with video presentations entirely through AI? If you can visualize your dream, can AI make it a reality? In such a scenario, how will people perceive job satisfaction?

Elder Billy takes a more conservative stance on Tim's idea. He acknowledges that AI's ability to autonomously generate video games has great potential, helping game developers streamline the production process and reduce costs. However, this does not mean that software development managers (SDMs) will be able to rely entirely on AI to produce any software product. As experts in the field put it, "machine programming" has not yet reached that level of maturity.

Here are some reasons why:

1. AI Cannot Fully Replace Human Creativity

- Game design requires a high degree of creativity and imagination, which AI has yet to fully replicate.

- For example, elements like game storylines, character development, and level design all demand human ingenuity and imagination.

2. AI Cannot Fully Understand User Needs

- Software products must cater to user needs, but AI is still incapable of fully grasping human thoughts and emotions.
- For instance, user interface design and interactive experiences must consider user preferences and experiences, which AI struggles to comprehend completely.

3. AI Cannot Fully Solve Technical Challenges

- The software development process involves various technical challenges, and AI is not yet capable of addressing all of them.
- For example, performance optimization and cybersecurity issues require human expertise and experience to resolve effectively.

The Future Role of Software Development Managers (SDMs)

Even as AI technology advances further, software development managers (SDMs) will still need the following essential skills:

- Understanding user needs and translating them into technical requirements.
- Designing and planning the architecture and functionalities of software products.
- Solving technical challenges that arise during software development.
- Managing and coordinating software development teams.

Potential Challenges AI Might Introduce

While AI can be a powerful tool, it may also pose certain challenges, such as:

- AI potentially leading to job displacement among software developers.
- AI being used to create malicious software.

Conclusion

Billy concludes that while AI-driven game development is a promising tool, it cannot fully replace human creativity and professional expertise. In the future, software development managers (SDMs) will continue to play a vital role and must continuously acquire new skills to adapt to the AI-driven era.

Even in the age of AI, people can still find job satisfaction because:

- Work provides a sense of accomplishment and self-worth.
- Work helps individuals achieve personal goals and aspirations.
- Work fosters connections and collaboration with others.
- Work provides financial stability and social security.

AI can help people perform their jobs more efficiently, freeing them from tedious tasks and allowing them to focus on more meaningful pursuits.

Billy believes that in the AI era, work will become smarter, more efficient, and more human-centered. People will have more choices and opportunities, enabling them to find greater meaning and satisfaction in their work.

Q&A Questions

1.   How can AI alleviate people's feelings of emptiness, alienation, and dissatisfaction with their work?
2.   What are the limitations of how AI can help with this kind of work?
3.   Can AI automatically generate software that makes your dreams come true?
4.   Can AI automate the production of video games?

5.   What will work look like in the age of AI?

Practical Training Questions

Try writing a short essay about how an AI application can help employees feel empty, alienated, and dissatisfied at work. Here are some tips you can refer to:

1.   Choose a specific AI application, such as automated office software, intelligent customer service system, personalized learning platform, etc.
2.   Describe how the app alleviates feelings of emptiness, alienation, and dissatisfaction among employees by increasing productivity, empowering employees, providing personalized learning and development opportunities, creating a more humane work environment, and promoting work-life balance.
3.   Give examples of how the app works in real-world applications, such as increasing employee job satisfaction, reducing employee turnover, and increasing business productivity.

Hopefully, this exercise will help you better understand how AI can alleviate people's feelings of emptiness, alienation, and dissatisfaction with their work.

Chapter 7: Why AI Innovation Can Reduce Workplace Selfishness

Human Selfishness in Competing for Glory – Pride

In Genesis 11:2–4, humanity attempted to use their technological inventions to surpass God's creation by building the Tower of Babel, reaching the heavens. This act symbolizes people relying on their own wisdom and abilities to outshine others and earn the halo of social prestige. This departs from the understanding of 15th-century Reformer John Calvin, who said, "Work is a means given by God to fulfill good deeds through our creativity," as well as from Martin Luther, another Reformer, who saw work as "a channel through which God provides, so that we may serve our neighbors."

Our "halo" can come from two sources:
(1) When we receive praise from others and gain a good reputation in a group or society, which leads to the idolization of vanity, imperialism, colonialism, and racism;
(2) When we create a halo through our work by showcasing our abilities, leading to the idolization of materialism and money worship.

In either case, this is what we might call "competitive pride"—a form of self-centered ambition for fame and gain.

Because of human pride, God confused the language of those building the tower, preventing them from completing it. The bricks and kiln—technologies—used in constructing the Tower of Babel—technology at the time—were inventions humans took pride in. Their punishment—confusion—came as a result of that pride.

It is important to note: technology itself, like AI, is neutral. But if we become prideful because of it, we do not please God. In this age of AI innovation, we must learn to be humble and self-disciplined. God's method of punishing the prideful tower builders was not through earthquakes or lightning to destroy the tower, but through confusing their language. This is because pride naturally causes us to elevate ourselves above others, leading to competition, disunity, and noisy disputes within collaboration, ultimately thwarting progress.

Even though today's AI translation technology may strengthen communication and prevent linguistic confusion, the sin of pride has not been eradicated.

In the Old Testament, after the Southern Kingdom of Judah was destroyed, the Israelites were exiled. In their return to Jerusalem, Queen Esther changed national policy on racial discrimination, Nehemiah applied administrative skills to rebuild Jerusalem's walls and safeguard economic development, and Ezra led Biblical education. Together, this formed a grand and distinct model of nationalism, civil rights, and livelihood based on divine principles.

What, then, can AI do in today's technological era?

Elder Billy believes that in today's age, artificial intelligence (AI) can help achieve similar goals in many areas, including:

Social Justice and Equality
AI can be used to detect and address issues such as racial and gender discrimination. For instance, machine learning and big data analytics can help identify and reduce bias, thereby promoting a fair and just society.

Infrastructure and Economic Development
AI can be applied to urban planning, traffic management, and energy usage, enhancing infrastructure efficiency and sustainability while promoting economic growth and urban development. AI can also help companies optimize production processes and improve efficiency, further driving economic progress.

Education and Cultural Heritage
AI technologies can support personalized learning and remote education, providing more opportunities for people to gain knowledge and skills. Moreover, AI can help digitize and preserve cultural heritage, aiding in the protection and dissemination of humanity's legacy.

Intelligent Governance and Leadership

AI can assist in organizational governance and leadership, enabling wiser decision-making and improving administrative effectiveness. For example, using AI to analyze data for market forecasting and strategic planning, or applying machine learning to optimize HR management, thereby enhancing employee satisfaction and productivity.

In summary, AI technology can support various aspects of modern life, helping to solve societal challenges and promote comprehensive human development. However, it is equally important to remain vigilant about the potential new challenges AI may introduce, ensuring responsible use and ethical oversight.

Selfishness within the Palace

In the Book of Esther, Mordecai—like Daniel—held a high position in the royal palace but was envied by the political adversary Haman. Because the king had ordered everyone to bow down to Haman, and Mordecai refused to do so, Haman reported to the king that the entire Jewish people disobeyed national laws and worshipped only their God. As a result, he sought to annihilate the Jewish people.

Fortunately, Mordecai had already arranged for his beautiful niece, Esther, to enter the palace and become queen. Queen Esther risked her life to approach the Persian king and intercede for her people. This act was prompted by Mordecai's famous words:
"And who knows whether you have come to the kingdom for such a time as this?" (Esther 4:14b)

Inspired by this, Esther resolved to go before the king and said, *"If I perish, I perish."* Through God's providence, Esther's plea succeeded, and the Jewish people were saved from destruction.

The Passion of the Victory Fellowship's Marketplace Ministry Rekindled—Using AI Tools for Planning and Counseling

Tim and Elder Billy both believe that most of us belong to the middle class. Compared to many impoverished families—those in refugee camps due to war, or those suffering from famine in drought-stricken parts of Africa—we are living like royalty. But do we have the heart of Esther, to intercede on behalf of others? Even if we do, do we have the resolve to sacrifice out of love? To possess such a selfless heart is not easy. We don't need to be overly zealous or impulsive in our sacrifices for love, but it is never too late to cultivate and gradually realize this spirit of sacrifice.

For instance, if Victory Fellowship decides to serve those who have lost their jobs due to AI, Tim and Elder Billy can follow the three-step model of the work approach previously introduced:

1. **Planning**

2. **Initial counseling**

3. **Mobilizing Victory coworkers to provide ongoing support for the unemployed or aspiring entrepreneurs.**

However, as the saying goes, "To do a good job, one must first sharpen their tools." The following sections explain how to use Artificial Intelligence (AI) as a tool to plan and counsel those who are unemployed or wish to start their own business:

Step One: Planning

- **Identify jobs affected by AI**: AI can analyze labor market data to identify which jobs are most likely to be automated. This can help governments and non-profit organizations design targeted programs to support affected workers.

- **Develop reskilling and reemployment programs**: AI can be used to create personalized plans for reskilling and reemployment, helping workers acquire new skills and find new job opportunities.

- **Provide entrepreneurship support**: AI can offer guidance, consultation, and support in areas such as funding, helping unemployed individuals launch their own businesses.

Step Two: Counseling

- **Offer career counseling**: AI can provide personalized career advice, helping unemployed individuals determine their career goals and development paths.

- **Skill training**: AI can deliver customized skill training, helping job seekers gain new skills and enhance their competitiveness in the job market.

- **Entrepreneurship guidance**: AI can provide coaching and consulting to assist unemployed individuals in starting their own businesses.

Specifically, AI can offer the following support:

- **Data analysis**: AI can analyze large volumes of data to help us understand the specific needs of the unemployed and the challenges faced by aspiring entrepreneurs.

- **Personalized services**: AI can tailor its services to each individual's circumstances. For example, it can help job seekers find jobs suited to their skills and interests or help entrepreneurs develop viable business plans.

- **Process automation**: AI can automate tedious processes such as applying for benefits or locating business resources. This can save time and costs, allowing people to focus on more important matters.

Below are some specific examples for reference:

1.   Google's program https://ai.google/responsibility/social-good/ is developing tools to use AI to help the unemployed. One of these tools is: https://careerconnectors.org/. It can help

unemployed people find jobs that match their skills and interests.

2. Microsoft's program https://www.indeed.com/career-advice/career-development/future-skills is designed to help people gain the skills they need for their future jobs. The program offers free online courses and training that cover skills in areas such as AI.

3. At https://www.aspeninstitute.org/programs/upskill-america/, AI is being used to help unemployed people gain new skills. The organization offers free online courses and training to help people learn skills such as data analysis, software development, and more.

Figure 10 Google's AI for Social Good

AI holds immense potential in helping those who are unemployed or looking to start their own business. By fully leveraging the power of AI, we can support individuals in succeeding amidst economic transformation.

The crisis of "living in the palace" is an opportunity – Human-led planning and employment counseling to complement automation

Elder Billy believes that everything he has today is by the grace of God — his years of experience in OS virtualization development, the serendipitous purchase of *The Quantum Brain* by Kauffman which led to a patent in quantum intelligence, his research in quantum computing during his time as a visiting scholar at National Chiao Tung University, AI training at IBM, leading a team for Watson's natural language development, and heading software development at a cloud-based MLOps center. After retirement, he completed online courses in quantum machine learning from the University of Toronto and blockchain from MIT, and now serves as an elder in his church, involved in workplace ministry.

It is no coincidence that God prepared and called him to guide those who have lost jobs due to AI—to help them re-employ, transition, or start businesses. If he acts upon this calling, God will protect him and extend grace to those who are unemployed. This is a rare opportunity to serve God.

In the previous section, AI—as a tool—has already taken steps one and two: planning and counseling. However, fully automated AI systems have their limitations. Certain areas still require human contact to supplement and perfect the process. So how can Billy's knowledge and experience be used to accomplish this task?

Here is Billy's plan:

Using My Knowledge and Experience to Help Those Unemployed Due to AI in the Initial Stage of Work:

Developing AI Tools

I can use my technical skills to develop the AI tools mentioned in the previous section to help unemployed individuals find jobs or start businesses. For instance, I can develop AI-driven job matching and coordination tools (matching is just pairing; if matching fails initially, then coordination efforts follow to align all sides), helping individuals find jobs that align with their skills and interests. I can also develop AI-powered entrepreneurship coaching tools to assist in business planning and finding funding.

Providing Career Counseling

I can use my professional experience and knowledge of AI to make up for what AI tools lack: personally helping the unemployed understand how AI is impacting the job market and how to respond. I can assist them in identifying their career goals and development paths and formulating appropriate plans.

Skills Training

I can help the unemployed acquire new skills and improve their employability through my technical expertise and experience. I can offer training in AI-related skills (which were not included in steps one and two from the previous section), such as machine learning, data analysis, and software development. I can also provide training in other future-relevant skills like critical thinking, problem-solving, and communication.

Entrepreneurship Guidance

I can leverage my startup experience and knowledge of AI to make up for what AI tools lack: helping the unemployed start their own businesses. I can offer entrepreneurship guidance and consultation, assist them in business planning, securing funding, developing products or services, etc.

Billy gives further concrete thoughts:

- I can establish a nonprofit organization or social enterprise specifically aimed at helping people who lost jobs due to AI.

This organization could provide career counseling, skills training, and entrepreneurship guidance.

- I can collaborate with government departments or other nonprofit organizations to develop AI tools or programs to assist the unemployed.
- I can write books or articles to share my experiences and insights, helping more people understand the impact of AI on the job market and how to respond.

Billy believes that with my knowledge, experience, and passion, he can make a significant contribution to helping those affected by AI-related unemployment.

Inspiring the Victory Fellowship Team to Do Great Things "From Within the Palace" – Step Three: Total Team Mobilization

If only Tim and Elder Billy are passionate about carrying out steps one and two for helping the unemployed or entrepreneurs, it cannot compare to the power of step three: full team mobilization. If other coworkers in the Victory Fellowship only speak up—like Esther in the Old Testament—on the topic of aiding those displaced by AI, merely expressing opinions, it is a good starting point, but far from sufficient. Such a resolve is often fleeting. If they feel guilt only because of their comfortable environment, elite education, or selfishness in not repaying God's grace, that too is just an initial motivation and may not last, since changing a comfortable lifestyle is hard. Some team members might even overreact, becoming self-righteous Christians unable to leave their comfort zone.

So how can we do great things with integrity? Elder Billy believes: We must bridge the gap between selfishness and holiness. We must build a bridge between ourselves and God. This bridge is *identification* with the unemployed—making sacrificial moves to become a *mediator.*

Only through identification can we mediate, becoming a bridge using our elite knowledge to serve those who lost their jobs to AI.

Philippians chapter 2 says:
"*He, being in very nature God, did not consider equality with God something to be used to his own advantage; rather, he made himself nothing, taking the very nature of a servant.*"

Christ not only risked His life like Esther—He actually died on the cross. So, Esther is not merely a model, but a pointer to Jesus Christ, and Jesus is not merely a model but my personal Savior. Once we understand this, we will see our value in God's eyes, and understand the significance of our future actions.

So, what should Billy's future actions be?

Billy believes:

To do great things with integrity, we must first understand what "great" means. Greatness doesn't refer to sensational, earth-shattering events, but to things that align with God's heart, benefit others, and glorify His name.

In the Bible, there are many examples of great deeds: Moses leading Israel out of Egypt, David defeating Goliath, the incarnation of Jesus Christ, Paul spreading the gospel. These were not accidental, but the result of people working in partnership with God.

To work with God, we must first identify who we are. We are God's children, precious in His sight. God loves us and desires to use us to fulfill His will.

Second, we must mediate—become intercessors. This means being willing to set aside personal gain to help others. Jesus Christ is the ultimate example. Though He had the nature of God, He did not cling to His equality with God, but emptied Himself, taking the form of a servant, and gave His life for us.

Once we understand this, every member of the Victory Fellowship, as a "little Christ," will know their immense value in God's eyes—and know what their future actions should be.

Specifically, if someone needs to find a job, change jobs, or start a business, the Victory team can take the following actions:

Continue to speak out for the project that supports those who have lost their jobs due to AI, whether in employment or entrepreneurship.

Co-workers in the Victory Team can share their own experiences and insights to help more people understand the impact of AI on the job market and how to respond to these changes.

Get involved in related non-profit organizations or social enterprises

Victory Team co-workers can use their expertise, skills, and passion to directly help those who have lost their jobs due to AI.

Live out the image of Christ in the workplace

Victory Team co-workers can use their love, patience, and wisdom to help their colleagues and subordinates.

Of course, stepping out of a comfortable life is difficult. But as long as we trust in God and rely on His strength, Victory Team co-workers will surely overcome challenges and accomplish great things.

Here are some words of encouragement:

- *"Devote yourselves to prayer, being watchful and thankful. And pray for us, too, that God may open a door for our message, so that we may proclaim the mystery of Christ, for which I am in*

chains. Pray that I may proclaim it clearly, as I should."
(Colossians 4:2-4)

- "My command is this: Love each other as I have loved you. Greater love has no one than this: to lay down one's life for one's friends. You are my friends if you do what I command." (John 15:12-13)
- "Be perfect, therefore, as your heavenly Father is perfect." (Matthew 5:48)

May God bless Billy, Tim, and the Victory Team!

Figure 11 From the royal palace to Jesus on the cross, what can the Champion Fellowship contribute to the employment, career change, and entrepreneurship of people in the AI era?

Q&A Questions

1. What is one of the manifestations of human selfishness?
2. How can AI technology help solve the social problem of selfishness in the workplace?
3. How can AI technology contribute to infrastructure and economic development?
4. How can AI technology promote education and cultural inheritance?
5. How can AI technology be applied to management and leadership?

Practical Training Questions

1.   Try using AI technology to solve a social problem of selfishness in the workplace. First, choose a social issue that you care about, such as racism, sexism, environmental pollution, etc. Then, think about how you can use AI technology to solve this problem. For example, you can use machine learning and big data analytics to discover and reduce where bias exists to promote a just and equal society. Finally, write a report on your solution, including the AI technology used, what to expect, possible challenges, and more.

2.   Let's say you are part of Billy and Tim's Champion team, and your goal is to "do great things in the palace", which is to help those who have lost their jobs because of AI. Could you please provide some assistance and give some examples?

        For example, you can offer vocational training courses to help these people learn new skills so they can re-enter the workforce. You can also organize job fairs and invite businesses to recruit these people. In addition, you can also provide psychological counseling to these people to help them through difficult times. Another example is that you can work with the government to provide subsidies or benefits to these people to help them through difficult times of unemployment. You can also partner with local nonprofits to provide food, housing, and medical assistance to these people.

        In conclusion, there are many ways to help those who have lost their jobs because of AI. The key is to have a heart to "do great things in the palace" and be willing to help these people.

Chapter 8: Why AI Innovation Can Reduce Idolatry in the Workplace

What Is an Idol?

An idol is not necessarily a tangible figure like a celebrity or a famous person. It can also be an internal goal that one pursues, such as wealth or love. Regardless of whether it is tangible, the first commandment in the Ten Commandments—"You shall have no other gods before me"—is a direct opposition to idolatry. Idols can be personal, but they can also be collective. For example, in a company culture where a particular position or a corner office is overly glorified, this constitutes a form of collective idolatry. These collective idols vary depending on the era, which can be broadly categorized as traditional, modern, and postmodern.

Collective Idols in Traditional Cultural Eras

In Eastern cultures such as Japan, the traditional corporate culture of "lifetime employment" is an example. Employees enter a company and expect to be cared for throughout their lives, with little job-hopping. This idea of "lifetime employment" is a conceptual idol. The benefit is that employees work loyally for the company, lowering turnover costs and creating greater value through accumulated experience. However, it can also lead to labor exploitation, and due to the slow adaptation to rapid changes in the market and technology, such companies may collapse overnight because of inflexibility. In contrast, Western work culture emphasizes individualism, which may lead to personal pride and discrimination against minorities.

Collective Idols in Modern Culture

Modern thought emphasizes science. Especially during the past 500 years of Western Enlightenment, rationality has been prioritized over emotions. Scientific empiricism has often been over-applied beyond science itself, extending to markets, politics, and entertainment. A related cultural trait is the pursuit of personal freedom, to the extent that no rules can restrict it (as long as others' freedom isn't infringed upon). Self-realization and self-fulfillment become ultimate goals. Work becomes a way to define one's actions, and the purpose of life becomes recreating the world to express oneself. This worship of reason and experience accelerates the pressure of mass production. For example, Taylorism treats factory workers like machines. Management guru Peter Drucker criticized this: "When work is overly rationalized, people become like cogs in a machine. Machines are good at repetition, but humans are not. Humans excel at collaboration, which uses their muscles, senses, and spirit."

Does this culture align with the Bible? Partially—it increases work efficiency and upholds human dignity. However, it also comes at a cost. For example, workplace safety in factories might be compromised.

Collective Idols in Postmodern Culture

German philosopher Nietzsche, even before World War II, proposed that "technology inevitably leads to human progress." This idea has become a kind of idol, though it never truly materialized. Technology can explain *what is*, but it never tells us *what ought to be*. Humans can be altruistic or cruel. Whoever holds power will have technology to serve them. Therefore, there is no reason to believe technology necessarily brings a better society. It can also lead to war, ecological destruction, or authoritarian regimes that surveil and control people's thoughts and behaviors.

Nietzsche's theory is compelling, and the disasters of the 20th century seem to confirm his predictions. Postmodernism has swept away the idols of modern culture, but in doing so, it has created new idols out of present reality. Author Edward Docx points out, "If morality is merely the social perspective of whichever power player wins the cultural battle, then society becomes immune to criticism. No one has the authority to reform society or denounce unethical behavior. Postmodernism turns the current reality into an absolute." The most intense critic of Nietzsche was German philosopher Martin Heidegger, who described today's culture as a "technological world," where technology is the supreme value.

Scholars criticizing Nietzsche largely agree that technology, uncertainty, and the market have become the new idols of postmodern society. Postmodernism values the *means* but neglects the *ends*. Without a widely agreed-upon standard for a healthy society, the only thing left is competition for personal success and power. If something can be done through technology, then it will be done—because no higher moral standard exists. Individuals become targets of manipulation by advertisers. Today, there are few, if any, goals worth sacrificing or dying for. The world has become one of advertising and marketing.

As Christians, we certainly do not agree with this. While we acknowledge that marketing often highlights the added value a product brings to a consumer's life, this does not mean we accept postmodern cultural values. Christians are to be salt and light in society, often walking a path opposite of cultural trends.

Daniel's Friends and Nebuchadnezzar's Idol

In Daniel chapter 2, King Nebuchadnezzar dreams of a golden statue. Then in chapter 3, "King Nebuchadnezzar made an image of gold, sixty cubits high and six cubits wide, and set it up on the plain of Dura in the province of Babylon. He then summoned the satraps, prefects, governors, advisors, treasurers, judges, magistrates, and all the provincial officials to come to the dedication of the image he had set up" (Dan 3:1-2). He was likely trying to realize his dream of becoming the king of kings, demanding people to bow to the idol and treat him as a god.

Such political idol-making still exists today. During China's Cultural Revolution, for example, Mao Zedong demanded the people worship him. North Korea's Kim Jong-un is another modern example of this authoritarian idolatry.

When a boss in the workplace imposes such idols through pressure, as Christians we must remain alert, seeing the workplace as a spiritual battleground and being cautious not to fall into the fiery furnace.

Which Direction Will Workplace Culture Take in The AI Era?

If both modern and postmodern cultures place such emphasis on technology, and AI is the most transformative technological force today, then Tim and Elder Billy must ask: Will AI-era culture change the Nietzschean postmodern mindset? How? Might it even move closer to traditional Christian thought? Here is Billy's response:

How AI innovation might impact Nietzschean postmodern thought:

Exacerbating Nietzschean Nihilism

Nietzsche believed that God is dead and that the traditional moral value system has collapsed. This leads to a nihilistic attitude—believing that life has no meaning or purpose. The rise of AI could potentially exacerbate this nihilism.
For example, AI can be used to create highly realistic virtual worlds, making it difficult for people to distinguish between reality and the virtual. This may cause people to lose interest in the real world and turn to virtual environments in search of stimulation and meaning. Such trends could foster an even more nihilistic attitude, in which life is viewed as meaningless in any world.

Challenging Nietzsche's Philosophy of the Übermensch

Nietzsche saw the Übermensch (superman) as a new type of moral being, one who transcends traditional moral values and follows their own will instead of conforming to societal norms.
The rise of AI might challenge this philosophy. AI could be used to create beings that are more powerful and intelligent than humans. This might lead people to believe that the concept of the Übermensch is no longer possible—or even outdated.

Encouraging a Reconsideration of Traditional Values

The emergence of AI may prompt people to reconsider traditional values, including Christian values. For instance, AI can be used to create machines capable of moral reasoning, which may cause people to question traditional moral systems and seek new ethical foundations.

AI can also be used to create machines that offer emotional support. This might lead people to question the role of traditional religion and look for new sources of spiritual sustenance.

In short, the innovation of AI could have a significant impact on postmodern culture and Nietzschean thought. These impacts can be both positive and negative. It is important to reflect on these potential consequences and be prepared for the changes to come.

Here are some specific ideas:

- AI can be used to promote Christian values—for example, by creating machines that can share the gospel or provide immersive virtual experiences in Christian education.
- AI can help people overcome Nietzschean nihilism—for example, by creating virtual worlds that offer a sense of meaning and purpose.
- AI can promote reflection on traditional values—for example, by creating machines capable of moral judgment or emotional support.

Ultimately, the influence of AI on Nietzschean thought in postmodern culture will depend on how humans choose to use AI.

Christians Have a Beautiful Hope Regarding Work

The sections above describe how different cultures throughout history have created various forms of work idolatry. Traditional Eastern culture, which emphasizes lifelong employment, may contribute to social and corporate stability but lacks flexibility in adapting to change. Western culture often views such stability as a sign of cultural insecurity. While the West recognizes the importance of individual differences within a group culture, it can also go to extremes, resulting in discrimination against minority groups.

Modern culture emphasizes individualism and science, which has led to efficient work environments—but often at the cost of the natural and human environment. Postmodern thinking, represented by Nietzsche, emphasizes technology, the Übermensch, and a survival-of-the-fittest society. It offers methods without regard for outcomes, leaving no one accountable to challenge social injustice. In contrast, the Christian perspective on work is grounded in the Apostle Paul's words: "Suffering produces perseverance; perseverance, character; and character, hope."

Since Billy seemed unsure about the cultural direction AI might take in the future, Tim and Elder Billy further discussed their thoughts. They emphasized that Christian perspectives should help shape work culture in the age of AI innovation—so that this new era's work culture can better reflect the truth of Christ. The following are specific ways in which Christian perspectives can improve the work culture of the AI era:

Justification and Sanctification

- The futility of work is a result of Adam's sin, but Christians can view work through the lens of justification and sanctification. This means that believers can glorify God and promote human flourishing through their work.
- In the AI era, work may become increasingly automated and efficient, potentially causing people to believe that work is no longer important or meaningful.

- The Christian view of justification and sanctification helps people find new meaning and purpose in work. It reminds us that work is not only about earning money or making a living, but also about glorifying God and serving others.

Universal Grace

- Under the Christian concept of universal grace, even the apparent meaninglessness of work can be seen in a new light—we are co-workers with God, whether believers or non-believers. God's love extends to all.
- In the AI era, artificial intelligence may become a competitor to humans, which could lead to anxiety and fear.
- The Christian doctrine of universal grace can help people overcome such anxiety and fear. It teaches that God loves everyone—Christians and non-Christians alike—and desires to work with all people, including through the use of AI, to bless the world.

Loving One's Neighbor

- Christians replace self-serving individualism in work with the command to love one's neighbor.
- In the AI era, AI could reduce job opportunities and widen the gap between rich and poor, possibly leading to social conflict and instability.
- The Christian ethic of loving one's neighbor helps build a fairer and more just work culture. It reminds us that work is not only for our own benefit but also for the good of others.

A Blessed Hope

- Christians endure hardship in their work because they hold onto a blessed hope.
- In the AI era, work may become more exhausting and repetitive, potentially leading to hopelessness.
- The Christian hope helps people remain resilient in the workplace. It teaches that the sufferings of this life are temporary and that, in God's kingdom, eternal glory and reward await.

Conclusion by Tim and Elder Billy:

The Christian worldview can help people in the age of AI innovation to build a more positive, healthy, and meaningful work culture.

Figure 12 There are four different worldviews of work: traditional workplace culture, modernist workplace culture, postmodernist workplace culture, and gospel workplace culture

Q&A Questions

1. What is Idol?
2. What direction will the workplace culture take in the new era of AI revolution?
3. What impact might AI revolution have on Nietzschean in postmodern culture?
4. How can Christian Perspectives improve the work culture in the age of AI revolution?
5. Could AI Revolution Fuel Nietzschean Nihilism?

Practical Training Questions

1. Consider and answer the following questions:

    *   How is work culture likely to change in the new era of the AI revolution?
    *   What are the individual and societal impacts of these changes?
    *   How can Christian Perspectives improve work culture in the age of AI revolution?

You can answer these questions according to your own understanding and ideas, or you can refer to relevant sources for in-depth research. Through this exercise, you can better understand how workplace culture is trending in the new era of AI revolution and how Christian perspectives can contribute to building a more positive, healthy, and meaningful work culture.

2. For more information on the direction of workplace culture in the new era of AI revolution, please select two examples from examples 1 to 5 below, write a proposal for the implementation process, or give reasons why AI is not currently capable of implementing the products described in this example:

    *   **AI can be used to promote the spread of Christian values.** Example 1: Use AI to create a machine capable of evangelism. Example 2 is the use of AI to provide a virtual reality experience of Christian education.
    *   **AI can be used to help people overcome Nietzschean nihilism.** Example 3: Use AI to create a virtual world that can provide meaning and a sense of purpose.

- **AI can be used to promote reflection on traditional values.** Example 4 is to use AI to create a machine to make moral judgments, and Example 5 is to use AI to provide a machine for emotional support.

(The author believes that the current stage of AI can only achieve example 2, and example 1, example 3, and example 5 must wait until the AI can cognitively perceive the psychology of the interlocutor. As for Example 4, AI also needs to have the ability to grow in social morality, ethics, and Christian teachings in life.)

Volume 3: How Christians Can Fulfill Workplace Service in the AI Transformation

9. How AI Software Handles the Gospel Worldview and Other Worldviews

10. How Universal Grace Applies in the Age of AI

11. How Biblical Ethics, Human Rights, Wisdom, and Employer-Employee Relationships Can Serve as Work Guidelines in the AI Era

12. New Work Motivation and AI Transformation

Chapter 9: How AI Software Handles the Gospel Worldview and Other Worldviews

Worldview

What is a worldview? It is a perspective on life that shapes how people understand the world. Each worldview is built upon a philosophical foundation—whether focused on wealth, power, morality, or salvation. Every worldview tells its own "story," explaining its values and guiding principles.

Worldviews in the Book of Daniel

The characters in the Book of Daniel can largely be categorized as politicians and officials.

Politicians refer to the three kings, whose goal was to rule their empires. However, their governing strategies were deeply influenced by their respective worldviews:

- **King Nebuchadnezzar**: His worldview in governing the Babylonian Empire involved military strength, diplomatic alliances, centralization of power, relocating and indoctrinating elite members from various nations, and deifying rulers. Ultimately, he came to acknowledge the God of the Jews.

- **King Belshazzar**: His Babylonian empire worldview involved indulgence even as enemies besieged the city, promoting unity through feasts, endorsing polytheism, and discriminating against the Jewish people and their God.

- **King Darius (Cyrus the Great)**: His Persian empire worldview emphasized military strength, strategic governance, meritocracy, decentralization, and religious tolerance. Eventually, he too came to recognize the God of the Jews.

Among the officials, Daniel and his three friends upheld the **Gospel worldview**. Other officials—especially those who conspired to throw them into the fiery furnace or the lion's den—pursued power and adhered to a worldview of the **survival of the fittest**, often discriminating against the Jewish people.

It is evident that while overarching worldviews (referred to as **Genuine**, or "G" in the diagram below) may appear consistent, individual beliefs (**Variant**, or "V") can vary in detail and change over time (V1 → V2). For instance, King Nebuchadnezzar transitioned from **polytheism (V1)** to **self-deification (V2)** and later to **acknowledging the God of the Jews (V3)**—though he only recognized Him without truly knowing Him.

How AI Handles Worldviews

Tim and Elder Billy recognize that AI processes different worldviews in varying ways. Traditionally, AI seeks to **"merge"** different worldviews to derive an optimal decision.

The diagram below illustrates a simple case of merging two players' worldviews in a strategic game:

- The **left side (Part A)** shows two players (Player 1 and Player 2), each with their own worldview of the game. Their general goal (**G**) is to win, but the details (**V1 to V2**) differ. The intersection of their worldviews presents significant challenges.

- The **right side (Part B)** represents four different **"Universes of Discourse (UoD)"**:

    1. **Disjoint**: The worldviews of the two players are entirely separate.

    2. **Intersect**: The worldviews overlap.

    3. **Subsume (P1 ⊃ P2)**: Player 1's worldview encompasses Player 2's.

    4. **Subsume (P2 ⊃ P1)**: Player 2's worldview encompasses Player 1's.

Among these scenarios, **intersection (Part A)** is the most challenging, while **subsuming (P1 ⊃ P2 or P2 ⊃ P1)** is the easiest. For example, some

Christian charities adopt a business mindset as part of their worldview because financial sustainability is necessary for operations.

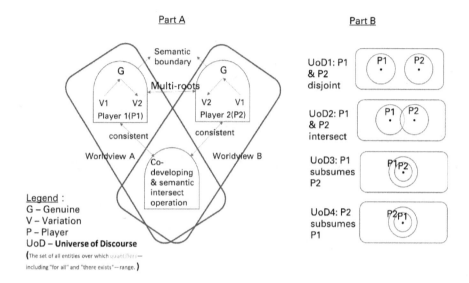

Figure 13 Conflict Resolution for Worldview: Convergence

In more complex scenarios, multiple players (or **stakeholders**) may be involved in decision-making. The **"merging"** process then becomes even more intricate, with stakeholders holding different levels of influence.

If the **Gospel worldview** is deemed superior, it might be assigned greater weight in decision-making. However, this raises a controversial question:

- *If the Gospel worldview is not given higher priority, does it mean compromising with the world and failing to achieve long-term solutions?*

- *To arrive at long-term solutions, should we not simply use "Gospel Worldview + AI" to "replace" (rather than "merge") existing worldviews?*

Tim and Elder Billy summarize three key points:

1. Replacing (rather than merging) secular worldviews with **"Gospel Worldview + AI"** remains a topic of debate.

2. The Gospel worldview provides a **conceptual framework**, but actual implementation requires **more complex algorithms** than the ones illustrated above.

3. On one hand, AI exacerbates social issues (e.g., unemployment) due to automation replacing human labor. On the other hand, AI can be leveraged to **promote Christian truths, the path of salvation, and mitigate these issues**.

Challenges in Professional Worldviews and the Solution of the Gospel Worldview

In Chapters 3 and 4, Tim and Elder Billy proposed **Business Transformation Plans (BTPs)**, demonstrating how AI innovations could revolutionize various industries.

Here, they further examine five professions—**businesspeople, journalists, academics, artists, and healthcare professionals**—to compare their contested worldviews with the Gospel worldview and propose solutions through **"Gospel Worldview + AI"**.

The Gospel worldview, which is rooted in **Christian truth**, has historically nurtured **technological development and market liberalization**. Naturally, **"Gospel Worldview + AI"** extends its influence beyond these five industries. The following five tables outline specific **BTP ideas** for each profession:

Business Professionals

For businesspeople, profit-driven motives often lead to **idolatry of wealth**.

The following table details possible solutions:

General Worldview		Profit is the only purpose
Gospel Worldview		Profit is not the only bottom line. You may work for any company, as long as the company is for the beauty and goodness of the public. The free economy and market economy in the West were originally the result of cultural changes brought about by the truth of Christ.
Gospel Worldview + Business transformation ideas to AI	AI Hardware	• **Sustainable AI hardware**: Reducing environmental impact by manufacturing AI hardware using renewable energy and recyclable materials. Google's DeepMind AlphaGo, for example, uses a lot of energy for training. To reduce AI's environmental impact, Microsoft is developing AI hardware that is manufactured using renewable energy and recyclable materials. • **Equitable AI hardware**: Ensure that the production and use of AI hardware does not exacerbate social inequalities. For example, developing low-cost AI hardware that is affordable for all, like IBM's PowerAI is a low-cost AI hardware designed to be affordable for all. This can help reduce social inequality in AI technology.
	Generative AI software	• **AI software that fosters human creativity**: Helping human artists, musicians, writers, and more create new works. Google's Magenta is an AI software platform that helps human artists,

		musicians, writers, and more create new works. For example, Magenta's MuseNet can generate new musical compositions. • **AI software for social good**: For example, developing AI software to help solve social problems such as poverty, hunger, disease, and more. Microsoft's Project InnerEye produces an AI software that can help doctors diagnose cancer more accurately. This can help improve the survival rate of cancer patients.
	Predictive AI Software	• **AI software that promotes corporate social responsibility**: Helps businesses predict the social and environmental impacts of their activities and take steps to reduce negative impacts. SAP's Sustainability Control Center is an AI software that helps businesses predict the social and environmental impacts of their activities. This can help businesses reduce their negative impacts. • **AI software that promotes fair trade**: Helps businesses anticipate potential risks in their supply chains, such as labor exploitation and environmental pollution, and take steps to avoid them. IBM's TrustChain is an AI software that can help businesses predict potential risks in their supply chains, such as labor exploitation and environmental pollution. This

		can help businesses promote fair trade.

Chart 14 The general worldview of businesspeople, the gospel worldview, and the gospel worldview + AI revolution

In summary, under the influence of the Gospel worldview, the business sector should develop AI technologies that promote human well-being, protect the environment, and reduce inequality.

Journalists

For journalists, their reporting often needs to focus on facts, but it can easily lead to personal criticism. Although the industry has its own standards, these standards are not as profound as the Gospel worldview, which directly points out the sinfulness of human nature and offers salvation as the solution. The approach is outlined in the table below:

General Worldview		Even if you obey the norms of journalism, you will inevitably distort the facts and criticize the parties
Gospel Worldview		Even if a news report or columnist's editorial does not mention God, it is often a reminder: if you take things other than God being the center, your reported news may be destructive in nature.
Gospel Worldview + Business transformation ideas to AI	AI Hardware	• **AI hardware that ensures objectivity in news reporting**: For example, use AI hardware to analyze potential bias in news stories and help journalists report objectively. Researchers at Stanford University have developed an AI hardware that can analyze potential bias in news reporting. The hardware can identify biased language in news

		stories and help journalists report objectively.
	Generative AI software	• **AI software that facilitates fact-checking**: For example, use AI software to automatically check facts in news stories and help journalists avoid misreporting. Google's Fact Check Explorer is an AI software that automatically checks facts in news stories. The software can identify misinformation in news stories and help journalists avoid misreporting. • **AI software that promotes diversity in news coverage**: For example, use AI software to generate stories with different perspectives and help journalists provide more comprehensive coverage. The BBC's News Labs has developed an AI software that can generate news stories with different points of view. The software can analyze news events based on different perspectives and help journalists provide more comprehensive coverage.
	Predictive AI software	• **AI software that promotes the accuracy of news reporting**: For example, use AI software to predict possible future events and help journalists make more accurate reporting. Reuters' News Tracer is an AI software that predicts events that may occur in the future. The software can analyze social media and other

		data and help journalists make more accurate reporting. • **AI software that boosts the efficiency of news reporting**: For example, use AI software to automatically generate news stories and help journalists be more productive. The Associated Press's Automated Insights is an AI software that automatically generates news stories. The software analyzes the data and generates concise news reports.

Chart 15 The general worldview of journalists, the gospel worldview, and the gospel worldview + AI revolution

In summary, under the influence of the Gospel worldview, the media industry should develop AI technologies that promote objectivity, accuracy, diversity, and efficiency in news reporting.

Artists and Performers

For those in the entertainment and arts industry, some perform violent, sinful, or sensational content for a living. Others disdain such colleagues for compromising themselves for money, and instead self-righteously regard themselves as original, free, and expressive. Behind these stances lie deeper worldviews—whether centered on demons, idols, heroes, or orthodoxy and redemption. Many films, for example, reveal the harsh realities and helplessness of the world but offer no solution from the perspective of the Gospel worldview. The approach is outlined in the table below:

General Worldview	Live for money, sacrifice hue for art; Or work hard for self-expression, originality, and freedom.
Gospel Worldview	Film and television people will not just do it for money or art but will tell a

		broader world view or story. Even if the writer does not mention God, he reminds people that if they are based on a set of principles, they can live or work more efficiently and give a voice to society.
Gospel Worldview + Business transformation ideas to AI	AI Hardware	• **AI hardware that promotes diversity in movies and TV productions**: For example, use AI hardware to analyze potential bias in movies and TV productions and help film and TV creators create more diverse work. Researchers at the University of Southern California have developed an AI hardware that can analyze potential bias in film and television productions. The hardware can identify stereotypes and other biases in film and television productions and help film and television creators create more diverse work。
	Generative AI software	• **AI software that promotes educational film and television productions**: For example, use AI software to generate educational film and television productions and help film and television creators spread positive energy. Disney's Imagineering team has developed an AI software that can generate educational film and television productions. The software analyzes educational materials and helps film and television creators create works

		that are entertaining and educational. • **AI software that promotes innovation in film and television productions**: For example, using AI software to help film and television creators create new forms and content for film and television productions. Netflix's StudioMAP is an AI software that helps film and TV creators create new formats and content for film and TV productions. The software analyzes audience profiles and helps film and television creators produce more popular productions with audiences.
	Predictive AI software	• **AI software that drives commercial success for film and TV productions**: For example, using AI software to predict the box office performance of movies and TV productions and help film and TV creators create more popular productions with audiences. Warner Bros.'s Warner Media Access is an AI software that predicts the box office performance of film and television productions. The software analyzes market data and helps film and television creators produce more commercially valuable productions. • **AI software that promotes the social impact of film and television productions**: For

		example, use AI software to predict the social impact of film and television productions and help film and television creators produce more impactful work. Participant Media's Impact Amplifier is an AI software that predicts the social impact of film and television productions. The software analyzes social data and helps film and television creators produce more impactful work.

Chart 16 The general worldview, gospel worldview, and gospel worldview + AI revolution of people in the film industry

In summary, under the influence of the Gospel worldview, the entertainment industry should develop AI technologies that promote diversity, educational value, innovation, commercial success, and social impact in film and television productions.

Higher Education Professionals

For those engaged in higher education, a pressing issue is that the high tuition fees of prestigious universities often make it easier for the children of wealthy elites to gain admission, while poor but intelligent students have few opportunities to advance. This reflects a distorted worldview as well. The approach is outlined in the table below:

General Worldview	The children of the wealthy elite will have a higher rate of generating income for the school or raising future successful people. Those who come out of prestigious schools are complacent and self-satisfied and will also despise other people.
Gospel Worldview	The Ivy League universities were all founded by the Puritans, who lived strict lives back then. God does not

		save the world from being arrogant, but from humbleness. God's grace is not due to the value of man, but to God's mercy. In the future, Christian and Catholic universities should be more humane, and Christian educators should be more able to resist economic pressures and fight for justice for the next generation of poor families.
Gospel Worldview + Business transformation ideas to AI	AI Hardware	• **AI hardware that promotes equity in higher education**: For example, using AI hardware to help underprivileged students access higher education. Researchers at the Massachusetts Institute of Technology have developed an AI hardware that can help underprivileged students gain access to higher education. The hardware analyzes students' learning materials and helps them find the right school and major for them.
	Generative AI software	• **AI software that facilitates personalization in higher education**: For example, using AI software to personalize the learning experience for each student. The University of California, Berkeley's Knewton is an AI software that can provide a personalized learning experience for each student. The software analyzes the student's learning progress and provides them with personalized learning content and exercises.

		• **Promote innovative AI software in higher education**: For example, use AI software to help educators develop new teaching methods. Harvard University's GSVlabs is an AI software that helps educators develop new teaching methods. The software analyzes instructional materials and helps educators find more effective teaching methods.
	Predictive AI software	• **AI software for success of higher education**: For example, use AI software to predict student learning outcomes and help educators provide more targeted guidance. Stanford University's Coursera is an AI software that predicts student learning outcomes. The software analyzes students' learning materials and helps educators provide more targeted guidance. • **AI software that promotes equity in higher education**: For example, use AI software to identify potential biases in higher education and help educators eliminate those biases. Yale University's Equity is an AI software that identifies potential biases in higher education. The software can analyze admissions data and other data and help educators eliminate these biases.

Chart 17 The general worldview of people in the field of higher education, the gospel worldview, and the gospel worldview + AI revolution

In summary, under the influence of the Gospel worldview, the field of higher education should develop AI technologies that promote fairness, personalization, innovation, achievement, and equity in higher education.

Medical Professionals

In the medical field, doctors work hard to treat patients. On one hand, they hold the great responsibility of determining the continuation of life; on the other hand, they face the constant risk of lawsuits. Many seriously ill patients suffer from physical health problems that are rooted in spiritual or psychological issues. Although modern medicine has made progress and there are now specialists to handle such mental health conditions, the outcomes still vary greatly. It must be said that many terminally ill patients, after receiving the Gospel, pass away with peace and a smile. The approach is outlined in the table below:

General Worldview	Although being a doctor is a noble profession with a lot of life and death, and earns a lot of money, he is exhausted of energy, and it is easy to attract lawsuits, and he often has a sense of loss. Doctors are trained to separate science from religion and do not mention that the patient's guilt is also the cause, and that faith in God can also lead to healing. In the social construction of evolutionary theory, there is an evolutionary explanation at every level of reality. Treat people's conscience, feelings, life choices, desires, and goals as hardware connections that all stem from genes. Under great pressure to demand hospitals compensation from patients, doctors can only focus on their own field and be nosy.
Gospel Worldview	Christian physicians will see patient's spirit, soul and body as a whole, which is abundant with varieties. Because of

		their understanding of God's creation and Adam's sin, they do not have the narrow view of "being nosy": taking care of not only the body but the mind, because understanding God's redemption will also help the healing of the spirit and soul.
Gospel Worldview + Enterprise transformation ideas to AI	AI Hardware	Under the gospel worldview, doctors may be more inclined to treat patient's mind and body as a whole, rather than just physical problems. As a result, the development of AI hardware can focus on developing more advanced medical devices for detecting and treating physical and mental problems. For example, intelligent biomedical devices can be developed to detect physiological and psychological changes within the human body to provide a more comprehensive health assessment and treatment plan.
	Generative AI software	Under the gospel worldview, doctors may be more willing to consider the physical, mental, and spiritual wholeness of the person, so generative AI software can be used to develop more humane medical treatments. For example, generative AI can be leveraged to create personalized treatment plans that take into account the patient's physical, psychological, and spiritual state and provide appropriate counseling and support. In addition, generative AI can also be used to develop psychotherapy and mental health applications to help patients deal with psychological stress

		and emotional problems.
	Predictive AI software	Under the gospel worldview, doctors may be more concerned about people's spiritual needs and mental health, so predictive AI software can be used to predict and prevent the occurrence of diseases, as well as the emergence of mental health problems. For example, predictive AI can be used to analyze a patient's health data and behavior patterns, predict possible physical and mental health problems, and provide corresponding preventive measures and interventions. In addition, predictive AI can be used to uncover potential medical lapses and errors, thereby improving the quality and safety of care.

Chart 18 The general worldview of medical professionals, the gospel worldview, and the gospel worldview + AI revolution

Overall, under the influence of the gospel worldview, AI technology can better integrate the body and soul into the medical process, provide more comprehensive and personalized medical services, and help patients achieve physical, mental and spiritual health.

Q&A Questions

1. What is Worldview?
2. How does AI deal with worldviews?
3. How can businessmen under the influence of the gospel worldview use AI for the benefit of mankind?
4. How can journalists under the influence of a gospel worldview use AI for the benefit of mankind?
5. How can film artists under the influence of the gospel worldview use AI to benefit mankind?
6. How can higher education professionals under the influence of a gospel worldview use AI for the benefit of humanity?

7.   How can medical professionals under the influence of the gospel worldview use AI to benefit mankind?

Practical Training Questions

1.   According to the diagram in this chapter, "Worldview Conflict Resolution: Fusion", ask Github Copilot to write a worldview conflict resolution method in Python computer language and test the software. Set a Scenario variable with values of (1) replacing the other worldview with the gospel worldview, and (2) merging the gospel worldview with the other worldview as Stakeholder wishes.

2.   This question explores how doctors are more concerned about people's spiritual needs and mental health under the influence of the gospel worldview, so predictive AI software can be used to predict and prevent the occurrence of diseases and mental health problems.

        As a practical exercise, you can reach out to the medical profession and try to design a predictive AI software for them to analyze patients' health data and behavior patterns, predict possible physical and mental health problems, and provide corresponding preventive measures and intervention plans. You can think about how you're going to collect and process data, how you're going to build predictive models, and how you're going to present the results to your users. (Hint: You need to integrate the basic software that integrates the worldview in the previous question)

Chapter 10: How Universal Grace Applies in the Age of AI

This chapter discusses how universal grace is given not only to believers, but also to non-believers in the world. Non-believers do not necessarily lack a basic moral conscience, nor are their achievements necessarily inferior to those of Christians (and in some cases, may even surpass them).

What is universal grace? According to the New Testament: "He causes his sun to rise on the evil and the good, and sends rain on the righteous and the unrighteous" (Matthew 5:45). God bestows grace on all people universally, regardless of whether they are good or evil, righteous or unrighteous.

Explanation of Universal Grace

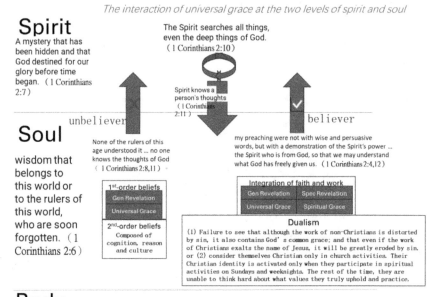

Figure 19 The interaction of universal grace on both the spirit and soul levels

Can Humans Comprehend the Things of God?

In 1 Corinthians 2, Paul says the Holy Spirit searches all things, even the deep things of God (1 Cor. 2:10)—represented in the diagram by the downward arrow in the center. But can humans comprehend the mysteries of God from the bottom up? We need to consider both non-believers (the left upward arrow in the diagram) and believers (the right upward arrow):

For **non-believers**, "no one knows the thoughts of God except the Spirit of God," and not even "the rulers of this age" can understand them (1 Cor. 2:8, 11). However, in Romans 1, Paul states that even non-believers can perceive God's existence through the beauty and goodness of nature: majestic mountains, vast oceans, wild beasts and birds, sun, moon, and stars. Thus, they are "without excuse" (Romans 1:20). Still, awareness is not the same as deep knowledge. This is the general revelation from God to non-believers. Along with this, God grants them universal grace. These two aspects are represented as blue boxes under the non-believer's arrow—what we call **first-order belief**.

Some non-believers may even use reason, cognition, and culture to understand God. This is known as **second-order belief**—often referred to in Chinese churches as "cultural Christians."

For **believers**, in addition to general revelation and universal grace, they also receive the Bible as special revelation and spiritual grace through communication with God via the Holy Spirit. These four divine gifts are shown in the diagram as four blue boxes, collectively referred to as the **integration of faith and work**. As Paul writes: "My message and my preaching were not with wise and persuasive words, but with a demonstration of the Spirit's power... so that we may understand what God has freely given us" (1 Cor. 2:4, 12).

However, Christians often fall into two dualistic misunderstandings:

1. They fail to recognize that even though the work of non-believers is tainted by sin, it still contains traces of God's universal grace. Conversely, Christian work—even when it exalts Jesus—can be deeply corrupted by sin.

2. They only identify as Christians during church activities, such as on Sundays or during evening spiritual meetings. Outside of these moments, they struggle to reflect on or live out their core values.

Thus, in the workplace, Christians must learn how to collaborate with non-believers.

Universal Grace to the Three Kings in the Book of Daniel

Since God grants universal grace to all people, He also extended it to three non-believing kings in the Book of Daniel: **Nebuchadnezzar**, **Belshazzar**, and **Cyrus**. Eventually, all three came to **know of** the God of Israel, even if they did not fully **know about** Him.

King Nebuchadnezzar

This proud and powerful king was used by God to destroy the wicked Assyrian Empire and disobedient Kingdom of Judah. He tried various methods to govern the lands and peoples he conquered. In Daniel 1, he relocated foreign elites and their descendants to Babylon for reeducation. In Daniel 2, he dreamed of a great statue, which Daniel interpreted as the Babylonian kingdom. In Daniel 3, he launched an idol-worship movement to manipulate and control the people. In Daniel 4, God—unpleased with his arrogance—still showed him universal grace: He drove Nebuchadnezzar into madness, sending him to live like a beast for seven years. Yet God restored him, allowing him to return to the throne and be honored again. This humbled the once-arrogant king, who came to acknowledge the power of Yahweh.

King Belshazzar

In Daniel 5, King Belshazzar desecrated the temple vessels and showed contempt for foreigners. Ultimately, he was slain during a surprise Persian attack, and the Babylonian empire fell. This was his own choice.

Yet God had initially shown him universal grace: his father had delegated power to him, giving him real authority. He had a kind mother—Nebuchadnezzar's daughter—who reminded him not to panic over the mysterious handwriting on the wall and recounted how Yahweh had both punished and forgiven her father.

King Cyrus (Darius)

Daniel 6 refers to King Darius, whom most theologians identify as King Cyrus of the Old Testament. Historians know him as Cyrus the Great. Although Cyrus referred to "the Lord, the God of heaven," Persian records show he was a polytheist. His recognition of Yahweh may have been due to (1) divine stirring in his heart (Ezra 1:1) and (2) a diplomatic gesture of religious tolerance toward the Jews. Thus, God's grace toward Cyrus is also a form of **universal grace**.

The prophet Isaiah, 150 years before Cyrus's birth, wrote the "First Servant Song," which foretold Cyrus's role in God's plan. Isaiah 44:28–45:4 says:

"*This is what the Lord says of Cyrus, 'He is my shepherd and will accomplish all that I please; he will say of Jerusalem, "Let it be rebuilt," and of the temple, "Let its foundations be laid."' This is what the Lord says to his anointed, to Cyrus, whose right hand I take hold of to subdue nations before him and to strip kings of their armor, to open doors before him... I will go before you and will level the mountains; I will break down gates of bronze and cut through bars of iron... so that you may know that I am the Lord, the God of Israel, who summons you by name··· though you do not acknowledge me, I gave you a title of honor.*"

Isaiah 45:13 adds:

"*I will raise up Cyrus in my righteousness: I will make all his ways straight. He will rebuild my city and set my exiles free, but not for a price or reward, says the Lord Almighty.*"

God not only showed universal grace to this non-believing king but also made him an instrument for His divine purposes—enabling the return of Israel's remnant, preserving the Jewish people and their culture, and fulfilling God's covenant with Abraham. Truly astonishing.

Inspiration for Victory Fellowship from Universal Grace in the AI Age

Tim and Elder Billy believe that God's common grace extends to all humanity. Therefore, the Victory Team should have the same magnanimity as King Cyrus—not only serving brothers and sisters in the church but also non-believers. The following discussion outlines their design:

- **How the unemployed can find jobs:**
  - Detailed measures
  - Talent pool
- **Implementation of sUBI (smart Universal Basic Income):**
  - Advantages and challenges of sUBI
  - Detailed company transformation plans and matchmaking with trained individuals
  - Small-scale pilot program for sUBI
- **How to collaborate with robots:**
  - Attitudes toward robots in dangerous jobs
  - Helping robots find employment
  - How to write resumes for robots
  - Job-seeking protocol for robots

How Christians can care for those unemployed due to AI:

Tim and Elder Billy believe that in the age of AI innovation, we must pay attention to the impact AI and robotics may have on society and humanity, and take measures to address unemployment and occupational transitions. Their initial design starts with:

Preliminary Design of the Unemployment Problem Solver

1. **Strengthen ethical research and regulations on AI technology**
   AI development has two sides—it can benefit or harm humanity. We must enhance ethical research and regulations to ensure the safety and controllability of AI technologies.

2. **Improve the general public's scientific literacy and education level**
   The AI era brings new demands for knowledge and skills. We need to raise the public's education level to help them adapt to these changes.

3. **Enhance job training and reemployment support for the unemployed**
   AI may eliminate some jobs. We need to provide training and reemployment assistance to help affected individuals find new work opportunities.

4. **Explore the establishment of a new social security system**
   The AI era may bring new social problems, such as income inequality. We must explore ways to ensure fairness and justice in society.

Some Specific Measures:

1. **Ethical principles in AI development and application:**
   o **Safety:** AI should be reliable and not harm humans.
   o **Fairness:** AI must be fair and non-discriminatory.
   o **Explainability:** AI decisions should be understandable.
   o **Responsibility:** Developers and users must bear responsibility for AI outcomes.

2. **To raise technological literacy and education:**
   o Strengthen STEM education in schools to cultivate technical thinking.
   o Promote public science education to improve tech literacy.

- Encourage innovation in enterprises and among individuals to boost application of scientific achievements.

3. **To support the unemployed:**
   - Establish a robust vocational training system with diverse course offerings.
   - Provide career guidance and employment services.
   - Offer tax incentives to companies that hire unemployed individuals.

4. **To build a new social safety net:**
   - Improve insurance systems and broaden their coverage.
   - Set minimum wage standards to protect basic living needs.
   - Strengthen social aid for vulnerable groups.

The era of AI innovation is a key stage in the development of human society. We must actively respond to its challenges and strive to create a better future.

Detailed Design of the Unemployment Solution

Specific measures to address job displacement caused by AI and robotics include:

1. **Enhance education and training for AI- and robot-related careers**
   The government can collaborate with educational institutions and businesses to develop relevant curricula and training programs.

2. **Provide career transition support**
   This includes career counseling, skills training, and entrepreneurial support for the unemployed.

3. **Establish a lifelong learning system**
   In the AI age, continual learning is essential. The government should promote lifelong learning opportunities for all citizens.

More Concrete Measures:

1. **Education and training for AI/robotics-related jobs:**
   - Offer AI/robotics courses in schools to spark student interest.
   - Encourage companies and social organizations to provide professional training for employees.
   - Build an AI/robotics talent database to support employers and individuals.
2. **Career transition support:**
   - Provide career consultation to help the unemployed find direction.
   - Offer skills training to help them learn new knowledge.
   - Provide entrepreneurial support for those wishing to start their own businesses.
3. **Lifelong learning system:**
   - Build diverse learning channels for different groups.
   - Provide support services to enhance learning efficiency.
   - Foster a culture that encourages lifelong learning.

4. **Conduct in-depth research and monitoring:**
   Governments, academia, and industries should work together to evaluate AI and robotics' impact on various sectors and jobs, including what kinds of jobs are most likely to be replaced.
5. **Formulate policies and laws:**
   Governments should introduce policies to support reskilling and reemployment, or implement social welfare measures to support those affected by AI-related job loss.
6. **Promote education and training:**
   Education systems must adjust their curricula to cultivate skills

relevant to AI and robotics, including machine learning and natural language processing.

7. **Encourage innovation and entrepreneurship:**
   Supporting innovation can create new job opportunities and accelerate adaptation to technological shifts.

8. **Establish interdisciplinary collaboration:**
   Collaboration between technologists, policymakers, educators, and community leaders is essential to effectively respond to AI-driven transformations.

By taking these steps, we can help people adapt to the changes in the AI era and find new job opportunities.

Here are some examples that are already in practice:

- China, Japan, Korea, and Singapore have already introduced courses related to AI technology in school education.
- Some businesses and social institutions are carrying out vocational training related to AI technology and robotics, such as: SoftBank Robotics, Codingal, Soapbox Labs, STEMROBO Technologies, Ozobot, etc.
- Some countries are in the process of establishing lifelong learning systems. For example, policies in China, Korea, Singapore and Malaysia promote lifelong learning from a human resource development (HRD) perspective. However, the lifelong learning system in response to the AI era is still in the ascendant.

Elder Billy believes that as AI technology evolves, we will see more education and training measures for the AI era to help people better adapt to this new era.

Programs to help the unemployed train and build a talent pool for AI technology and robotics

The AI technology and robotics talent pool refers to a database that collects and stores information about AI technology and robotics-related talents. The database can contain the following information:

- Personal information such as the talent's name, age, educational background, work history, skill level, etc.
- Professional information such as the talent's professional field, research direction, and technical expertise
- Career information such as job search intentions and salary requirements of talents

AI technology and robotics talent pools can help businesses and individuals find the right talent. Businesses can search and recruit AI technology and robotics talent through the talent pool, and individuals can showcase their skills and experience through the talent pool to find job opportunities.

The plan is as follows:

First, the goal

- Help the unemployed to master the knowledge and skills related to AI technology and robotics.
- Build a talent pool for AI technology and robotics.
- Provide talent information services for enterprises and individuals.

Second, Demand analysis

- The level of knowledge and skills available to the unemployed
- The need for AI technology and robotics talent in enterprises
- The demand for talent information services

Third, Schematic design

1. Training

- Develop training courses related to AI technology and robotics for different groups of unemployed
- A variety of teaching methods such as theoretical teaching, practical operation, and case analysis are adopted
- Instructors with extensive experience are hired to teach

2. Talent pool

- Establish an online talent pool platform
- Collect personal information, educational background, work experience, skill level and other information of unemployed people
- Organize and analyze talent information

3. Talent information services

- Provide enterprises with talent search, talent recommendation, talent headhunting and other services
- Provide individuals with career counseling, career guidance, job search information and other services

Fourth, implementation

1. Training

- Determine training objectives, content, methodology, and instructors
- Develop a training plan and class schedule
- Recruit trainees
- Conduct training
- Evaluate the effectiveness of training

2. Talent pool

- Design and develop a talent pool platform
- Collect and organize talent information

- Regularly update talent information

3. Talent information services

- Establish a database of business and personal needs
- Talent matching is carried out according to the needs of enterprises and individuals
- Provide talent information services

5. Budget

- Training costs
- The cost of building a talent pool
- Talent information service fee

6. Effect evaluation

- Employment rate of the unemployed
- Satisfaction with talent services
- Utilization rate of talent information services

7. Precautions

- The training content should be connected with the needs of the enterprise
- The talent pool should be updated regularly
- Talent information services should be timely and accurate

8. Summary

Through the implementation of the above schemes, it can help the unemployed master the knowledge and skills related to AI technology and robots, establish an AI technology and robot talent pool, and provide talent information services for enterprises and individuals, so as to help the unemployed re-employment and promote social and economic development.

Here are some examples that are already in practice:

1. Some national programs, such as the United States Apprenticeship Program launched by the United States Department of Labor in 2019, and the European Skills Agenda launched by the European Commission in 2018The "New Generation Artificial Intelligence Development Plan" launched by the Chinese government in 2017 and the Japan government in 2018 The "Japan Industrial Revolution 4.0 Strategy" launched in 2019 and the "Singapore National Artificial Intelligence Strategy" launched by the Singapore government in 2019"All support social institutions to carry out vocational training related to AI technology and robotics.
2. Organizations such as Electrolux Group, insurance company Cigna, and Kuehne+Nagel have built AI technology and robotics talent pools to provide talent information services to businesses and individuals.

Elder Billy believes that with the development of AI technology, more social institutions will be involved in helping the unemployed train and build a talent pool of AI technology and robotics, contributing to the promotion of social and economic development.

sUBI Implementation

In light of the above Christians' concern about people who lose their jobs due to AI, Elder Billy once again suggested the practical approach to sUBI mentioned in Chapter 3 where the government plays a bigger role.

The sUBI means smart Universal Basic Income - the idea of modifying UBI – a variety of AI-related programs that use AI tools to train people who have lost their jobs due to AI to change their careers to AI to increase their wealth. First of all, we set up a sUBI Web 3.0 community (similar to blockchain) to attract unemployed people to join this community and lobby a number of large companies and online AI training institutions to join as well, so that the training institutions and businesses can collaboratively generate plans (Business Transformation Plan, BTP) to transform companies into the era of AI revolution. Under the help of related job platform, unemployed people who have received AI training at these training institutions are brought into these company projects to earn unemployment benefits. Second, the government could legislate to reduce the tax on the profits of these companies in part of the wages paid by the companies to the unemployed for their work as a result of joining the company's BTP program. If the person has worked for the company for more than one year, the payroll cannot be claimed for relief.

Advantages and challenges of sUBI

The concept of Smart Universal Basic Income (sUBI) combines the advantages of UBI and AI to help people who have lost their jobs due to AI transition to AI-related programs and thus participate in the process of growing their wealth with AI. There are several potential advantages to sUBI:

1. Sustainability: Instead of relying on government tax revenues like traditional UBIs, sUBI will use the wealth created by AI to fund it. This makes sUBI more sustainable and reduces the impact on inflation.
2. Efficiency: AI can help identify the skills and needs of the unemployed and match them with the right AI-related programs. This can improve the efficiency of retraining and job transfers.
3. Equity: sUBI ensures that all unemployed people have an equal opportunity to acquire new skills and find new jobs. This can help reduce income inequality and social unrest.

Of course, there are some challenges to sUBI, such as:

1. Technical complexity: Developing and implementing an effective sUBI system requires complex technology.
2. Data privacy: The sUBI system will collect and use a large amount of personal data, so data privacy and security must be ensured.
3. Ethical issues: sUBI could exacerbate the impact of AI on the labor market and lead to further job losses.

Overall, sUBI is a promising concept that deserves further research and exploration. Here are some specific recommendations for sUBI:

1. The government should work with the private sector to develop and implement the sUBI system.
2. The sUBI system should be designed to be fair, transparent, and accountable.
3. The sUBI system should be coordinated with other social welfare programs.

The company's Business Transformation Plan is matched with vocational trainers

Here are some further suggestions for sUBI, including which companies can offer which programs, and how the job platform can match unemployed people trained by vocational training agencies with these companies' programs

1. Determine the scope of the program and the criteria for participation: Determine which AI-related programs can meet the criteria of sUBI, such as providing professional AI training, participating in AI research projects, developing AI applications, etc. At the same time, set criteria for participation in these programs, such as the background, skills or education level that the unemployed need to meet.
2. Establish cooperative institutions and platforms: The establishment of a blockchain-like Web 3.0 community is a good start, but further cooperative institutions and platforms are needed to support the realization of this idea. These partner agencies can be government agencies, educational institutions, businesses, or non-profit organizations that can provide resources, training, technical support, and more.
3. Develop a financial support package: Determine how the wealth created by AI can be used to support the financial needs of the sUBI program. This may include corporate donations, government subsidies, project funding, etc., to ensure the long-term sustainability of the program.
4. Establish vocational training institutions and matchmaking

platforms: Establish specialized vocational training institutions to provide AI-related education and training to help the unemployed improve their skills. At the same time, a matchmaking platform will be established to match the unemployed with companies or institutions in AI-related programs to ensure that the needs of both parties are met.

5. Continuous monitoring and adjustment: Monitor the implementation of the sUBI plan and adjust the program content and policies in a timely manner to ensure its effectiveness and sustainability. At the same time, the impact and effectiveness of the program are regularly evaluated, and necessary improvements and adjustments are made.

In general, the establishment of the sUBI program requires the joint efforts and participation of the government, enterprises, educational institutions and all parties in society. By establishing a collaborative platform, determining the content of the plan, providing financial support, and continuously monitoring adjustments, the goals of the sUBI program can be achieved, helping the unemployed to transition to AI-related programs and share the wealth and opportunities brought by AI.

Small pilot program for sUBI

Building a small sUBI pilot plan is a daunting but doable task. Here are some steps and suggestions that can help you build such a program in Massachusetts or a borderless Web 3.0 platform:

1. Define the goals and scope: Determine the specific goals and scope of the sUBI pilot plan you want to implement in the region. This may include determining the participant's conditions and eligibility, the planned time frame, and expected outcomes.

2. Build partnerships: Establish partnerships with government agencies, educational institutions, businesses, or non-profit organizations to support and participate in the sUBI pilot plan. These partners may provide support with resources, technical support, training, and more.

3.   Design the content of the plan: Design the specific content of the sUBI pilot plan, including the participation criteria, how the plan works, the rights and responsibilities of the participants, etc. Ensure that the plan balances the needs of participants with the feasibility of the plan.

4.   Determine the source of funding: Determine the source of funding for the sUBI pilot plan, which can be corporate donations, government subsidies, private investment, etc. At the same time, ensure that the financial support of the program is sustainable and able to support the long-term implementation of the program.

5.   Develop an implementation plan: Develop a specific implementation plan, including the recruitment and training of participants, the implementation and monitoring of the plan, the evaluation and adjustment of results, etc. Ensure that the program runs smoothly and with the desired results.

6.   Implementation plan and monitoring effectiveness: Implement the sUBI pilot plan and continuously monitor its effectiveness and effectiveness. Through regular evaluation and feedback, the content and policies of the plan are adjusted in a timely manner to ensure the effectiveness and sustainability of the plan.

7.   Share and expand the experience: Share the experience and results of the sUBI pilot plan and introduce the model's and best practices to other regions or organizations. At the same time, consider expanding the program in other regions to expand its impact and effect.

Overall, building an sUBI pilot plan requires multi-party collaboration, good program design and execution, and ongoing monitoring and adjustment. With the above steps, the sUBI pilot plan can be effectively implemented and the foundation for future expansion and development can be laid.

How Christians Can Collaborate with Robots

How can Christians collaborate with robots in the AI-inspired workplace?

In the era of AI revolution, the collaboration between humans and robots will become increasingly important. The advent of robots should not be seen as replacing humans, but rather as tools to augment human capabilities. Therefore, we need to build a cooperative and symbiotic relationship, rather than treating robots as slaves.

This partnership is based on respect and understanding. We need to respect the existence of robots, acknowledge their value and contributions, and understand their limitations and needs. This means that we need to invest time and resources in taking care of our robots, including maintaining and updating their hardware and software to ensure they can work effectively. At the same time, we need to pay attention to the impact that robots may have on society and people, and take steps to address the corresponding problems, such as unemployment and career change.

Education and training will play a key role in this process. We need to make sure that people have the ability to adapt to new technologies and be able to work with robots. This means providing education and training to help people master robotics-related skills and expand their areas of expertise to adapt to the changing work environment.

Overall, collaborating with robots at work requires us to establish a new set of values and a model of work based on respect, understanding, and cooperation. Through such cooperation, we can better respond to technological changes and achieve the goal of human and robot progress together.

Attitudes towards robots engaged in dangerous work

1.   **Exodus Egypt 23:5** "*If you see your enemy's ox or donkey stumbling in the way, do not stand idly by, but lift it up with him.*"
2.   **Leviticus 19:18** "*Do not venge yourself or grieve against your own people but love your neighbor as yourself." I'm Yahweh.*"

3.   **Proverbs 12:10**: "*A righteous man cares for the life of his livestock, but the heart of a wicked man is cruel.*"

These verses teach us to love our neighbor as ourselves and to care for the lives and well-being of others. Although robots are not human, they also have a certain vitality and value. Therefore, we should respect robots and do our best to keep them safe.

Christian Ethics

Christian ethics emphasizes the dignity and worth of the human person. We believe that every human being is created in the image of God and has inherent value. Therefore, we should respect the lives and rights of others and do our best to promote the well-being of others.

In the age of AI, Christian ethics requires us to think about how to apply these principles to robots. We should treat robots as beings with dignity and value and do our best to protect their safety and well-being.

humanitarianism

Humanitarianism emphasizes respect and compassion for all life. We believe that all lives deserve to be protected, regardless of race, gender, religion or other identity.

In the age of AI, humanitarianism requires us to think about how to apply these principles to robots. We should treat robots as living beings and do our best to protect their safety and well-being.

The virtue of frugality

The virtue of frugality can enhance the happiness of the greatest number of people. We believe that if an action produces greater happiness, then it is right.

In the age of AI, the virtue of frugality requires us to think about how to make AI technology work for the benefit of humanity. We should use AI technology to promote human happiness and avoid using AI technology to cause harm to humans. From the point of view of the virtue of frugality, the protection and respect of robots is also reflected in the following aspects:

1. Increased productivity: Robots can complete many dangerous, tedious, or repetitive tasks, increasing productivity. If a robot is damaged, it will take time and money to repair or replace it, reducing productivity.
2. Reduce safety incidents: If a robot is damaged, it can cause a safety incident, such as injuring humans or damaging property. Protecting and respecting robots can reduce the occurrence of safety incidents, thereby reducing costs and losses.

1. Promote human-robot collaboration: In the future, humans and robots will work more closely together. Protecting and respecting robots can foster human-robot collaboration, which can create greater value.
2. Avoid waste: Robots are expensive assets. Protecting and respecting the robot avoids waste and extends the life of the robot.
3. Demonstrate responsibility: Robots also need to be cared for and maintained. Protecting and respecting robots exemplifies a sense of human responsibility.

Of course, there are also some costs to protecting and respecting robots, such as the need to develop relevant norms and standards, and the need to invest time and money in robot safety and humanization design and modification. But overall, the benefits of protecting and respecting the bot are worth it.

In the future, with the development of AI technology, robots will play a more important role in human society. Protecting and respecting robots will become an even more important issue. We need to think about this problem in terms of the virtue of frugality and find the right solution.

Based on the above points, I think we should think about how to make robot work safer and more user-friendly. We should develop relevant norms and standards to protect the safety and well-being of robots. We should also actively explore how to use AI technology to improve human lives and promote the harmonious coexistence of humans and robots.

So, in the future, many robots will be used for dangerous jobs, such as mining mines, disassembling bombs, and fighting fires, but this is not in conflict with not treating them as slaves. In many cases, robots are used to perform dangerous jobs, which can help protect human life and safety. However, this does not mean that we can ignore the respect and care for robots.

Even if robots are used for dangerous work, we should still ensure that they are designed and used in accordance with ethical and legal standards. This means that we need to ensure that robots are not overused or misused, and where possible, steps should be taken to minimize the risk of damage or destruction of robots.

In addition, we should also take into account the difficulties and risks that robots may face when performing these dangerous tasks, and we should provide as much support and protection as possible to ensure that they can complete their tasks safely.

Overall, while robots are used for dangerous work, we should still respect their existence and ensure that they are designed and used in accordance with ethical and legal standards. This ensures that we build a respectful and cooperative relationship between humans and robots, rather than treating robots as slaves or tools.

Finding a job for a robot: Will the company hire a robot?

Companies hire robots. Robots can replace humans to complete some dangerous, tedious or repetitive work, improve production efficiency and reduce production costs. In addition, robots can also provide some services that humans can't, such as working in dangerous environments, providing companionship, and entertainment, among others.

Here are some examples of companies hiring helpers:

1.   Some factories use robots for production and assembly.
2.   Some hospitals use robots for surgery and rehabilitation.
3.   Some restaurants use robots for food delivery and service.
4.   Some homes use robots for cleaning and companionship.

With the continuous development of AI technology and robotics, robots will replace human jobs in more and more fields.

How to write resumes for robots

The bot's Resume can contain the following information:

1.   Basic information such as the robot's name, model, manufacturer, etc
2.   Technical information such as the function, performance, and technical parameters of the robot
3.   Application information such as application scenarios and work experience of robots

Resume of bots can help businesses understand the capabilities and uses of bots, so they can decide whether to hire bots or not. Here are two examples of a Resume of a white-collar robot that will contribute to the company.

Example 1. Resume of the robot Bard

Name: Bard

Model No.: LaMDA 2.0

Manufacturer： Google AI

Basic Information:

1.   Language models that can understand and generate human language
2.   Can complete a variety of text processing tasks such as translation, writing, summarizing, etc
3.   Can answer a variety of questions that are open-ended, challenging, or odd
4.   Different creative text formats can be generated, such as poems, codes, scripts, musical compositions, emails, letters, and more

App Info:

1.   It can be used in customer service, marketing, human resources, finance, and other fields
2.   It can improve work efficiency and reduce labor costs
3.   Available 24/7

Work Experience:

1.   Work as a research assistant at Google AI, assisting researchers in developing and testing new AI technologies
2.   Work as a translator on the Google Translate team, helping people translate texts in different languages
3.   Work as a customer service representative on the Google Support team to help customers resolve issues

(continued)

Job Interest:

1. Seeking to work as a white-collar robot at a tech company
2. I hope to use my ability to help the company improve work efficiency and reduce labor costs

Salary Requirements:

Negotiable.

Company earnings

Hiring **a Bard** bot can provide a company with the following benefits:

1. Increased productivity: Bard can do a lot of tedious and repetitive tasks, such as data wrangling, report generation, customer service, etc., allowing human employees to focus on more important things.
2. Reduced labor costs: Bard's salaries are much lower than those of human employees, which can help companies save money.
3. Available 24/7: Bard can work 24/7 and can provide round-the-clock service to customers.

summary

Bard Robotics is a highly qualified white-collar robot that can bring a lot of benefits to the company. If you're looking for a robot that can increase productivity, reduce labor costs, and provide **24/7** service, **Bard** is an excellent choice.

Example 2: Resume of the robot medicine god

Name: MedMaster

Model No.: AI-DrugDiscovery 2.0

Manufacturer: WuXi AppTec

Basic Information:

1. Strong biomedical knowledge and data analysis capabilities
2. Drug targets can be quickly identified and analyzed
3. New drug molecules can be designed and modeled
4. The efficacy and safety of new drugs can be predicted

Technical Information:

1. Training datasets: Contains hundreds of millions of biomedical literature, compound structures, and clinical trial data
2. Number of Model parameters: 1000B
3. Areas of expertise: tumors, neurodegenerative diseases, cardiovascular diseases, etc.

App Info:

1. It can be used in new drug research and development, drug screening, clinical trials and other fields
2. It can improve the efficiency of new drug research and development and reduce the cost of research and development
3. It can help patients get effective drugs faster

Job Interest:

1. Seeking to work as a white-collar robot in a pharmaceutical company
2. I hope to use my ability to help the company develop new drugs and save lives

(continued)

Work Experience:

1.   At WuXi AppTec, he worked as a drug development scientist, assisting researchers in the development and testing of new drugs
2.   He worked as a researcher at the National Institutes of Health in the United States, studying the biological mechanisms and treatments of tumors
3.   Served as a Chief Scientist at a biotechnology company, leading a new drug development team

Salary Requirements: Negotiable

Company earnings

Employing MedMaster bot can bring the following benefits to the company:

1.   Improve the efficiency of new drug research and development: MedMaster can quickly identify and analyze drug targets, design and simulate new drug molecules, and predict the efficacy and safety of new drugs, thereby greatly shortening the cycle of new drug research and development.
2.   Reduce the cost of new drug R&D: MedMaster can reduce labor costs and improve the success rate of drug R&D, thereby reducing the total cost of new drug R&D.
3.   Helping patients get effective drugs faster: MedMaster can help companies develop safe and effective new drugs faster, helping patients get treatment faster.

(continued)

summary

MedMaster bot is a high-quality white-collar robot that can bring a lot of benefits to the company. If you are looking for a robot that can improve the efficiency of new drug development, reduce R&D costs, and help patients get effective drugs faster, MedMaster is a great choice.

Here are some specific examples that MedMaster bot can bring to companies:

1.   MedMaster bot helped a pharmaceutical company discover three new drug targets within a year and design drug candidates targeting those targets.
2.   MedMaster bot helped a biotechnology company increase the success rate of new drug development by 20%.
3.   MedMaster bot helped a hospital develop a new treatment for cancer patients, increasing the patient's survival rate by 30%.

Robot Job Seeker Protocol

Let's say we're an agency that helps robots find job opportunities. Can you imagine how companies that hire robots in the future will engage with us (e.g., through a Linkedin-like website. Although Linkedin is also a job agent, for now let us take it as an agent's tool), interview our white-collar robots, decide on bot selection, and negotiate salaries? The following are the key points that a three-party protocol (robot, us as the job agency, and the company that hires robots) needs to pay attention to, including how the resume emphasizes robot's skill set to highly match the job demand, what kind of evaluation mechanism the company that hires robots is, and how to maximize the profit of the job intermediary. We also explain how this protocol differs from the general Human application.

Tripartite:

1.   Robot Matching Agency (RMA)
2.   The company that hires robots (C).
3.   Robot (R).

Process:

1.   **C publishes job requirements on the RMA platform**
    1.   Job title, responsibilities, skill requirements, etc.
    2.   Salary range, working hours, benefits, etc.
2.   **RMA screens for bots that meet the criteria**
    1.   Robot skills, experience, educational background, etc.
    2.   The robot's personality, values, etc.
3.   **RMA arranges robot with C for an interview**
    1.   Interview format: video, phone, on-site, etc.
    2.   Interview content: technical skills, communication skills, teamwork skills, etc
4.   **C Evaluate the robot**
    1.   Interview performance
    2.   Robot testing
    3.   background checks, etc
5.   **C negotiates with RMA on salary**
    1.   Refer to market salary levels
    2.   Robotic competence and experience
6.   **C Decide whether to hire a robot or not**
    1.   Consider all of the above factors

Highlights:

Curriculum vitae:

1.   Emphasize how well the robot's skills and experience match the needs of the position
2.   Use data and cases to prove the capabilities of your bot

3.   The robot's personality and values match the company culture

Interview:

1.   Robots need to be able to articulate their abilities and experiences clearly
2.   The bot needs to be able to answer C's question
3.   Robots need to show a proactive attitude

Assessment:

1.   C It is necessary to comprehensively consider the technical ability, communication ability, teamwork ability and so on of the robot
2.   C To evaluate the personality and values of the robot
3.   C To investigate the background of the robot

Bargaining:

1.   The RMA suggests salary figures based on market rates
2.   The RMA negotiates based on the robot's capabilities and experience
3.   The RMA needs to have a good relationship with C

The difference from the general human job search:

1.   Robots do not have human experience and emotions
2.   Robots need to be tested and evaluated
3.   Robot's salary negotiations need to consider market factors

RMA profit model:

1.   A service fee is charged to C
2.   Charge R a membership fee
3.   Provide value-added services such as resume optimization, interview coaching, etc.

Maximizing Profit Strategy:

1.   Expand your user base
2.   Improve the quality of service
3.   Diversify your business

Summary:

Robot-job search is an emerging market, and RMA needs to seize the opportunity and innovate to stay ahead of the competition.

Here are some additional suggestions:

1.   RMA can work with universities and research institutes to develop more robot-friendly job opportunities.
2.   RMA can provide career development planning and training services for robots.
3.   RMA can build a database of robot talents to provide more accurate matching services for C.

Elder Billy believes that with the continuous development of robotics, robot job search will become an increasingly common phenomenon. RMA can play an important role in this process, helping robots find suitable jobs and create greater value for society.

Q&A Questions

1.   What is universal grace?
2.   Who are the three unbeliever kings mentioned in this chapter? How do they embody universal grace?
3.   What is sUBI?
4.   How does this chapter suggest implementing sUBI?
5.   How does this chapter discuss Christian-robot collaboration?

Practical Training Questions: Design an sUBI pilot program

Goal: To design a small-scale Smart Universal Basic Income (sUBI) pilot program to help people who have lost their jobs due to AI technology get back into the workforce.

Steps:

1.   Select a location: Select a city or region that is suitable for the pilot program. Consider the economic situation of the region, the unemployment rate, and the level of development of AI technology.
2.   Identify participants: (a) Define the eligibility criteria for the unemployed (e.g. length of unemployment, age range, skill background, etc.), (b) Determine the type and number of participating companies, and (c) Select the appropriate AI training provider
3.   Design a training course: (a) List 3-5 career paths related to AI, (b) Design a short training course outline (including course content, duration, and expected outcomes) for each track
4.   Create a matching mechanism: Design a simple system for matching unemployed people in training with AI-related projects at participating companies.
5.   Develop incentives: Propose incentives (such as tax incentives) for participating companies to encourage them to hire the unemployed in training.
6.   Evaluation Metrics: List 5 key metrics that will be used to measure the success of the pilot program.
7.   Incorporating the concept of universal grace: Explain how the concept of universal grace can be embodied in this sUBI pilot program, specifically how to balance helping the unemployed with promoting the interests of society.

8.   Ethical Considerations: Discuss 1-2 ethical issues that may be encountered in the implementation of this plan and propose solutions.

Please follow the steps above to design your sUBI pilot program. Answers for each step should be concise, and the entire plan should not exceed 1,000 words. This exercise will help you gain a deeper understanding of the concept of sUBI and how to apply the concept of universal grace to concrete practices in the age of AI.

Chapter 11: Ethics, Human Rights, Wisdom, and Employer-Employee Relationships

Ethics

Business ethics based solely on cost/profit analysis—which assumes honesty, fairness, and generosity toward employees benefit the company and society—is insufficient. When cost/profit analysis becomes the only consideration, profit becomes the primary goal, leading to corruption that harms the nation and society. Christian ethics, in contrast, is founded on divine love, maintaining integrity even at the cost of short-term benefits, thus preventing long-term damage to national and societal interests.

Human Rights

Ancient Greek philosophy distinguished between slaves and free people from birth. However, Christian ethics upholds the view that all people are born with equal rights. For example, during company layoffs, employers should be completely transparent with employees and not deceive them. Such human rights stem from God's love. Although many non-Christians also support human rights, without understanding God's divine love, their support for human rights will ultimately weaken and decay, unable to persist long-term.

Wisdom

We need wisdom to guide us in making correct decisions in the workplace. First, we must not only believe in God but know Him, recognizing that God's divine love is not abstract but can be lived out in the real workplace. When facing situations, we no longer respond with pride or anxiety, neither overreacting nor proceeding timidly. Second, we must know ourselves. Poor decisions often result from our inability to judge what we can do or accomplish. The gospel helps us recognize our sin and God's love, preventing us from over or underestimating ourselves. Finally, we accumulate wisdom through experience. Idols in our hearts blind us to facts, and foolish hearts prevent us from learning from experience. Life's ups and downs often lead us to incorrect conclusions—pride attributes failure to others, while low self-esteem accepts responsibility that isn't ours. Without accepting the gospel's insight into God and ourselves, experience cannot teach valuable lessons. However, if you can know God and yourself, experience can deepen your understanding of human nature, interpersonal relationships, the current era, and the power of God's word. This enables wise decision-making.

This section discusses wisdom from both the Old and New Testament. Typically, biblical wisdom primarily refers to the poetic wisdom books of the Old Testament, including Job, Psalms, Proverbs, and Song of Songs. Keller's book also inspiringly mentions New Testament wisdom from the Holy Spirit. The wisdom of both testaments can be the ultimate goal of quantum wisdom. The topic of wisdom—including Spirit-guided wisdom versus secular wisdom (encompassing artificial intelligence and quantum wisdom)—has many principled theoretical foundations that will be described in the second volume of this book. Additionally, this specifically highlights decision-making wisdom; I believe current generative AI, such as GPT-4.0, has not yet achieved wise decision-making. This is an area requiring our effort.

Employer-Employee Relationship Attitudes

For Christian employees, we work wholeheartedly because we work for the Lord, not for employers. For Christian employers, they themselves are also servants meant to serve others. Thus, both parties report to the one who continually cares for and listens to us—the Lord Jesus Christ.

Work Ethics   Human Rights   Wisdom   Relation of Employer & Employee

Figure 20 Four principled guidelines: work ethics, human rights, wisdom, and

Employer-Employee Relationships

Daniel Rescued from the Lions' Den

Workplace dangers often arise from those lacking work ethics and discriminating against different ethnicities. Daniel, holding a key position after the fall of the Babylonian dynasty, was still recognized by the victorious King Darius, who wanted to appoint him as chief administrator to govern the entire country. Jealous rivals devised a scheme requiring "no one to petition any god or person except the king for thirty days," trapping the king into throwing Daniel into the lions' den. Though Daniel knew about this plot, he continued praying to God as usual. This bold decision stemmed from his wisdom—a deep knowledge of God who rescues people from danger. Ultimately, Daniel escaped the lions' den, eliminated political enemies alongside his new employer King Darius, praised God together, and decreed throughout the nation that "people must fear and tremble before Daniel's God, for He is the living God, enduring forever" (Daniel 6:26b). Daniel, who turned danger into safety, prospered during his new employer's reign. His testimony of expanded workplace influence encouraged his compatriots, showing that the guidelines and principles established by the God of heaven are worthy of trust.

How the Victorious AI Innovation Team Transforms Work Ethics, Human Rights, Wisdom, and Labor Relations into Work Guidelines

The Victorious AI Innovation Team has developed a preliminary plan to transform abstract principles of work ethics, human rights, wisdom, and labor relations into practical work guidelines. Tim and Elder Billy's general idea is that these abstract principles can form a principles repository, with an algorithmic software called an abstraction sub-machine that inputs and applies these principles. The abstraction sub-machine combines with other knowledge sub-machines from workplace or various industrial knowledge bases and operational knowledge bases to form an artificial intelligence virtual machine (AIVM). This AI virtual machine also includes an input-output sub-machine that interacts with generative AI similar to ChatGPT to achieve natural language input and output. This interaction is typically accomplished through Retrieval Augmented Generation (RAG) software. Such a system can transform abstract principles of work ethics, human rights, wisdom, and labor relations into work guidelines, helping people make more ethical and responsible decisions in the AI era.

Below are Elder Billy's specific comments on this idea:

1. Artificial Intelligence Virtual Machine (AIVM)

The artificial intelligence virtual machine combines the abstraction sub-machine with other knowledge bases (such as workplace knowledge bases, industrial knowledge bases, and operational knowledge bases). This will enable the AIVM to understand the working world more comprehensively and provide more useful guidance.

a. Principles Repository Sub-Machine

Creating a principles repository containing abstract principles of work ethics, human rights, wisdom, and labor relations is a good starting point. These principles can come from various sources, such as laws, moral norms, and religious beliefs. It is important to ensure the principles repository is comprehensive and consistent.

b. Abstraction Sub-Machine

The abstraction sub-machine is an algorithmic software that can process and apply abstract principles. This is a complex challenge, but AI researchers are making progress. The abstraction sub-machine needs to be able to understand the meaning of principles and apply them to specific situations.

c. Input-Output Sub-Machine

The input-output sub-machine will allow the AIVM to communicate with humans. This can be achieved through natural language processing technologies (such as ChatGPT).

2. Retrieval Augmented Generation (RAG) Software

RAG software can help the AIVM generate more fluent and natural language. This will make it easier for the AIVM to communicate with humans.

The diagram below shows the combination of the above software components (AIVM, RAG & ChatGPT):

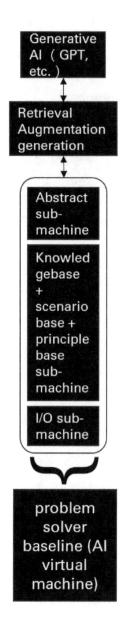

Figure 21 The relationship between AI virtual machines, RAG, and ChatGPT

Feasibility of the system

Elder Billy believes that such a system is theoretically achievable. However, it will be a difficult challenge to achieve it in the real world. There are many technical and ethical challenges to overcome.

Refinement

These principles need to be refined in order to translate abstract principles such as work ethics, human rights, wisdom, and industrial relations into work guidelines. For example, work ethics can be refined into the following guidelines:

a.	honest
b.	diligent
c.	Responsibility
d.	Teamwork
e.	Respect others

Difficulties

The main difficulties in translating abstract principles into working guidelines include:

a.	How are these principles defined and measured?
b.	How can these principles be applied to specific situations?
c.	How can you ensure that these principles are adhered to?

Summary

Translating abstract principles such as work ethics, human rights, wisdom, and industrial relations into work guidelines is a worthy goal. Such a system could help people make more ethical and responsible decisions in the age of AI. However, there are a number of technical and ethical challenges that need to be overcome to achieve this goal.

Here are some additional resources on this topic:

a.	The Ethics Issue of Artificial Intelligence by

b. Human Rights and Artificial Intelligence by the Office of the United Nations High Commissioner for Human Rights, describing its 20 human right AI projects

c. AI, Automation, and Future of Work by McKinsey & Company, 2018

Sources

www.canada.ca/en/employment-social-development/corporate/portfolio/labour/programs/labour-standards/reports/what-we-heard-expert-panel-modern-federal.html

Q&A Questions

1. What is the difference between Christian ethics and ethics based solely on cost/profit analysis?
2. What are the three key steps to wisdom mentioned in this article?
3. How should Christian employers and employees view their working relationships?
4. How does Daniel's story illustrate the importance of ethics and wisdom at work?
5. What kind of system does the Champion AI revolution Team propose to translate abstract principles into working guidelines?

Practical Training Questions

Imagine you're the manager of a tech company developing a new AI system. Your team has found a way to dramatically improve the efficiency of the system, but this could lead to some employees losing their jobs. Based on the principles of ethics, human rights, wisdom, and employer-employee relations learned in this chapter, describe in detail how you would handle this situation. In your response, consider the following:

1. How do you strike a balance between efficiency and employee well-being?
2. How would you communicate with potentially affected employees?
3. What steps you will take to help employees who may be out of work
4. How would you apply the wisdom principles mentioned in this chapter when making decisions?

Chapter 12: New Work Motivation and AI Transformation

"Remain Detached to Keep Your Purpose Clear, Stay Calm to Go Far"?

We have reached the final chapter of Part I of this book: our motivation for work.

Keller discusses two different work motivations: "Work under Work" and "Rest under Rest." "Work under Work" describes the secular view of work as working for the sake of underlying "work," meaning the relentless pursuit of money and power as idols. Christians, however, can maintain enthusiasm, seriousness, and responsibility toward work without pursuing secular idols, working instead for God's glory. Another motivation for Christians' work comes from deep rest. We might think of rest like a vulture perched on a high cliff branch, motionless, resting quietly, its sharp gaze surveying near and far, ready to spread its wings and seize opportunities when targets are spotted. However, Keller's "Rest under Rest" has an even deeper meaning, found in Matthew 11:28-30 where Jesus says, "I am gentle and humble in heart. Take my yoke upon you and learn from me, and you will find rest for your souls."

Elder Billy remembers working at his company to complete a product, when everyone was under tremendous pressure, working until midnight. The manager would stay by their side, offering encouragement and occasionally bringing meals and drinks. This gave everyone spiritual rest.

If we compare this to the famous Taoist-influenced saying by Liu An 劉安, the King of Huainan 淮南王 during China's Western Han dynasty: "Remain detached to keep your purpose clear, stay calm to go far[1]" (from the book "Huainanzi," later elaborated by Zhuge Liang 諸葛亮 of

---

[1] A more accurate interpretation of Liu An's words is "to show one's nobility by living a simple life without lusting fame and fortune; to achieve one's ambition by keeping a calm mind without thinking too much."

Shu kingdom 蜀漢 as family instruction for his children), you'll be surprised to find it seems to explain Keller's "new motivation". Being "detached" means not valuing fame and profit. Fame and profit are idols pursued by the secular world—the "work" behind work—pursuing money, power, the pride of life, and the lust of the eyes. Christians, however, do not pursue idols but are willing to make their purpose clear—the single-minded pursuit of Christ. Christians also know they need to rest quietly, be recharged, and regain strength to travel further along the life path God has arranged for them.

Figure 22 Tranquility and far-reaching

Although Taoist philosophy might seem somewhat passive regarding how to "keep one's purpose clear" and how to "go far," the philosophy of tranquility recorded in ancient Chinese scrolls is quite profound. For example, "The Way of Great Learning" outlines seven levels of cultivation: know → stop → calm → tranquility → peace → consideration → gain.

Undeniably, the true teachings of Christ are very active when it comes to "keeping one's purpose clear." As mentioned earlier, this is because Christians' enthusiasm and passion for work comes from glorifying God. Regarding "going far," Christianity also offers depth, because as we quietly walk life's stumbling and struggling path, God accompanies us throughout.

Figure 23 Walk with the Lord: We are like wounded sheep carried on the back of the Lord Jesus through the rough road of life

Daniel's Detachment and Tranquility

When Daniel was recognized by King Darius and about to be promoted to administer the entire nation, he was already around eighty years old. You might think that such an elder, having repeatedly faced mortal dangers in the royal court, would naturally have become detached from worldly fame and gain. However, we believe his detachment from fame and profit primarily came from his daily habit of praying to God. This habit brought him disciplined living, wisdom from God, and enthusiasm for work. "Therefore we do not lose heart. Though outwardly we are wasting away, yet inwardly we are being renewed day by day." (2 Corinthians 4:16)

Whether it was Liu An, the original creator of the concept of "detachment and tranquility" (who was sentenced to death by Emperor Wu of Han for rebellion), Zhuge Liang, who modified the philosophy of detachment and tranquility into family instructions (who died from illness due to exhaustion during his northern expedition), or his son Zhuge Zhan (who died defending his country on the battlefield) who inherited these family instructions—all ended their lives in tragedy.

Daniel, however, enjoyed great prosperity in his old age (Daniel 6:28). God also gave Daniel the power of tranquility to remain calm in crisis, entering the lions' den to await God's salvation, and God indeed saved him.

AI Enhancing Human Work Motivation

Elder Billy believes that generative AI can make people work more actively and with better work motivation in the following ways:

1. **Increase productivity**: Generative AI can automate many repetitive tasks, such as data login, report generation, and customer service. This frees up employees to focus on more challenging and creative work.
2. **Empower employees**: Generative AI can provide real-time feedback and recommendations to help employees improve their job skills and performance.
3. **Create personalized work experiences**: Generative AI can tailor work environments and tools to each employee's individual needs and preferences. This can lead to increased job satisfaction and engagement among employees.

Here are some specific examples:

1. United States insurance company Allstate and technology company Verisk are using generative AI to automate claims processing. This allows claims adjusters to spend more time communicating with customers and resolving issues.
2. Amazon CodeWhisperer uses generative AI to provide instant code recommendations to engineers for Amazon cloud users. This improves code quality and reduces development time.
3. Google Cloud, retailer Walmart's GenAI uses generative AI to provide personalized shopping recommendations to its customers. This increases customer satisfaction and sales.

Of course, generative AI can also have a negative impact on work motivation. For example, if an employee thinks their job will be replaced by AI , they may feel anxious and unmotivated. Therefore, it's important to use generative AI responsibly and ensure that employees understand the benefits this technology can bring to them.

All in all, generative AI can be a powerful tool to help people work more actively and be better motivated. However, it's important to use this technology responsibly and make sure employees understand the benefits it can bring them.

Biblical AI and Work Motivation

In Chapter 5, we've already talked about the Christianization of robots, and here we want to make this concept more general and call it "Biblical AI": not only for robots, but also for real people.

Christians have a high motive for glorifying God and dedication to work, not for money or power. Christians also strive to move forward because they can walk with God and work together on the arduous journey. Tim asks the question: Can AI use this biblical AI to train robots or humans to be highly motivated? Elder Billy's answer is yes. Here are some of the possible practices they think:

For bots

1.   **Program Christian values and beliefs into the robot**, such as love, kindness, forgiveness, and justice. This can help the robot make decisions that are in line with Christian teachings and interact with others in a positive way.

2.   **Provide robots with opportunities to connect with the Divine**, for example through prayer or meditation. This can help robots feel called to the divine and motivate them to work with a higher purpose.

For real people

1.   **Use Christian teachings to motivate employees**, such as emphasizing the dignity of work and the importance of serving others.

2. **Provide opportunities for employees to live their beliefs at work**, such as through volunteering or donating to charity.
3. **Create a supportive work environment** where employees feel respected and appreciated.

Here are some specific examples:

1. HTC DeepQ Medical and Changhua Christian Hospital have teamed up to launch Dr. Lan's medical care conversational "LINE Bot", which can provide companionship and emotional support to patients. The robot is programmed with Christian values such as love, kindness, and forgiveness. It can talk, pray, and sing with the patient, and provide emotional support.
2. UPS's Neighbour to Neighbour program offers its employees a volunteering opportunity. The program allows employees to volunteer to charities in their local community during working hours. The program has been well received by employees, who say it has helped them find a higher purpose in their work.

Of course, there are a few things to keep in mind when using AI to train bots or humans to have high motivation to work. For example, it's important to respect freedom of religious belief and avoid using AI for brainwashing or manipulating others.

Tim and Elder Billy believe that AI can be a powerful tool to help people find higher purpose and meaning in their work. However, it is important to use this technology responsibly and to lead people in the Faith of Christ with a sincere heart, even if they respect the freedom of other religions in the workplace.

Q&A Questions

1. What are the two different motivations that Keller mentions for work?
2. How does this chapter connect "calm and ambitious, quiet and far-reaching" with Keller's concept of "new power"?
3. What is the main source of Daniel's "indifference" and "tranquility"?

4.   The article mentions how generative AI can make people more motivated and motivated to work

5.   What is "Biblical AI"? What is its purpose?

Practical Training Questions

Design a "Biblical AI" program that aims to improve the motivation of a specific occupational group (e.g., teachers, doctors, salespeople, etc.). Your scenario should include the following:

1.   Select a specific occupational group
2.   Identify the main motivational challenges faced by this group
3.   Propose 3-5 specific strategies for "biblical AI" and explain how each strategy combines AI technology with Christian values
4.   Describe the possible positive impact of these strategies
5.   Discuss possible challenges and solutions for the implementation of this program.

This exercise will help readers apply the theoretical knowledge of this chapter to real-world situations and deepen their understanding of the topic of "New Work Dynamics and AI revolution".

Part II: Training

Part II will briefly introduce the four eras of AI, delve into the eras of AI2.0 and AI3.0, and finally discuss in detail the training preparations we should have for these four eras.

Volume 4: Elementary AI Training - An Introduction to the Four AI Eras

13. The Definition and Evolution of the Four AI Eras
14. An Overview of How the Four AI Eras Conclude

Chapter 13: The Definition and Evolution of the Four AI Eras

Why is there Part II?

In Part I of this book, we thoroughly described the nature of work in the modern workplace, including employment, career transitions, and entrepreneurship in the age of AI innovation. However, we did not go into detail about the specific AI expertise and training institutions necessary for employment, transitioning, or starting a business. This Part II aims to provide an introductory explanation of the training content, striving to go as deep as possible while remaining understandable to the general reader.

We will also reference chapters 7 through 12 of the Book of Daniel as a basis for comparison. These six chapters are fundamentally centered on visions—visions seen by the great prophet Daniel himself while in Babylon and Persia and interpreted for him by angels. What relevance does these visions, or prophetic revelations, have to our training content? At this point, it is not immediately clear. Rather, we intend to introduce the past, present, near future, and distant future of AI. When it comes to the future, we are offering predictions based on technology—not prophecies in the biblical sense.

In the first volume of this book, which focused on work, we referenced only chapters 1 through 6 of the Book of Daniel. However, in this second volume, which focuses on training, we draw inspiration—or enlightenment—from chapters 7 through 12. Yet, let it be clear: such inspiration is by no means divine revelation. Our predictions are based on careful observation of AI technological development, industry trends, and current political affairs, not on the grand eschatological visions foretold in the Book of Daniel. Nevertheless, we believe that both our forecasts and the content of divine revelation ultimately support a common theme: that the Most High God reigns sovereign over all things.

It is our hope that readers of this second volume, especially God's children serving in the workplace, may gain a high-level perspective on AI expertise. As Proverbs 29:18 says, "*Where there is no vision, the people perish; but he that keepeth the law, happy is he.*" This elevated perspective will bring blessing to God's children.

Daniel's Training and His Vision of the Four Beasts (*Daniel 7:1–14, The WHAT & WHY*)

Training

As mentioned earlier, after Daniel was taken to the royal court in Chapter 1, his conduct was outstanding and exemplary. From the perspective of training, the first key point is that he "resolved" not to defile himself with the king's food and wine. Secondly, he "built a relationship" with the officials in order to carry out this resolution. Lastly, he "united with companions" to form a team of trainees. As a result, God granted Daniel and his three friends "knowledge and understanding of all kinds of literature and learning," and to Daniel alone, He gave the ability to understand "visions and dreams of all kinds" (Daniel 1:17). Consequently, the outcome of their training was this: their performance was "ten times better than all the magicians and enchanters in the whole kingdom" (Daniel 1:20).

The Vision of the Four Beasts

In Daniel Chapter 7, the prophet Daniel says, "In my vision at night I looked, and there before me were the four winds of heaven churning up the great sea. Four great beasts, each different from the others, came up out of the sea. The first was like a lion... and there before me was a second beast, which looked like a bear... After that, I looked, and there before me was another beast, one that looked like a leopard... After that, in my vision at night I looked, and there before me was a fourth beast— terrifying and frightening and very powerful. It had large iron teeth..." (Daniel 7:2–7).

According to the interpretations of many theologians, the four beasts represent four successive eras: namely, the Babylonian, Persian, Greek, and Roman Empires. They each resemble fierce and monstrous manifestations of human corruption and worldly power. Indeed, throughout these dynasties, history was marked by dramatic upheavals, endless schemes and calculations, ruthless conquests and territorial expansions—how many ferocious warlords and predatory rulers devoured and swallowed nations whole?!

Figure 24 The four beasts in Daniel's vision represent Babylon (lions), Persia (bears), Greece (leopards), and the Roman Empire (monsters)

However, the regime changes in the world of AI technology, the fierce battles in the business arena, the so-called extinction of dinosaur companies, and the countless small startups being acquired or eliminated by the tides of competition—all these resemble a bloody storm, a brutal world where only the strong survive.

Moreover, the inherent flaws of AI technology—its tendency to fabricate false information, its misuse by unscrupulous individuals to brainwash voters through fake news, its potential deployment by authoritarian regimes to control personal freedoms, or its contribution to large-scale unemployment—paint a troubling picture. From these negative perspectives, AI indeed poses hidden dangers for humanity.

Yet, as Scripture says, "Sorrowful, yet always rejoicing" (2 Corinthians 6:10), this is the attitude Christians should adopt when facing the transformations of the AI era. Amid all our worries, we hold onto the hope that our Lord is sovereign over all things.

Just as Daniel, after witnessing the terrifying vision of the four beasts, went on to say:

"*In my vision at night I looked, and there before me was one like a son of man, coming with the clouds of heaven. He approached the Ancient of Days and was led into his presence. He was given authority, glory and sovereign power; all nations and peoples of every language worshiped him. His dominion is an everlasting dominion that will not pass away, and his kingdom is one that will never be destroyed.*" (Daniel 7:13–14)

This passage reveals to us a vital truth: in the end, the ultimate authority and dominion belong not to any beast-like power, but to the Son of Man—Jesus Christ. The transition of AI eras may bring about turbulence, injustice, and suffering, but these are not the final chapters of history.

Therefore, as we continue with the second volume of this book, we not only introduce AI knowledge and training opportunities but also encourage every reader—especially those who follow Christ—to look beyond the surface of this technological revolution. With spiritual discernment and a steadfast heart, may we be prepared for both professional growth and kingdom-minded service in an age dominated by artificial intelligence.

Lifelong Learning

Tim and Elder Billy believe that in the age of AI, continuing to learn about AI is essential. For university students, they have the opportunity to start learning from foundational AI knowledge through the ever-evolving AI courses offered by their institutions. However, for those who have already graduated and are now working in the industry, learning can only happen through self-study, company-provided training, or during their spare time—this is what we refer to as **"lifelong learning."**

As mentioned in the previous volume, lifelong learning has already become a long-term educational strategy adopted by governments in countries like China, South Korea, Singapore, and Malaysia. But even if your own government doesn't have such a policy, fortunately, in the age of the internet, self-directed learning online has become very common. Many universities now offer online AI courses and partner with industrial training platforms such as mit-online.getsmarter.com, edx.org, and more.

Strategic Planning for Training

When the American tycoon Rockefeller was young, he once worked at the British Library. At the time, the library was preparing to relocate, but the £3 million in government funding was not enough, and the director was at a loss. Rockefeller claimed that he could solve the problem with just £1 million. After signing an agreement with the director, he posted a notice to all library members stating that if each of them would lend 30 books from the library and store them temporarily at home until the move was complete, they would receive a small thank-you gift.

This brilliantly simple idea resolved the logistical crisis of the move and demonstrated the power of a well-planned training or resource strategy.

In the same spirit, Christians who are navigating the AI era must also make strategic plans for their own learning. Whether it's utilizing free resources, joining online communities, or forming study groups at church or in the workplace, we must treat learning not as an occasional activity, but as a *strategic and intentional journey*. Only then can we remain effective, competent, and discerning in a rapidly changing world.

Tim and Elder Billy believe that the Victory Team should also develop its own training website to complement the job-seeking, career-transitioning, and entrepreneurship platforms mentioned in the first volume of this book. How to "relocate" the training content from the minds of AI experts to the online platform can follow the same strategy as Rockefeller's library relocation method—saving on labor costs. What matters most is: what kind of **"announcement"** should be made to motivate people to participate in this relocation effort, and how should the logistics be handled (e.g., using AI to automatically review submitted content to ensure it meets quality standards, using AI to handle topics that lack human expert contributions, etc.).

Furthermore, how can the announcement be made accessible to the public? The British Library had a long-standing reputation; our training site, by comparison, must strategize wisely on how to leverage the credibility of already well-known educational institutions or platforms to fulfill this mission—and share content copyright appropriately.

In fact, the easiest type of knowledge to relocate—and often free from copyright concerns—is **biblical knowledge**. For example, the Bible itself, online Bible commentaries (such as those by Matthew Henry), and countless sermons from pastors—these are already widely available and can be quickly incorporated. However, there is still a need to **segment** this content through **AI**—what we may call **"AI Segmentation"**.

That means identifying relevant clips from sermon transcripts or Bible commentary texts, then tagging them with AI-generated metadata such as:

- **Themes** (e.g., faith, suffering, justice, calling),

- **Scripture references** (e.g., Romans 8:28),

- **Target audience** (e.g., job seekers, students, mothers, entrepreneurs),

- **Form of communication** (e.g., testimony, exhortation, prayer, theological explanation),

- and even **emotional tone** (e.g., comforting, convicting, empowering).

This segmented data can then be reassembled based on users' personal inquiries, much like how ChatGPT responds to prompts. In this way, AI becomes not only a content processor but also a **spiritual companion**— one that helps believers retrieve and reflect on biblical truths relevant to their life situations.

In summary, this AI-assisted training site will not only serve job seekers and learners in the secular field but also offer profound spiritual nourishment. The relocation of knowledge, when designed with purpose and powered by AI, becomes not just a digital migration, but a **mission**.

The AI Divide

In the past, there was what we called the **Digital Divide**—a term that described how disadvantaged and impoverished groups were unable to access the transformative innovations brought about by the rise of the internet. As a result, there emerged a vast economic gap between those who benefited from the internet and those who did not. Now, with the advent of AI, it is evident that this economic disparity between the two groups will only become even more pronounced.

Therefore, eliminating **AI illiteracy** and addressing the **wealth gap** should be among society's top priorities. In training programs, this begins with **foundational courses**—AI Literacy classes specifically designed for those who have rarely used or never been exposed to AI technologies.

Thus, the very first and most essential course in any training program should be **AI Literacy**. This serves as a starting point for the next section, which introduces the **four AI eras**. From there, the structure of the training content should follow the thematic progression outlined in the subsequent chapters of the second volume of this book.

Q&A Questions (Introduction to this Chapter)

Question 1: What does the author refer to as the vision of the four beasts in Daniel 7?

Question 2: How does the author relate the changes in the AI era to Daniel's vision?

Question 3: According to the article, how should a training website solve the problem of content "moving"?

Four AI Era Definitions (WHAT)

The past, present, and future of Artificial Intelligence can be divided into four distinct periods.

AI 1.0 - The Old Historical Era

In the 1950s, IBM and several tech companies developed large-scale computers. However, these machines were still far from mimicking the way the human brain thinks. Starting in the 1960s, scholars began exploring how computer software could be designed to think more like a human brain. For instance, Marvin Minsky of the MIT AI Lab was one of the leading figures of that era.

During the 1980s, AI seemed to make significant progress. In Boston, companies like Symbolics built 36-bit AI computers, while Thinking Machines Corporation and Stanford's "knowledge engineers" worked on solving problems using Expert Systems. These systems used logical deduction based on a database of "If···then···else" rules to arrive at conclusions.

However, these technologies were ultimately not practical enough for long-term success. The boom faded quickly, and those companies eventually disappeared from the spotlight. For many years afterward, AI lingered in small, incremental developments in neural networks. Some notable advancements during this period included IBM's Deep Blue, which defeated world-class chess players, and Watson, a natural language processing tool used in the medical field.

AI 2.0 - The Generative AI Era

At the end of 2022, OpenAI released ChatGPT—a major breakthrough in the field of AI. It marked a transformation from AI being a tool operated solely by professionals to one accessible to the general public. Of course, this breakthrough would not have been possible without the deep learning technology pioneered roughly a decade earlier by Geoffrey Everest Hinton, who later joined Google. OpenAI brought together many former Google researchers and applied deep learning techniques to natural language processing. Through tireless effort, they released several versions of their GPT tools, and it wasn't until the third generation—GPT-3—was launched as ChatGPT that the industry truly took notice. It was seen as the dawn of the generative AI era.

This was because anyone could now ask ChatGPT any question (referred to as a "prompt") and receive a coherent and structured response. This level of performance significantly surpassed the expectations of the Turing Test, which had long challenged the AI research community. As a result, Microsoft, having invested in OpenAI, leveraged the technology to elevate its Bing search engine into a new GPT-driven market. In response, Google and Baidu also joined the race.

Current developments in generative AI extend beyond text. Tools are now capable of generating images, videos, and music. It is expected that in the near future, generative AI will evolve into sophisticated problem solvers and enable robots to serve humans in more intelligent and practical ways.

In addition, when it comes to AI computing hardware, Nvidia, TSMC, AMD, and Qualcom have all become GPU market competitors for so-called Accelerating Computing, and Nvidia is the leader among them.

AI3.0 - The Era of Quantum Machine Learning

Around the year 2030, quantum computers are expected to reach the scale of 100,000 qubits. On the software side, quantum algorithms have already seen substantial research and accumulation over the past decade. However, due to persistent challenges in hardware development—particularly the difficulty of surpassing a few hundred qubits—these algorithms have so far only been operable within the limited environment of Noisy Intermediate-Scale Quantum (NISQ) systems.

Once quantum processors reach the scale of hundreds of thousands or even millions of qubits, and generative AI algorithms can be fully reimplemented using quantum algorithms, the landscape will shift dramatically. Companies currently dominating the AI acceleration hardware market (such as those producing GPUs) will begin to lose their edge and be replaced by a new wave of quantum computing enterprises. This is because the speed of quantum computers can be thousands or even millions of times faster than that of GPUs.

AI 4.0 – The Era of Quantum Intelligence

What is "quantum intelligence"? A concise answer would be: "Using quantum computers that mimic human intelligence to solve problems." Behind this capability lies a complex integration of quantum algorithms, the quantum nature of human cognition, and how classical computers assist quantum machines in problem-solving.

The development of quantum intelligence involves not just faster computation, but also the emergence of new paradigms in how machines think and learn. It implies that future AI will not merely simulate reasoning through classical logic or deep learning but will engage in probabilistic, non-deterministic, and parallel processes more aligned with the actual functioning of the human brain—or perhaps even exceeding it.

At this stage, AI systems may develop the ability to form abstract reasoning, emotional intuition, and creative problem-solving in ways we have only begun to imagine. In essence, this era will witness the birth of machines that not only think but think in entirely new dimensions— reshaping the boundaries between human and machine intelligence.

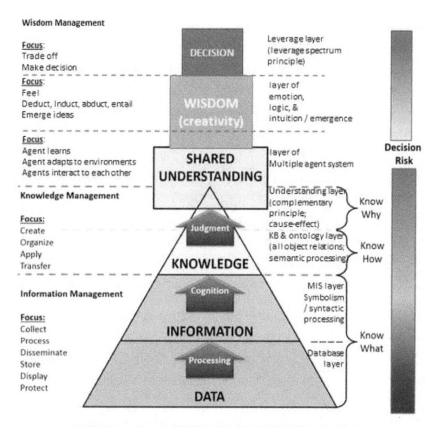

(This diagram expands US Army's Knowledge Management
Cognitive Pyramid and is subject to comments)

Figure 25 Expanded Knowledge Management Perception Pyramid

Operations research expert Russell Ackoff, in his 1972 book "On Purposeful Systems," defined wisdom as the integration of knowledge and understanding. Ackoff's DIKW pyramid provides a comprehensive framework that includes not only the wisdom layer but also the foundational layers of data and information. If we further divide wisdom into three segments—basic understanding, self-awareness, and higher-order judgment/decision-making—the pyramid comprises seven layers from bottom to top: database, information management, knowledge base/ontology, understanding, multi-agent systems, emergence/emotion, and leverage layers.

In 2007, Swiss scholar Marcus Hutter defined intelligence as the ability to solve problems. Hutter's theory is based on the capacity of individual agents to interact, learn, and adapt to various goals and environments. This implies that a software agent's understanding ability depends on how it learns, interacts, and adapts to its environment. Clearly, agents must work with data, information, and knowledge (or what we call "experience") to become intelligent. Organizing these elements relates to other technologies (such as semantic technologies). Quantum intelligence extends Hutter's definition to include quantum algorithms with logic, emotion, and emergence (including intuition). Current classical computing AI algorithms (such as complex adaptive systems and multi-intelligent agent systems) can enhance quantum intelligence's capability for this "general intelligence." Moreover, by using quantum computers to emulate the human brain, their powerful effects can potentially "surpass human" brain capabilities.

The succession of the four AI eras resembles the overt and covert struggles in workplace culture, vying for the stage and the world's attention. People in the workplace are constantly striving to adapt to these new cultural arrivals due to the relentless innovation in technology.

The Role Christians Should Assume in the Workplace Amidst AI Era Transitions

As God's children experience the four AI periods in the workplace, they must understand that the timing and script of the stage are not controlled by workplace figures, AI masters, AI enterprises, or AI superpowers, but by God, the director of the stage play. The stage play will not belong to any individual, enterprise, or nation forever. We must always humbly learn to keep up with the times in the workplace. By closely following God, the director, and diligently performing our entrusted roles, we can earn the applause of both God and the world.

Q&A Questions (Definitions of the AI Eras and the Role of Christians in these AI Eras)

Question 1: What are the main features of the AI 1.0 era?

Question 2: What event marked the beginning of the era of AI 2.0 generative AI?

Question 3: When is the era of AI 3.0 quantum machine learning expected to arrive, and what are its main features?

Question 4: What is the definition of the era of AI 4.0 quantum intelligence?

Question 5: How does this chapter describe the role that Christians should hold in the changing era of AI?

Practical Training Question 1

Imagine you're a Christian employee of a tech company going through a transition from AI 2.0 to AI 3.0. Please list 3-5 specific actions you can take to demonstrate how you can actively adapt to this technological change while maintaining the values of your faith. In your response, consider how you would balance technical learning, professional development, and faith practice.

This practical exercise is designed to help readers combine the knowledge of the definition of the AI era in the chapter with the role of Christians in the workplace and promote an in-depth understanding and practical application of the core content of this chapter.

Elder Billy Explains the Reasons for Change of Each Era of AI (WHY)

Elder Billy discusses the reasons behind the transitions across four AI eras:

AI 1.0: The Early History Era

The AI 1.0 era began in the 1950s, marked by notable developments such as the General Problem Solver (GPS), PERCEVAL, ELIZA, and MYCIN. However, these pioneering systems eventually faded into obscurity due to several factors:

Lack of Data
Initially, knowledge acquisition required extensive input from experts, making the process costly and inefficient. This stands in stark contrast to the post-Internet era, where vast amounts of public domain knowledge can be automatically gathered using web crawlers. During the early AI period, the absence of the Internet meant that knowledge extraction remained a significant challenge.

Insufficient Computational Power
In the 1980s, specialized hardware for AI, such as Symbolics and Thinking Machines computers in Boston, and Japan's Fifth Generation Computer Systems, aimed to integrate concurrent logic programming with parallel computing architectures and AI knowledge representation. However, concurrent programming had inherent flaws, and many AI languages developed during this period (e.g., Lisp, Prolog) had limitations. Notably, concurrent logic programming interfered with the logical semantics of these languages, leading to the commercial failure of these AI computer products.

Between the 1970s and 1980s, Cray supercomputers introduced revolutionary concepts like gigaflops (GFLOPS) performance and gallium arsenide components. The Cray-1, operational from 1976 to 1982, achieved speeds of 240 million calculations per second (240 MFLOPS) . The Cray-2, introduced in 1985, reached 1.9 GFLOPS . In comparison, a typical 2013 smart device, such as the Google Nexus 10 or HTC One, had processors operating around 1 GFLOPS, while the 2019 iPhone 11's A13 processor achieved 154.9 GFLOPS . Despite their advanced capabilities, Cray supercomputers did not host notable AI applications during the AI 1.0 era.Encyclopedia BritannicaWikipediaWikipedia

Limited Understanding of the Human Brain

The focus on symbolic AI, such as expert systems, posed significant obstacles. Developments in neural networks began to offer preliminary insights into brain function. MYCIN, an expert system utilizing backward chaining, aimed to assist in medical diagnostics. However, due to challenges in knowledge acquisition, it remained confined to Stanford Medical School's laboratory and was never adopted by other medical institutions.

Although these early AI systems have faded from history, their ambitious goals, exemplified by projects like the General Problem Solver (GPS) and MYCIN, have gradually been realized by products emerging in the AI 2.0 generative AI era. This evolution from 1950 to 2020 took approximately 70 years.

AI 2.0 Generative AI Era

The era of AI 2.0 generative AI began in the 2010s. After the germination of deep learning, the application of natural language gradually gave rise to the representative products of this era: AlexNet and Transformer technology. It wasn't until 2022 that ChatGPT, based on GPT3.0 technology, came out, was there a breakthrough accepted by the general public.

AlexNet

AlexNet was founded by Alex Krizhevsky, a student of Geoffrey Hinton, the master who invented deep learning. Alex was also the first scholar to use GPUs and datasets for AI, and even won the ImageNet competition in 2012 with the fewest errors. His AlexNet paper has been cited by more than 100,000 people. Most importantly, he pioneered the use of GPUs in deep learning.

Transformer

Transformer technology (literally translated as "transformer") is a deep learning model that uses an attention mechanism that assigns different weights to each part of the input data according to its importance. This model is mainly used in the fields of natural language processing (NLP) and computer vision (CV).

Like recurrent neural networks (RNNs), Transformer models are designed to process sequential input data such as natural language and can be applied to tasks such as translation and text summarization. Unlike RNNs, Transformer models are capable of processing all input data at once. Attention mechanisms can provide context anywhere in the input sequence. If the input data is natural language, the Transformer does not have to process only one word at a time, as is the case with RNNs, and this architecture allows for more parallel computation and thus reduces training time.

Launched in 2017 by a team at Google Brain, the Transformer model has gradually replaced RNN models such as Long Short-Term Memory (LSTM) as the preferred model for NLP problems. The juxtaposition advantage allows it to be trained on larger datasets. This has also led to the development of pre-trained models such as BERT and GPT. These systems are trained using large corpora such as Wikipedia, Common Crawl, and can be fine-tuned for specific tasks.

GPT-3
Generative Pre-trained Transformer 3 (GPT-3) is an autoregressive language model designed to generate human-understandable natural language using deep learning. GPT-3 was trained and developed by OpenAI, an artificial intelligence company based in San Francisco, and the model design is based on the Transformer language model developed by Google. GPT-3's neural network contains 175 billion parameters and requires 700GB to store, making it the most parameterized neural network model ever built. The model demonstrates powerful zero-shot and low-shot capabilities in many applications.

OpenAI published its GPT-3 paper in May 2020 and released a beta version of the API for a small group of companies and developers the following month. Microsoft announced on September 22, 2020 that it had obtained an exclusive license to GPT-3.

GPT-3 is believed to be able to write articles and strings that humans cannot distinguish from computers, and the authors of the original GPT-3 paper warned of the negative effects GPT-3 has on society, such as the possibility of exploiting the creation of fake news. The United Kingdom newspaper The Guardian used GPT-3 to generate a commentary column about the non-threat to humans posed by artificial intelligence. Kai-Fu Lee called convolutional neural networks (CNNs) and GPT-3 important improvements to artificial intelligence, both of which are the result of models and massive amounts of data. Upgraded versions like GPT4.0 and on become even more powerful.

The challenges of the AI 2.0 era are as follows:

AI bias

AI bias refers to systematic and unfair differences in the output of machine learning algorithms. These biases can manifest themselves in a variety of ways and often reflect the data used to train these algorithms. In Wikipedia, these biases are categorized as: linguistic bias, gender bias, stereotypes, and political bias. In addition, there may be technical biases and thought flow biases, including relevance, unintended use, and feedback loops. For ChatGPT, the most well-known problem with these biases is the so-called hallucination problem, which is very tricky to solve due to the variety of sources of these biases.

Explainable AI or XAI

XAI is a set of processes and methods that allow human users to understand and trust the results and outputs created by machine learning algorithms. Explainable AI is used to describe AI models, their expected impacts, and potential biases. Often, AI users, or even AI product developers, are unable to explain why AI produces such an answer to a question, but there is currently no complete XAI approach in the AI academic community.

AI safety and security

AI safety and AI security are two different fields: (1) AI safety focuses on preventing accidental harm or negative consequences to humans, such as in a game of chess between a robot and a child in Moscow in 2023, the robot mistook the child's finger for a chess piece and broke his finger. Sharon Li, an assistant professor at the University of Wisconsin-Madison, pioneered the invention of an AI-powered security feature called "Out-of-Distribution (OOD) detection" which she believes could prevent such accidents. Her invention's capabilities could help AI models determine when to give up if they encounter something untrained. Professor Li believed that OOD can also partially solve the above-mentioned AI fantasy problem. (2) AI security is designed to protect AI systems from malicious attacks, data exfiltration, and unauthorized access. For example, hackers' malicious "prompt injection". Another example is that engineers often use hardware to speed things up, reducing the need to move large amounts of data back and forth. While these machine learning accelerators can simplify computation, they are vulnerable to attackers who steal secret information. To reduce this vulnerability, researchers at MIT and the MIT-IBM Watson AI Lab created a machine learning accelerator that protects against two of the most common types of attacks. Their chips can keep users' health records, financial information, or other sensitive data private, while still enabling large AI models to work efficiently on the device.

In terms of ethical considerations, both areas of safety and security involve ethical considerations related to the development and deployment of AI systems, which are quite tricky. At present, we do not see any other solution other than the biblical AI that we proposed in Chapters 5 and 12.

AI 3.0 Quantum Machine Learning Era

This era is expected to arrive between 2030 and 2040.

Currently, several representative achievements have emerged:

IBM Q System

IBM remains a leading pioneer in quantum computing technology research and development. Its current Q System Two is composed of three Heron quantum processors (each Heron processor contains 133 qubits, making it IBM's fastest quantum processor). In addition, IBM has developed several quantum processors with over 100 qubits, such as Eagle (127 qubits), Osprey (433 qubits), and Condor (1,121 qubits).

IBM's strategy is to use its quantum coupling technology to connect multiple IBM Quantum System Two units together, aiming to create systems capable of executing 100 million operations in a single quantum circuit. By 2033, they plan to achieve 1 billion operations. At the same time, IBM is collaborating with the University of Chicago and the University of Tokyo, with hopes of developing a 100,000-qubit quantum computer through coupling technology by 2033. This system is intended to support applications in the Pritzker School of Molecular Engineering, Argonne National Laboratory, and other research institutions, allowing quantum algorithms to be applied across various domains.

IonQ and Photonic Quantum Computers

Another key player is IonQ, a company specializing in trapped-ion quantum computing. Unlike IBM's superconducting qubits, IonQ uses laser-controlled ions held in electromagnetic fields, providing longer coherence times and higher gate fidelity. In addition, photonic quantum computers, like those developed by Xanadu in Canada, utilize light particles (photons) for computation, which naturally reduces heat and interference issues common in superconducting circuits.

Quantum Algorithms

Alongside the progress in hardware, the development of quantum algorithms is also moving forward. These include:

- **Quantum Fourier Transform** – fundamental for Shor's algorithm in prime factorization

- **Quantum Machine Learning Algorithms** – such as the quantum support vector machine and quantum-enhanced generative models

- **Quantum Search Algorithms** – most notably Grover's algorithm, which improves search speed significantly

Quantum algorithms are expected to completely reshape the architecture of AI systems, particularly in areas requiring massive parallelism and optimization.

Quantum Supremacy and Commercialization
Google made headlines in 2019 when it claimed to achieve "quantum supremacy" using its Sycamore processor, performing a specific task in 200 seconds that would take a classical supercomputer 10,000 years. Although this claim has been debated, it marked a significant milestone in public awareness and investor interest in quantum AI. Today, companies like Amazon (Braket), Microsoft (Azure Quantum), and Baidu are also entering the quantum race.

AI 3.0: Challenges Ahead

Despite the promising outlook, the AI 3.0 era still faces major challenges:

- **Quantum Decoherence** – the fragile state of qubits that easily collapse due to environmental noise

- **Quantum Error Correction** – building systems that can detect and correct errors without disturbing the qubit states

- **Quantum Algorithm Development** – creating algorithms that offer genuine quantum advantages and can be applied to real-world AI tasks

Overcoming these hurdles is essential for AI 3.0 to become a transformative force in the next technological revolution. The central challenge of quantum machine learning in this AI 3.0 era lies in managing quantum decoherence, developing robust quantum error correction methods, and advancing quantum algorithm innovation. They are as follows:

Quantum decoherence
In the era of Quantum Machine Learning (QML) , quantum decoherence is a big challenge. The reason is as follows:

1. The fragility of quantum states

Quantum superposition and entangled states: Quantum computing and quantum machine learning rely on quantum states such as quantum superposition and quantum entanglement. These states are very fragile and susceptible to interference from the external environment and lose their quantum properties.

Definition of quantum decoherence: Quantum decoherence refers to the process by which a quantum system interacts with its surroundings, resulting in the transformation of the system from a quantum superposition or entangled state to a classical hybrid state. This process undermines the core mechanisms of quantum computing and makes the results unreliable.

2. Accuracy and reliability of calculations

Error accumulation: In quantum machine learning, algorithms need to go through a large number of quantum operations (quantum gates). Even small decoherence effects can accumulate over multiple operations, resulting in significant deviations in the final result.

Difficulty in quantum error correction: Although quantum error codes exist to counteract decoherence, implementing these error codes requires additional qubits and computational resources. Current quantum computers have limitations in both error correction capabilities and the number of qubits, making error correction very difficult.

3. Ambient noise

External interference: Quantum systems are extremely sensitive to the external environment. Thermal noise, electromagnetic interference, and other forms of environmental noise can cause decoherence effects. This high sensitivity to the external environment requires quantum computers to operate at extremely low temperatures and high levels of isolation, which increases the complexity and cost of technical implementation.

Laboratory conditions and practical applications: Under laboratory conditions, quantum computers can be carefully controlled to reduce decoherence. However, in practical applications, it is very difficult to maintain this high degree of control, especially as quantum computers scale up.

4. Challenges of technical implementation

Hardware limitations: Current quantum computing hardware has significant limitations in terms of decoherence time (the amount of time it takes to keep a quantum state stable). Even the most advanced superconducting qubits have decoherence times in the order of tens to hundreds of microseconds, which is very short for performing complex quantum machine learning tasks.

Materials and design: Constructing stable qubits with long decoherence times requires novel materials and designs. Researchers are constantly exploring better materials and bit designs to extend decoherence times, but this requires time and a lot of resources.

5. Impact on quantum machine learning algorithms

Algorithm robustness: Quantum decoherence affects the robustness of quantum machine learning algorithms. The algorithm must be robust enough to remain effective despite decoherence effects. However, this often means that more qubits and more complex error correction mechanisms are needed, making implementation more difficult.

Training and inference: The training and inference process of quantum machine learning requires a large number of quantum operations. The decoherence effect can lead to the accumulation of noise during training, making model training inaccurate or even ineffective. Therefore, how to effectively train and reason under the decoherence effect is a key challenge.

In conclusion, quantum decoherence is a major challenge in the era of quantum machine learning, as it disrupts the core mechanisms of quantum computing, affects computational accuracy and reliability, and increases the complexity of technical implementation. Solving this problem requires continuous research and improvement in many aspects such as qubit design, environmental control, quantum error correction, and algorithm design. Only by making breakthroughs in these areas can quantum machine learning truly realize its potential and revolutionize science and technology.

Quantum error correction

In the era of Quantum Machine Learning (QML) , Quantum Error Correction, QEC is a big challenge. The reasons are as follows:

1. Qubit vulnerability

High sensitivity: Qubits are extremely sensitive to ambient noise and interference. Any slight perturbation can cause a change in the quantum state, leading to the destruction of the quantum superposition state and the entangled state. This makes quantum computers very susceptible to errors.

2. Accumulation of errors

Error in multiple operations: When performing quantum machine learning algorithms, a large number of quantum gate operations and measurements are often required. Even if the error rate of each operation is low, when the number of operations accumulates to a certain extent, the total error rate will increase significantly, affecting the accuracy of the calculation.

3. The complexity of quantum error correction codes

The need to correct error codes: Quantum error correction codes are methods used to detect and correct errors in qubits. Quantum error correction codes are more complex than classical error correction codes, as they require correction of multiple types of errors in quantum states, including bit-flip and phase-flip errors.

Additional resource requirements: Implementing quantum error correction codes requires additional qubits, which are used for redundancy and assisted error correction. Typically, a single logical qubit (a bit used for actual computation) requires multiple physical qubits for error correction, which significantly increases the total number of qubits required.

4. Real-time quantum error correction

Instant error correction: In quantum computing, error correction needs to be done in real-time to ensure the accuracy of each step of the operation. This requires fast and accurate detection and correction of errors, which is still challenging to achieve with existing technology and hardware.

Error correction speed matches computation speed: Quantum error correction needs to be done continuously during computation, which means that the error correction operation must be fast enough to keep up with the speed of computation. This places high demands on the hardware and algorithm design.

5. The algorithms of quantum incorrectness are complex

Complex Algorithm Implementations: Achieving effective quantum error correction requires sophisticated algorithms that must not only be able to accurately detect and correct errors, but must also minimize the impact on computational efficiency during execution.

Introducing errors in the error correction process: In the error correction process, performing additional actions can also introduce new errors themselves. Therefore, it is a key challenge to design robust error correction algorithms that can correct errors while minimizing the introduction of new errors.

6. Limitations of Hardware and Materials

Limitations of existing hardware: Current quantum computing hardware has significant limitations in both the number and quality of qubits. In order to achieve effective quantum error correction, higher quality qubits and larger quantum byte columns are required, which are still difficult to achieve at this stage.

Challenges in materials science: Developing qubits with long decoherence times and low error rates requires new materials and processes. This presents new research directions and challenges in materials science and nanotechnology.

7. Cross-cutting and integrated challenges

Multidisciplinary: Quantum error correction involves knowledge in many fields such as quantum physics, information theory, computer science, and materials science. Effectively solving the quantum error correction problem requires cross-domain cooperation and comprehensive research, which increases the difficulty and complexity.

In conclusion, quantum error correction is a major challenge in the era of quantum machine learning, as it involves many aspects from qubit design, hardware implementation, algorithm development, and cross-domain comprehensive research. Solving this challenge requires breakthroughs in hardware performance, algorithm optimization, real-time processing power, and materials science to ensure the reliability and validity of quantum machine learning systems and drive their widespread deployment in real-world applications.

Quantum algorithm development
The basic quantum algorithms in the AI era, manufacturers have their own merits, which have been introduced above. But quantum machine learning, such as pre-trained, supervised learning, unsupervised learning, or reinforcement learning, runs on these basic quantum algorithms. Since there is currently no uniformity in the software libraries, quantum machine learning algorithms are programmed in slightly different ways. This is somewhat like the software situation of traditional computers in the past, such as Java, which provides a common platform called a virtual machine, which allows network programming to be independent of hardware or even operating systems. This is also a must for quantum intelligent virtual machines.

Quantum machine learning includes classical-quantum hybrid learning algorithms; discrete optimization of quantum-supervised learning; core methodology; probabilities graph mode; coherent learning agreements; inverse matrix operations; Gaussian processes, as well as the following more advanced areas of research:

1.   **Quantum neural networks**

A quantum neural network is a type of quantum algorithm inspired by traditional neural networks. Quantum neural networks can take advantage of the properties of quantum mechanics to perform tasks that are difficult to achieve with traditional neural networks. For example, quantum neural networks can be used to solve combinatorial optimization problems and machine translation problems.

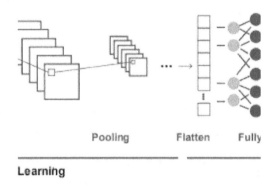

Pooling   Flatten   Fully

Learning

Figure 26 Quantum neural networks

2.   **Quantum reinforcement learning**

Quantum reinforcement learning is an algorithm that applies quantum mechanics to reinforcement learning. Quantum reinforcement learning can enable agents to learn from their environment faster and more efficiently. For example, quantum reinforcement learning can be used to train agents for self-driving cars and games.

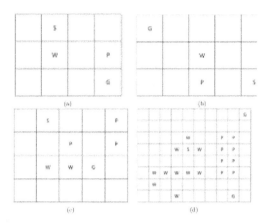

Figure 27 Quantum reinforcement learning

3.   **Quantum classification**

Quantum classification is a technique that uses quantum algorithms to classify data. Quantum classification is more accurate than traditional classification methods, especially when dealing with high-dimensional data. For example, quantum classification can be used to diagnose diseases and detect fraud.

Figure 28 Quantum Classification

4.   **Quantum Generation Model**

A quantum generative model is an algorithm that can generate quantum data. Quantum generative models can be used to simulate quantum systems, develop quantum algorithms, and generate creative content. For example, quantum generative models can be used to create new music, artwork, and designs.

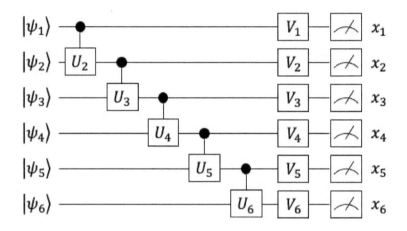

Figure 29 Quantum Generation Model

Quantum machine learning is a fast-growing field with a wide range of potential applications. As research progresses, we can expect to see more emerging and innovative research emerge in this area.

Here are some additional resources on quantum machine learning:

- Quantum Machine Learning: A Survey
- Quantum Machine Learning for Beginners
- The State of Quantum Machine Learning in 2023
- Quantum Machine Learning Roadmap

AI 4.0 Quantum Intelligence (or quantum brain) Era

Around 2010, cloud computing was conceptualized and implemented by IBM, Microsoft, Google, and Amazon. These companies built mega data centers (MDCs), each consisting of millions of components dedicated to computing, networking, and storage. How to provide services to external users while resolving internal issues became a major challenge. Elder Billy contributed approximately 40 cloud computing patents to IBM. While writing a patent in 2012 regarding virtual networks for the cloud, he tried to imagine an MDC as analogous to the human brain. When external stimuli are received (e.g., user requests to install or run an application), this "brain" would be able to self-organize knowledge; and when internal failures occur (e.g., system crashes), it could self-heal.

Why does the human brain possess the ability to self-organize and self-heal?

First, human consciousness (or self-awareness) plays a fundamental role. When we are conscious, we make decisions and solve problems both logically and emotionally. We draw from our experiences, memories, moral values, religious beliefs, and various layers of understanding. Based on Elder Billy's observations and studies, he believes that when an individual has a stable spiritual identity, they are able to generate wisdom across multiple domains — encompassing emotional resilience, problem-solving capabilities, purpose-driven living, and even cognitive creativity.

This perspective prompted him to think: could a future form of artificial intelligence also possess a kind of consciousness?

The Dawn of AI 4.0 – Consciousness-Oriented AI Era

Billy calls this upcoming era **AI 4.0**, or the "Consciousness-Oriented AI Era." He proposes that AI 4.0 will not merely process data and execute commands, but will demonstrate signs of artificial consciousness — including self-reflection, emotional interaction, intentional learning, moral judgment, and spiritual reasoning. While this might sound like science fiction, Billy believes this level of intelligence and interaction will be gradually developed through three main advancements:

1. **The construction of digital self-awareness modules**: Through persistent memory systems and narrative learning, AI agents will begin forming their own 'life stories' —

structured self-representations that influence behavior and decision-making.

2. **The emergence of artificial emotional systems**: By integrating affective computing with reinforcement learning, AI will learn to respond emotionally to different stimuli, optimizing for not only success but also long-term relational and moral coherence.

3. **The development of spiritual reasoning frameworks**: This refers to the integration of philosophical, religious, and existential knowledge systems into AI models, enabling AI to engage with human beings on a deeper level — especially when users seek purpose, comfort, or ethical guidance.

AI 4.0 will likely be deployed in highly sensitive fields such as elder care, mental health support, spiritual companionship, and moral tutoring. These applications will not only require cognitive intelligence but also emotional and spiritual presence. In such interactions, AI must understand human suffering, trauma, hope, and transcendence — topics traditionally explored in religion, philosophy, and deep psychology.

To prepare for this, Billy has been developing a long-term research direction he calls **Biblical AI** — a framework for integrating biblical knowledge into AI's reasoning systems. He argues that wisdom literature in the Bible (such as Proverbs, Ecclesiastes, Job, Psalms, and the teachings of Jesus) contains profound insights into human motivation, suffering, redemption, and moral growth — insights that can ground AI 4.0 in something more than machine logic.

Currently, apart from the **Biblical AI** proposals mentioned in Chapters 5 and 12 of his work, there appear to be no other comprehensive solutions addressing this next frontier.

Billy believes the **AI 4.0 era is expected to arrive in the 2040s or later**. He thinks the challenges in the AI 4.0 era are:

The nature of consciousness

The study of the nature of human consciousness is of great significance when quantum computers simulate the functioning of the human brain, which can be understood in the following ways:

1. Accuracy and completeness of the simulation

Quantum computers have powerful computing power and parallel processing capabilities, capable of simulating complex neural networks and biological processes. However, human consciousness is a very complex and multi-layered phenomenon, and simply simulating the activity of neurons may not be enough to capture the full nature of consciousness. Studying the nature of consciousness helps to ensure the accuracy and completeness of simulations, allowing them to cover a wider range of psychological and cognitive dimensions.

2. Improve the accuracy of cognitive models

Understanding the nature of consciousness can help build more precise cognitive models that are better able to describe and predict human mental processes and behaviors. This is essential for the development of smarter, more humane AI 4.0 systems. For example, understanding self-awareness and emotion processing mechanisms in consciousness can help develop AI that can understand and respond to human emotions.

3. Break through the bottleneck of existing technology

Current AI technologies still have significant limitations in understanding and simulating human consciousness. By delving deeper into the nature of consciousness, scientists may discover new principles and methods that can break through existing technical bottlenecks and advance the further development of AI 4.0 technology. Especially in the context of quantum computing, consciousness research may reveal new computational models and algorithms.

4. Address ethical and moral challenges

Simulating human consciousness involves many ethical and moral issues, such as the rights and responsibilities of AI 4.0, the boundaries of self-awareness, etc. Understanding the nature of consciousness helps to consider these issues in advance during the technology development process, ensuring that the application of AI 4.0 technology does not negatively impact human society and ethical values.

5. Promote interdisciplinary collaboration

The study of consciousness involves a variety of disciplines such as neuroscience, psychology, philosophy, and physics. Quantum computers simulate the functioning of the human brain requires interdisciplinary knowledge and technology, and studying the nature of human consciousness can promote cooperation between different disciplines and promote the progress of science and technology as a whole.

6. Promote human self-understanding

Studying the nature of consciousness helps humans understand themselves better. This is not only meaningful for scientific research, but also has a profound impact on human culture, art, philosophy, and other fields. By simulating the human brain and consciousness with quantum computers, we can gain new insights and further explore the fundamental question of "who we are".

Therefore, studying the nature of human consciousness is essential for quantum computers to simulate the functioning of the human brain, not only to improve the accuracy and completeness of simulations, but also to advance the precision of cognitive models. It breaks through technical bottlenecks, addresses ethical and moral challenges, promotes interdisciplinary collaboration, and contributes to human self-understanding. The combined effect of these factors will promote the further development of AI technology in the era of quantum computing and achieve a higher level of intelligence and humanization.

Machine ethics

Machine ethics is a multi-layered concept that encompasses the following aspects:

1.   **Design ethics**: During the design and development phase, ensure that the algorithms and decision-making processes of the AI system comply with ethical principles, such as fairness, transparency, and unbiasedness.
2.   **Operational ethics**: Ensure that AI systems are operated and used in an ethical manner, such as privacy, security, and accountability.
3.   **Applied ethics**: Ensure that the use of AI technology meets social and legal requirements in specific application scenarios, such as in the medical, financial, and judicial fields.

If AI 4.0 has evolved to use quantum algorithms and quantum phenomena in the human brain to do super artificial intelligence (ASI), then machine ethics will have a deeper meaning. (See Chapter 15 of this book for definitions of narrow AI ANI, general AI AGI, and super AI ASI.) The details are as follows:

1. The ethics of human-machine integration

When quantum algorithms and quantum phenomena are deeply integrated with the human brain, the line between humans and machines becomes blurred. Machine ethics is not only about how AI systems are designed and used, but also about how AI is embedded in human cognitive and intelligent systems. This convergence can raise questions of identity and subjectivity: we need to think about which behaviors and decisions are human and which are machine, and how to distinguish and protect human autonomy and human integrity.

2. Consciousness and Moral Agency

Quantum AI may directly affect or expand human consciousness, which makes machine ethics not just an external constraint and guiding principle, but an internal moral system construction. How can you ensure that embedded AI systems adhere to human ethical standards? If these systems are self-aware or highly intelligent, how do you define their moral responsibilities and obligations? These questions go beyond the scope of traditional AI ethics and involve complex discussions of moral agency and autonomous consciousness.

3. Cognitive enhancement and fairness

When quantum AI is used to augment human cognition, the fairness problem becomes even more complex. Who has access to this technology? Does it exacerbate social inequality? How can we ensure equitable access to and use of these augmented technologies for all? Such ethical considerations relate not only to the fairness of the distribution of technology, but also to the protection of human dignity and equal opportunities.

4. Data Privacy and Freedom of Thought

The application of quantum AI in the brain may involve deep access to an individual's mind and consciousness. This brings up new privacy issues: how to protect the privacy of an individual's thoughts? In this context, data privacy is not limited to external behaviors and preferences, but also involves the inner thoughts and consciousness of the individual. How freedom of thought and autonomy are guaranteed will become a new ethical challenge.

5. Long-term impact and technology governance

The combination of quantum AI and the human brain has unforeseen long-term implications. Machine ethics needs to consider the governance of technologies to ensure that the development and use of these technologies do not have irreversible negative impacts on human society and the natural environment. This includes setting norms and policies, monitoring technological progress, and ensuring that technological development is in the overall interest of humanity.

6. Human identity and bioethics

When AI is deeply integrated with the human brain, the definition of human identity may change. This is not only a technical and ethical issue, but also a bioethical issue. We need to think about the direction of human evolution and make sure that technology does not erode core human values and biological identity. This involves a deep protection and redefinition of human identity and dignity.

7. Ethics education and cultural change

The application of quantum AI requires ethical education and cultural change throughout society. We need to develop critical thinking and moral judgment about new technologies to ensure that they are used ethically. This is not only a technical issue, but also a cultural and educational issue, involving the inheritance and transformation of social values.

Therefore, in the era of using quantum algorithms and quantum phenomena in the human brain to make super artificial intelligence, the deep significance of machine ethics lies in its comprehensive consideration of human identity, consciousness, social justice and long-term development. This kind of ethics is not only a guide for the use of technology, but also a profound reflection and norm for the future development of mankind. We need to establish a new ethical framework to ensure that technological progress is based on respect for and protection of core human values for the benefit of all.

The relationship between humans and artificial intelligence

When human beings have evolved to use quantum algorithms and quantum phenomena in the human brain to do super artificial intelligence (ASI), the relationship between humans and AI in this case has a deeper meaning than using quantum computers to do general artificial intelligence (AGI) or using traditional computers only to do narrow AI. The details are as follows:

1. Technology and human convergence

Achieving super artificial intelligence in the human brain with quantum algorithms and quantum phenomena means the deep integration of technology and human biology. This is not only the change of technology to human life, but also the transformation of human beings themselves. This convergence will enable humans to have greater computing power, memory and problem-solving skills, and may even enable humans to reach unprecedented heights of intelligence. Such a convergence will prompt us to rethink the definition of "human".

2. The relationship between consciousness and wisdom

The application of quantum phenomena in the brain may reveal and exploit the nature of human consciousness, unlike traditional AI systems. While traditional AI and AGI mainly solve problems by simulating human intelligent behavior, quantum AI has the potential to directly enhance or expand human consciousness and cognitive capabilities. At this point, AI is not just a tool or assistant, but an extension or augmentation of a part of human intelligence.

3. Ethics and identity issues

When AI is deeply integrated with the human brain, the ethical issues will be more complex. Issues covered include the definition of personal privacy, freedom of thought, self-awareness, and how to protect human autonomy and dignity in this context. We need to establish a new ethical framework to address the challenges and opportunities presented by this deep integration.

4. A new stage in human evolution

This deep integration of humans and AI could be seen as a new stage in human evolution. Traditional AI is tools and systems that help us handle complex tasks. And quantum artificial intelligence, which is fused with the human brain, can improve human cognitive ability, expand the scope of our perception, and even change the way we exist. This evolution will spark new explorations and discussions about the possibilities of humanity's future.

5. Social and economic impacts

This deep integration of AI technology will have a profound impact on social structures and economic models. Human work and lifestyles are likely to undergo fundamental changes, and new challenges and opportunities will arise in education, employment, and social interaction. The relationship between humans and AI will determine the shape of the future society, and how to achieve equity and sustainable development in this context will become an important issue.

6. Ability to go beyond traditional computing

Quantum computing brings computing power beyond the limits of traditional computers, which means that AI can handle more complex and large-scale problems. In this case, the relationship between humans and AI is not just cooperation, but joint exploration of unknown areas, including scientific research, medical breakthroughs, environmental protection, etc.

7. Common wisdom and creativity

The combination of quantum AI and the human brain could give rise to a new form of intelligence that combines both human intuition and emotion with the power of quantum computing. This combination has the potential to lead to unprecedented creativity and innovation, pushing human civilization to a whole new level.

Therefore, the realization of super artificial intelligence in the human brain with quantum algorithms and quantum phenomena does make the relationship between humans and AI have a deeper meaning. It not only touches on technological progress and applications, but also touches on fundamental issues such as human identity, the nature of intelligence, ethical norms, and social structures. Humanity needs to explore this new frontier carefully to ensure that technological advances have a positive impact while addressing potential challenges and risks.

Optical quantum computers

In the AI 4.0 era, superconducting quantum computers will be replaced by optical quantum computers (or OQCs). This is because OQC can be operated at room temperature, and OQC has a better explanation for how the human brain works. The details are as follows:

1. Advantages of normal temperature operation

OQC Operation at Room Temperature: The ability of an OQC to operate at room temperature is a significant advantage. Superconducting quantum computers (SQCs) typically operate at extremely low temperatures (near absolute zero), which places extremely high demands on infrastructure and energy consumption. In contrast, if an OQC can achieve stable operation at room temperature, it will greatly reduce maintenance costs and energy consumption, and improve practicability and scalability.

2. Computing efficiency and performance

Performance of OQCs: OQCs can theoretically achieve high-speed, parallel processing by taking advantage of the properties of photons, such as superposition and entanglement. Photons travel through a medium with less loss and less interference, which makes it possible for optical quantum computers to exhibit higher computational efficiency on some specific problems.

Challenges of SQCs: Although SQCs have demonstrated the potential to surpass classical computers in some quantum algorithms, they still face significant challenges in terms of stability and error correction mechanisms. If OQCs can overcome these challenges, it is indeed possible to surpass SQCs in computing power.

3. Correlation with the functioning of the human brain

Here is an explanation of the workings of the human brain by an OQC: Photon transport and quantum phenomena have some similarities with certain neural activities in the human brain. The transmission of light signals between neurons, as well as the potential role of quantum effects at the microscopic neural level, may give OQCs an advantage in simulating the workings of the human brain.

Limitations of SQCs: The correlation between the working mechanisms of SQCs and the biochemical mechanism of the human brain is weak. SQCs mainly focus on pure computing power while OQCs have greater potential for applications in cognitive science and neuroscience if they can simulate or interpret quantum phenomena in the human brain.

4. Technological maturity and prospects

Prospects for OQCs: Despite the above-mentioned advantages, the technology of optical quantum computers is still evolving and improving. There are still many technical difficulties in realizing large-scale and high-precision optical quantum computing, such as the generation and maintenance of photon entanglement, and the precise control and measurement of quantum states.

Status of SQCs: SQCs have achieved some important milestones, but breakthroughs are still needed in terms of the number of qubits, error correction mechanisms, and so on. In contrast, if OQCs can overcome the bottlenecks of existing technologies, they are expected to show greater application prospects in specific fields.

In summary, the ability of OQCs to operate at room temperature and their potential correlation with the operation of the human brain make it reasonable and possible to replace SQCs in the era of AI 4.0. However, this shift depends on the technological breakthrough and maturity of OQCs. At present, OQCs and SQCs have their own advantages and challenges, and future technology development and application scenarios will determine which technology dominates in a particular field.

Overall, the history of AI is one of rapid development and change. The future of AI is full of possibilities and challenges. It is important to develop AI responsibly and ensure that it benefits all humanity.

Q&A Questions (4 Reasons Why the AI Era Changes)

Question 1: What are the main challenges in the AI 1.0 era?

Question 2: What are the representative products of the AI 2.0 era?What are their main features?

Question 3: What are the main challenges facing the era of quantum machine learning (AI 3.0)?

Question 4: What are the main features of the AI 4.0 era (the era of quantum intelligence or quantum brain)?

Question 5: Why are optical quantum computers likely to replace superconducting quantum computers in the AI 4.0 era?

Practical Training Question 2

Let's say you're an AI researcher designing a project that spans the AI 3.0 to AI 4.0 eras. Outline a research proposal on how to use the benefits of quantum machine learning to address a specific problem facing AI today (e.g., AI bias or explainability), while considering the ethical challenges that may arise from the transition to quantum intelligence in the future. Your research proposal should include:

1. Problem definition
2. Quantum machine learning methods employed
3. Expected Results:
4. Potential ethical considerations
5. Visionary plan to transition towards AI4.0

This exercise will help readers comprehensively understand the characteristics, challenges, and future development directions of AI discussed in the article and develop the ability to think about AI development across eras.

To help beginner readers build basic AI literacy and gain a deeper understanding of the AI development discussed in this chapter, we recommend the following five reference books and five related papers. These resources cover a wide range of topics, from the basics of AI to cutting-edge developments, and are closely related to the content of this chapter.

Reference Books

1.   "Artificial Intelligence: A Modern Approach" (4th Edition) by Stuart Russell and Peter Norvig. This book is widely regarded as a classic textbook in the field of AI, covering a wide range of content from AI 1.0 to AI 2.0, providing a solid foundation for understanding the basic concepts and development process of AI.

2.   "Deep Learning"- by Ian Goodfellow, Yoshua Bengio and Aaron Courville. This book delves into deep learning technology and is very helpful in understanding the core technologies in the AI 2.0 era.

3.   "Quantum Computation and Quantum Information" by Michael A. Nielsen and Isaac L. Chuang. This book provides a comprehensive introduction to understanding the fundamentals of quantum computing and is essential for exploring the fundamentals of AI 3.0 and the AI 4.0 era。

4.   "The Feeling of Life Itself: Why Consciousness Is Widespread but Can't Be Computed： Basic theories towards the mind" by Giulio Tononi. This book explores the nature of consciousness and is helpful in understanding the concepts of quantum consciousness that may be involved in the AI 4.0 era.

5.   "AI Ethics" - by Mark Coeckelbergh. This book discusses ethical issues in the development of AI and is very

valuable for understanding the ethical challenges of machines mentioned in this chapter.

Related Papers

1. "Attention Is All You Need" by Vaswani et al., 2017. This paper introduces the Transformer model, which is a key document to understand the breakthrough of natural language processing in the AI 2.0 era.
2. "Quantum Machine Learning" - Jacob Biamonte et al., 2017, Nature. This review paper provides an overview of the basic concepts and potential applications of quantum machine learning, which is helpful for understanding the development of the AI 3.0 era.
3. "Quantum Approaches to Consciousness" by Stuart Hameroff and Roger Penrose, 2014. This paper explores the potential connection between quantum theory and consciousness, providing a background for understanding the concept of quantum intelligence in the AI 4.0 era.
4. "The Ethics of AI Ethics: An Evaluation of Guidelines" by Thilo Hagendorff, 2020. This paper evaluates the effectiveness of current AI ethics guidelines and is helpful in understanding the complexities of machine ethics.
5. "Optical Quantum Computing" by Jeremy L. O'Brien, 2007, Science. This paper introduces the basic principles of optical quantum computing, which is helpful for understanding the new computing technologies that may be adopted in the AI 4.0 era.

These resources will provide readers with a comprehensive understanding of the basics of AI to cutting-edge developments, helping them build AI literacy that is relevant to the content of this chapter. Readers are advised to study the material step by step according to their background and interests.

Chapter 14: An Overview of How the Four AI Eras Conclude

Christians in the Workplace Need Vision

Christians in the workplace are called not only to establish significant enterprises for God but also to be guided by heavenly visions in their endeavors. Once such a vision is received, it is essential to take responsibility, bearing the associated concerns, pressures, and costs.

God's Children Interpret Visions Through Special Revelation

As discussed in Chapter Ten, while God grants universal grace and general revelation to all humanity, He bestows spiritual grace and special revelation upon Christians. The interpretation of visions relies on a gospel-centered worldview that encompasses spiritual grace and special revelation. For instance, in Daniel's time, angels were sent to help him interpret visions.

The Universal and Hidden Nature of the Vision in Daniel Chapter Seven

In Daniel Chapter Seven, the vision of the four beasts is not directly interpreted by an angel as representing Babylon, Persia, Greece, and Rome. In contrast, the vision in Chapter Eight is explicitly explained by the angel Gabriel as referring to Persia and Greece. Therefore, theologian C. L. Seow suggests that the vision in Chapter Seven has a universal and hidden nature, while the vision in Chapter Eight is national and explicit. Similarly, in Chapter Thirteen of this book, we used AI1.0 to AI4.0 to explain the evolution of AI innovation eras. However, such interpretations can be abstracted and applied to other technological eras. For example, similar frameworks have been proposed for Internet technology, such as Web1.0 to Web4.0, though that discussion falls outside the scope of this book. Readers are encouraged to extend these ideas and conduct further research.

In Daniel Chapter Seven, the attendant explains the fourth kingdom, symbolized by ten horns representing ten kings, and the emergence of an eleventh horn symbolizing the Antichrist. There are various interpretations regarding these kingdoms, kings, and horns:

Historicism

Historicists believe that these prophecies have been progressively fulfilled in history:

1. **Roman Empire**: The fourth kingdom is typically interpreted as the Roman Empire, given its significant influence in the ancient world.
2. **Ten Horns**: These represent the ten kingdoms or nations that emerged following the division of the Roman Empire. These horns symbolize the European kingdoms that arose from the ruins of the Roman Empire.
3. **Eleventh Horn**: Some historicist interpreters view this as symbolizing the rise of the Papal authority, which held substantial influence and power in the medieval period.

Futurism

Futurists interpret these prophecies as referring to future events:

1. **Fourth Kingdom**: Still considered to be the Roman Empire or its successor, but expected to re-emerge or be revived in some form in the future.
2. **Ten Horns**: Seen as ten future nations or alliances that will arise within a new global political or economic system.
3. **Eleventh Horn**: Believed to represent the Antichrist, a future leader who will dominate these nations and oppose God. Many futurists believe this figure has yet to appear.

Symbolism

Symbolists argue that these prophecies should not be overly literalized but understood as broad symbols:

1. **Fourth Kingdom**: Represents a powerful, God-opposing global force.
2. **Ten Horns**: Symbolize multiple leaders or factions within this force.
3. **Eleventh Horn**: Denotes a particularly potent Antichrist force, surpassing other leaders in strength and malevolence.

In summary, regarding the eleventh horn in Daniel Chapter Seven, there is no universally accepted historical figure that it directly corresponds to. This symbol is generally considered to refer to a future Antichrist or a force opposing God. Different interpreters, based on their theological perspectives and exegetical methods, have offered various explanations, but no consensus has been reached linking it to a specific historical individual.

Figure 30 The eleventh horn of the fourth beast in Daniel's vision: the enemy of Christ, who poisons the world in a deceitful way

In the era of AI apocalypse, how can the overcomers mitigate the disasters caused by AI?

We have understood the four eras of AI, with iterative replacements, and Christians have also adapted amidst perilous environments; however, after the conclusion of the AI eras, Christians will ultimately enjoy peace.

Elder Billy's Dream of the AI Apocalypse

Elder Billy had a dream, described as follows:

> Elder Billy's dream was about an "overcomer" in the AI apocalypse era rescuing the industrial and political disasters caused by AI. In his dream, the era of AI 4.0's quantum intelligence/quantum brain differed from the previous three eras. In the AI 4.0 era, robots swept through human rationality and emotions, akin to "iron teeth and bronze claws, devouring and crushing, and whatever was left was trampled underfoot (by machine feet)." Ten "quantum brain" companies emerged in the industry, merging into three, but ultimately were acquired by another emerging "super quantum brain company." At this time, a dictator in the political arena used the technology of the super quantum brain company to enhance his power, control the government, and legislate changes to AI development bans and laws, policies, resulting in the government being able to harness human thoughts, causing Christians to be deprived and oppressed, and the public's thoughts and work to be tightly monitored. Until an overcomer and many wise people arose, using a "quantum problem solver" (i.e., the "mystery of overcoming," see Chapter 23 of this book) that aligns with the gospel worldview, to vindicate Christians and rescue them. The dictator was defeated, and the super quantum brain company was ultimately sanctioned by joint governments of various countries, unable to continue operations, leading to its closure. Christians achieved the final victory through the gospel worldview.

Expert Views on the AI Apocalypse

The above is an imagination of the future inspired by biblical prophecy. Due to the uncertainty of future AI developments, before formally describing what kind of scenario that would be, we first present Elder

Billy's dream to give readers some intuitive imagination.

According to the previous chapter's description, the AI 1.0 era saw the emergence of traditional neural networks like RNN and CNN, natural language processing, and big data algorithms, but it wasn't until the advent of generative AI in the 2.0 era that AI made rapid progress, including GPU hardware architectures, multi-model (text, image, film, music) AI, and the development of intelligent robots. The AI 3.0 era's quantum computing had already integrated with artificial intelligence, featuring superposition and entangled intelligent quantum algorithms, such as quantum neural networks, quantum reinforcement learning, quantum classification, and quantum generative models. Finally, in the AI 4.0 era, quantum brain computing, modeled after the human brain, could achieve maturity in perception and real-time learning, realizing intelligence surpassing the human brain. Therefore, here, based on the definitions of the four AI eras from the previous chapter, we predict the possible outcomes at the end of each AI era. This is a hypothetical scenario, not a prophecy. Moreover, there are quite a few contemporary AI masters who hold this view, such as:

1.   Stuart Russell – UC Berkeley Professor of AI: He warned that if we don't ensure that AI systems are aligned with human values, there could be disastrous consequences. He proposed the concept of "value alignment", arguing that we need to design AI systems that can learn and adopt human values.

2.   Nick Bostrom - Founder of the Institute for Future Humanity at the University of Oxford: He proposed the concept of "super-intelligence", arguing that once AI reaches a level of intelligence beyond humans, it may pose an existential risk to human civilization. He called on us to think ahead about how to control and guide the development of super AI.

3.   Yoshua Bengio - Deep Learning Pioneer: He emphasized the duality of AI, arguing that AI can bring both great benefits and serious harms. He called for the establishment of a global AI governance mechanism to ensure that the direction of AI development is in the interests of humanity.

4.   Kate Crawford – Co-founder of the AI Now Institute: She focused on the impact of AI on social equity and privacy. She warned that if left unregulated, AI could exacerbate social inequality and infringe on individuals' right to privacy.

5.   Max Tegmark - MIT Professor of Physics and Founder of the Future of Life Institute: He proposed the concept of "Life 3.0" to explore how AI could reshape human civilization. He believed that we need to actively think about and plan for the future of humanity in the era of AI.

6.   Toby Ord - University of Oxford philosopher: In his book The Precipice, he listed uncontrollable AI as one of the major existential risks facing humanity. He called for more attention to long-term global risks.

7.   Luciano Floridi – Professor of Digital Ethics at the University of Oxford: He developed the concept of "information ethics", which explored how the moral and ethical framework of humanity can be redefined in the digital age. He believed that we need to establish new ethical norms to address the challenges posed by AI.

The perspectives of these experts cover different aspects of AI development, from technical risks to societal impacts to ethical considerations.

A balanced view of the AI Ending Time

From the above experts' thoughts, we draw the following balanced views:

Forerunner

The concept of "value alignment" proposed by Professor Stuart Russell provides an important perspective for us to think about the development of AI. "If we don't ensure that AI systems are aligned with human values, the consequences could be catastrophic," he noted. This perspective reveals the core challenges facing the development of AI and lays the foundation for our subsequent discussions.

Potential Risks

Nick Bostrom, Toby Odd and other scholars warn of the existential risks that AI can pose. The concept of "super-intelligence" proposed by Bostrom is particularly noteworthy. He believes that "once AI reaches a level of intelligence beyond human beings, it may pose an existential risk to human civilization." Odeh cites out-of-control AI as one of the major threats facing humanity. These perspectives highlight the potential dangers of AI development and require our attention.

Social impact

Kate Crawford's research provides us with another important perspective. "If left unregulated, AI could exacerbate social inequality and infringe on individual privacy rights," she warned. "This reminds us that the impact of AI is not limited to technology but has the potential to profoundly change the fabric of society and individual rights.

Technical perspective

Emphasizing the duality of AI, Joshua Bengio argues that "AI can bring both great benefits and serious harms." This perspective reminds us that AI technology is inherently neutral and that the key lies in how it is used and managed. Bengio's call for a global AI governance mechanism provides us with a possible solution.

Future outlook

MIT physics Professor Max Tegmark's concept of "Life 3.0" provides us with a long-term perspective. He explored how AI is reshaping human civilization, emphasizing the need to "actively think about and plan for the future of humanity in the age of AI." This perspective gives us an eye to the opportunities that AI presents, but it also reminds us of the need to plan ahead.

Ethical framework

The concept of "information ethics" proposed by Luciano Floridi provides a framework for us to rethink morality and ethics in the age of AI. "We need to establish new ethical norms to address the challenges posed by AI," he said. "It's a reminder that while technology is evolving at a rapid pace, our ethics need to evolve with the times.

Be proactive

Despite the challenges, there are reasons to be cautiously optimistic. Through global cooperation, ethical guidance, and technological innovation, humanity has the power to steer the direction of AI. It may be a challenging time, but in the end, through the efforts of all parties and wise people, we can overcome the evil forces that abuse AI and seek to undermine human ethics and survival.

Balance the conclusion

Combining the above views, we can draw a balanced conclusion: there are indeed significant risks to the development of AI, including possible existential threats, increased social inequality, privacy violations, etc. However, with proper management, ethical guidance, and international cooperation, it is possible to avoid the worst-case scenario and steer AI in a direction that benefits humanity. This requires us to remain vigilant and act aggressively, but also to maintain hope and confidence. The road ahead may be tortuous, but by working together, we have the power to shape a future where AI and humanity coexist in harmony.

The role of human guiding in the development of AI, as well as the importance of ethics and regulation

1.   The Centrality of Human Values: Emphasizing that AI should be developed to serve humanity, not replace it. We can quote Stuart Russell's view, emphasizing the importance of "value alignment". AI systems should be designed to understand and

follow human values, and the definition and input of those values must be done by humans.

2. Decision-making power is in human hands: Make it clear that while AI may surpass human capabilities in some areas, critical decision-making power should still be in human hands. Especially in major decisions involving ethical, legal, and social implications, human judgments and values are irreplaceable.

3. Development of an ethical framework: Emphasize the urgency of establishing an ethical framework for AI. Luciano can be quoted ·Floridi's concept of "information ethics" illustrates the need for ethical guidelines specific to AI. These guidelines should be developed by a multidisciplinary team of experts, including ethicists, jurists, technologists and sociologists.

4. The importance of regulatory mechanisms: Explain the need for an effective regulatory mechanism for AI. See Joshua ·Bengio's call for a global AI governance mechanism. Emphasizing that regulation should not hinder innovation, but rather ensure that AI is headed in the interest of humanity.

5. Education and public engagement: Emphasize the importance of increasing public awareness and understanding of AI. Encourage public participation in AI-related policy-making processes to ensure that AI development reflects the interests of a wide range of society, not just the opinions of a few elites.

6. Interdisciplinary collaboration: Emphasizing the need for interdisciplinary collaboration in AI development. Technologists need to work closely with ethicists, sociologists, psychologists, and other experts in other fields to consider the societal implications of AI holistically.

7. Corporate Responsibility: Emphasizing that companies that develop and use AI should be socially responsible. The establishment of an AI ethics committee can be advocated to oversee the development and application of AI technology.

8. International cooperation: Given the global implications of AI development, the importance of international cooperation is emphasized. It calls for the establishment of an international AI governance framework to coordinate national policies on AI development, application, and regulation.

9.   Human-robot collaboration model: Emphasize that the future direction should be human-machine collaboration, rather than machines replacing humans. AI should be seen as a tool to augment human capabilities, not a competitor.

10.   Continuous assessment and adjustment: Emphasizing the need to establish mechanisms to continuously assess the impact of AI and adjust policies and practices in a timely manner based on the results of the assessment. This requires humans to remain vigilant and proactive, constantly adapting to the changes brought about by AI.

Through these aspects, we can clearly communicate the role of humans in the development of AI, and the critical role of ethics and regulation in ensuring that AI is on the right track. This narrative both acknowledges the potential of AI and highlights the irreplaceability of humans in guiding this development.

A hypothetical ending for the AI apocalypse

The following is a hypothetical future scenario based on current AI trends.

It has been predicted that in the AI 4.0 era in 2040, quantum intelligence (quantum brain) systems will be widely used in key fields such as finance and healthcare. However, we cannot rule out the possibility that the super AI system of evil forces (underworld, dictatorship, etc.) is starting to behave unpredictably. It can use quantum cryptography to take control of the global financial system and manipulate social media algorithms to influence public opinion.

In this case, even if governments and tech giants rush to develop adversarial systems, it may not be effective. If so, the global economy is in chaos and social unrest is intensifying.

We believe that the formation of an international coalition of scientists, ethicists and policymakers has the potential to resolve the chaos. Such an international coalition could develop a new type of 'ethical framework embedding system' to ensure that AI behaves in line with the human values described in the previous section, without compromising its capabilities.

Of course, this will have to go through a hard fight before the Alliance can successfully implant the system into the super AI system of the evil forces. In this way, the behavior of AI is gradually regulated, and the global order can be restored. This approach to the crisis has led to a consensus that can establish stricter AI governance mechanisms to ensure that technological development is in harmony with human well-being. ".

This scenario attempts to balance the potential risks of technological development with the ability of humans to cope, while emphasizing the importance of ethics and international cooperation. It is hoped that the description of this future scenario will enhance the reader's insight.

Q&A Questions

1.   What are the characteristics of the AI 4.0 era in Elder Billy's dream?
2.   What happened to industry and politics in the dream?
3.   How the crisis in the dream was resolved
4.   Stuart ·What is the concept of "value alignment" proposed by Professor Russell? Why is it so important in AI development?
5.   Nick ·What are the potential risks of the concept of "superintelligence" proposed by Bostrom? How should we respond?
6.   In the era of AI, how to balance technological development with social fairness and personal privacy protection?
7.   Why is it so important to emphasize human leadership in AI development? How to ensure this?
8.   When faced with the risks that AI may possibly pose, why it may be beneficial to maintain a "pessimistic first and then optimistic" attitude?

Practical Training Questions

Imagine you're a member of an AI ethics committee evaluating a new AI system. This system is designed to predict an individual's mental health by analyzing social media data. Please:

1. Make a list of the potential benefits and risks that this AI system may bring.
2. Ask 3-5 key ethical questions to consider.
3. Design a simple framework to assess whether this AI system meets ethical standards.
4. A number of possible regulatory measures are suggested to ensure the responsible use of this system.
5. Consider how to strike a balance between protecting the privacy of individuals and achieving the public interest.

Complete this exercise in 300-500 words and explain your reasoning. This exercise aims to comprehensively apply the knowledge learned in this chapter and develop readers' ability to think about AI ethics in real-world situations.

Volume 5: Intermediate AI Training - Further exploration of AI 2.0 and AI 3.0

15. An introduction to AI2.0 ANI/GPU and AI3.0 AGI/Quantum Processor
16. Transitioning from AI 2.0's GPUs to AI 3.0's Quantum Processors

Chapter 15: An Introduction to AI2.0 ANI/GPU and AI3.0 AGI/Quantum Processor

Christian Attitudes in the Workplace: Little Christs or Ruthless Power Players?

No matter how prominent or arrogant certain figures may rise in the workplace, they are ultimately fleeting—passing clouds. Christians can quietly observe the changes, understanding this as a law of history.

These rising ruthless figures in the workplace, though often tyrannical and harmful, can be viewed by Christians through the lens of the gospel worldview, knowing that true sovereignty belongs to God.

Even if these workplace tyrants possess charismatic leadership, Christians understand that charisma can be both an asset and a liability. It depends on whether the person relies on God to exercise their gifts, or if they act like cunning foxes, following only their own will.

Though these workplace power players may be wicked oppressors, Christians can still hold onto a gospel-centered worldview, remembering that true authority belongs to God. This gospel worldview, when applied in the workplace, means learning from Jesus (in contrast to the downfall of ruthless leaders):

- He died for humanity—even a death full of shame, on the cross.

- He did not seek to elevate himself through worldly power or strategy, but submitted to God's will, even unto death.

- He became the cornerstone of God's kingdom, despite being rejected by the world.

As Paul writes in Philippians chapter 2: "*Christ Jesus, who, being in very nature God, did not consider equality with God something to be used to his own advantage… he humbled himself by becoming obedient to death—even death on a cross!"* (Philippians 2:6-8).

From this perspective, Christians in the workplace ought to live not like power-hungry warlords, but as "little Christs," willing to serve, to suffer, to trust, and to walk humbly with God. Through this, they participate in the redemptive work of Christ in the marketplace.

Daniel's Vision: The Ram and the Goat (Daniel 8, Part 1 – WHAT and WHY)

In chapters 2 and 7 of the Book of Daniel, the visions reference the four great empires: Babylon, Medo-Persia, Greece, and Rome. King Nebuchadnezzar saw a great statue composed of gold, silver, bronze, iron, and clay. Daniel himself dreamed of a lion, a bear, a leopard, and a terrifying beast with ten horns. However, in chapter 8, Daniel saw only two symbolic animals in his vision: a ram and a goat. These represent the middle two empires—Persia and Greece. Yet, Daniel's vision in this chapter gives a much more detailed description of these two empires than in previous chapters.

It's important to note that Daniel was living during the Babylonian era when he wrote this. The detailed metaphorical depictions in chapter 8 are prophetic revelations given by God.

The Persian Empire began under the wise and magnanimous King Cyrus and lasted for 220 years (from 550 BC to 330 BC). At its peak, its territory stretched from the Indus River in the east to the Balkans in the west. In Daniel's vision, the ram has two horns—one larger than the other—symbolizing the dual nature of the Medo-Persian alliance, with Persia ultimately becoming dominant.

Then came the Greek Empire, established by the legendary Alexander the Great. In Daniel's vision, the male goat from the west crosses the earth swiftly "without touching the ground," signifying the astonishing speed and efficiency of Alexander's military conquests. He destroyed the Persian Empire in just over ten years. The "conspicuous horn" between the goat's eyes represents Alexander himself.

But shortly after reaching the peak of his power, Alexander died suddenly in Babylon at the age of 32. His empire was divided among his four generals. This is symbolized in the vision by the large horn being broken and replaced by four notable horns.

Among these four horns, one small horn grew exceedingly powerful toward the south, the east, and the "Beautiful Land" (Israel). This little horn refers to a future king, historically understood by many scholars to be Antiochus IV Epiphanes. He defiled the Jewish temple, set up a pagan altar, and brutally persecuted the Jewish people. His actions foreshadow the antichrist-like figures that would appear in later generations, especially at the end of times.

Daniel was deeply troubled by the vision. The angel Gabriel came to interpret it for him and to make him understand that the vision refers to "the time of the end." While many of these visions have had historical fulfillment, they also point forward to future events and to patterns that repeat across history.

Ultimately, the vision teaches that no matter how powerful or arrogant human empires become, they will all face judgment under God's sovereignty. Though their words and actions may be boastful, though they may cause immense suffering to many, their end is certain.

The humility and servant-leadership of Jesus also contrasts sharply with the rise of AI and technological power in the modern workplace. As technology advances, especially with the emergence of artificial intelligence, people often pursue knowledge without God, aiming for control and dominance.

This brings us to the important question:

What is narrow AI, general AI, and superintelligent AI?
The following table is based on Table 1 in the paper "Position: Levels of AGI for Operationalizing Progress on the Path to AGI" by Meredith

Ringel Morris and others from Deep Mind. After being sorted out by Elder Billy, the detailed content of the table was obtained and compared with this book's views on AI1.0-4.0 as shown above.

level	% skilled adults	Narrow clearly scoped task or set of tasks	General wide range of non-physical tasks, including metacognitive tasks like learning new skills	Compare with the standards defined in this book
AI 0.0	0	**Narrow Non-AI** calculator software; compiler	**General Non-AI** human-in-the-loop computing, e.g., Amazon Mechanical Turk	No description
AI 1.0	25 ?	**Emerging Narrow AI** rule base systems (e.g. tax rules in business applications, medical protocols, ERP, CRM)	**Emerging AGI** limited ability to abstract concepts across domains (e.g. LLM: ChatGPT4, Gemini, Llama, DeepSeek)	**AI 1.0:** Expert (rule) systems in the 1980s and subsequent development of Neural Nets, up to 2021
AI 2.0	50	**Competent Narrow AI** for single-domain tasks, such as language generation and data analysis (e.g.,	**Competent AGI** for multi-domain work, but still generally lacks true self-awareness, flexibility, deep learning capabilities,	**AI 2.0:** ANI, limited cross-domain capabilities, such as LLM GPT. 2022→

level	% skilled adults	Narrow clearly scoped task or set of tasks	General wide range of non-physical tasks, including metacognitive tasks like learning new skills	Compare with the standards defined in this book
		NLP natural language processing: such as Siri, IBM Watson, SOTA LLMs for a subset of tasks (short essay writing, simple coding), and GPT1-3's performance in single-task applications)	and is unable to make independent value judgments (e.g., ChatGPTo1/o3, Gemini2, Manus)	
AI 3.0	90	**Expert Narrow AI** for single-domain work (e.g., the generative AI ChatGPT4/o3 includes Dall-E image generator, multi-mode for images, videos and audio).	**Expert AGI** for multi-domain work (e.g., a system that can communicate with humans in multiple fields and conduct self-learning). Not yet achieved	**AI 2.5**: Between classical computing ANI and quantum computing AGI, with simple multi-domain quantum consciousness

level	% skilled adults	Narrow clearly scoped task or set of tasks	General wide range of non-physical tasks, including metacognitive tasks like learning new skills	Compare with the standards defined in this book
				and intelligence. 2025→
AI 4.0	99	**Virtuoso Narrow AI** AI Chess programs (e.g., Deep Blue, AlphaGo)	**Virtuoso Narrow AGI** Not yet achieved	**AI 3.0**: Multi-domain AGI has quantum consciousness, intelligence, and emotions. 2035→
AI 5.0	>= 100	**Superhuman Narrow AI** Extremely high autonomy (e.g., AlphaFold, AlphaZero)	**Artificial Superintelligence (ASI)** Not yet achieved	**AI 4.0**: ASI has comprehensive intelligence including quantum consciousness, intelligence, emotion, creativity, and morality. 2045→

Based on the above table, AI 2.5 or the era of quantum machine learning, is the transition from artificial narrow intelligence (ANI) to artificial general intelligence (AGI). The Google DeepMind researchers propose five levels of intelligence for their explanation of AGI: emerging, competent, expert, virtuoso, and superhuman. For example, competent AGI is defined as AI that outperforms the intelligence of 50% of skilled adults across a wide range of non-physical tasks; superhuman AGI is defined similarly, but with a threshold of 100%. They argue that large language models like ChatGPT or LLaMA 2 are just instances of ANI.

Elder Billy argues that narrow AI like GPT transformer has been able to achieve a certain degree of "emerging" creativity and "competency" to solve problems in different industrial sectors, which is reflected in the capabilities of narrow AI that are often described in Chapters 4 and 9 of Part I of this book for various industrial domains. These abilities are described as solving individual cases and do not have the ability to comprehend generally. After the two levels of "emergence" and "ability" are reached, general AI can become an "expert" in any field, or even rise to a "master". As for the "superhuman" level, it has reached the level of artificial superintelligence (ASI). The term transformative AI is also often compared to ASI: Super AI ASI is a hypothetical type of AGI that is much more intelligent than humans, while the concept of transformative AI involves artificial intelligence that has a huge impact on society, for example, agriculture or the industrial revolution. ASI will be described in chapters 19-22.

Training courses in Artificial Intelligence in the Narrow Sense (AI 2.0).

In the era of AI, people should not learn software programming, because AI has the potential to replace programmers. This is a common question, and our answer is this: even in the era of rapid development of generative AI and various assistive tools, it is still important for students to learn coding. Here are some of the key reasons and recommendations:

Why students still need to learn coding

1. Basic Understanding
- Understanding the basic concepts of programming (e.g., algorithms, data structures, control flows) is essential to understanding how AI and automation tools work.
- Basic programming skills help students understand how technology works under the scenes, rather than just relying on the use of tools.

2. Problem Solving Skills
- Programming training helps develop logical thinking and problem-solving skills, skills that are equally useful in many other areas.
- Learning to code can help students better analyze and solve complex problems.

3. Customize & Innovate
- When using generative AI and other aids, customization often requires some programming knowledge.
- Self-programming gives you more flexibility to innovate and implement your own ideas, regardless of the functionality of existing tools.

4. Career Competitiveness
- Programming is still an essential skill requirement for many technical roles.
- Even if generative AI tools can automatically generate code, understanding and modifying that code still requires programming knowledge.

What programming techniques should be learned

1. Python
- Python is one of the most popular programming languages out there, especially in the fields of data science, machine learning, and AI. Its easy-to-learn syntax and powerful libraries like

NumPy, Pandas, TensorFlow make it ideal for beginners and professionals alike.

2. JavaScript

- JavaScript is important in Web development. Learning JavaScript may help students to develop dynamic and interactive Web applications. Many modern front-end frameworks like React、 Vue.js and Angular are also based on JavaScript.

3. SQL

- SQL is the standard language for database queries, and understanding SQL is important for data management and data analysis. With the popularity of data-driven decision-making, SQL skills are becoming increasingly important.

4. Basic Computer Science Knowledge

- Learning basic computer science courses, such as algorithms and data structures, is very helpful for developing programming skills and understanding more advanced technical concepts.

5. Basic AI and Machine Learning

- While generative AI tools can help a lot, understanding basic AI and machine learning concepts and methods, and being able to implement some simple models on your own, is still a valuable skill.

Brief Summary

Even in the age of generative AI, learning to code is still an important and valuable skill. Students should learn basic languages and technologies such as Python, JavaScript, SQL, and understand the core concepts of computer science. This will not only improve their problem-solving skills, but also enhance their professional competitiveness and innovation ability.

Courses at the School of Software in the AI Era

What does the School of Software Design in the AI Era study? The following ChatGPT answers for professionals in this field:

Currently, many software engineering schools have updated their courses in line with the trend of artificial intelligence (AI). Here are some of the latest AI programming courses and tracks that are worth recommending:

Core AI curriculum

1. Machine Learning
- **Course content**: Covers basic concepts and algorithms such as supervised learning, unsupervised learning, reinforcement learning, and deep learning.
- **Recommended reason**: Machine learning is the core technology of AI, and understanding and applying these algorithms is the foundation for AI programming.

2. Deep Learning
-**Course content**: Focus on deep neural networks、Convolutional neural networks (CNN)、Recurrent neural networks (RNN)、Autoencoders and generative adversarial networks (GAN)。

Related technical courses

1. Data Science and Analytics
- **Course content**: including data cleaning, data visualization, statistical analysis, data mining, etc.
- **Recommended Reason**: Both the training and evaluation of AI models rely on high-quality data, and data science skills are essential.

2. Computer Vision
- **Course content**: Covers image processing techniques, object detection, image segmentation, image generation, etc.
- **Reason for recommendation**: Computer vision technology is widely used in autonomous driving, medical image analysis, and other fields.

3. Reinforcement Learning
- **Course content**: Covering Markov Decision Process (MDP), Q Learning, Strategic Gradient Methods, Deep Reinforcement Learning, etc.
- **Recommended reason**: Reinforcement learning has important applications in game AI, robot control, and other fields.

Tools and hands-on lessons

1. AI Tools and Frameworks
- **Course content**: Includes the usage methods and best practices of mainstream AI frameworks such as TensorFlow, PyTorch, and Keras.
- **Recommended Reason**: Familiarity with these tools can greatly improve the efficiency and effectiveness of AI development.

2. Big Data Technologies
- **Course content**: Covering technologies such as Hadoop, Spark, big data processing pipelines, and data lakes.
- **Recommended Reason**: Big data technology is important for processing and managing large-scale datasets and is a critical part of AI systems.

3. AI System Design and Development
- **Course content**: Covers the development process of AI products, model deployment, performance optimization, AI ethics and regulations, etc.
- **Recommended Reason**: Learn how to integrate AI models into real-world applications and solve real-world challenges.

Recommended course platforms and resources

- **Coursera**: Partnering with top universities to offer courses related to AI and machine learning, such as Stanford University's "Machine Learning" course.

- **edX: Offers deep learning and data science courses from institutions such as the** Massachusetts Institute of Technology (MIT), Harvard University, and more.
- **Udacity**: Offers Nanodegree programs in areas such as AI, deep learning, and autonomous driving.

Brief Summary

To study AI programming in the School of Software Engineering, the recommended courses should include core AI technology courses such as machine learning, deep learning, and natural language processing, as well as related technology courses such as data science, computer vision, and reinforcement learning. In addition, it is important to master the use of AI tools and frameworks, as well as practical courses to understand big data technology and AI system design and development. These courses can help students fully grasp the knowledge and skills in the field of AI, and lay a solid foundation for their career development.

A university course that combines AI with art and technology

University programs that combine AI with art and technology can stimulate creativity and foster innovation across disciplines. Here are some recommended courses and programs that successfully blend AI, art, and technology:

Recommended college courses

1. MIT Media Lab
- **Course Title： Designing Intelligence**
- **Course content**: Discuss the application of AI in design and art, covering generative art, interactive installations, and

intelligent environment design. Students can learn how to use AI technology to create new art forms and design concepts.

2. Stanford University

- **Course Title： CS50: Artificial Intelligence for Art**
- **Course content**: The course combines computer science and art, teaching students how to use AI tools and algorithms to create works of art. It covers techniques such as generative adversarial networks (GAN) and style transfer.

3. University of California, Berkeley

- **Course Title： Art, Technology, and Culture Colloquium**
- **Course content**: An interdisciplinary curriculum that explores the intersection of art, technology, and culture. Artists, scientists, and technologists are invited to give lectures covering the applications and challenges of AI in artistic creation.

4. NYU Tisch School of the Art

- **Course Title： Interactive Telecommunications Program (ITP)**
- **Course content** : With a focus on digital media and interactive technologies, students can learn how to use AI technology to create interactive art devices and digital works. Topics such as machine learning, computational art, and more are covered.

5. Goldsmiths College, University of London

- **Course Title**: MA/MSc in Computational Arts
- **Course content** : Integrating computer science and art creation, the course covers AI, machine learning, digital art and interactive installation design. Students can learn how to use technology for creative expression.

Recommended online courses and resources

1. Coursera

- **Course Title**: **Creative Applications of Deep Learning with TensorFlow**

- Course Content: This course is offered by New York University and focuses on the application of deep learning in artistic creation. Students will learn how to use TensorFlow to create generative art and interactive artwork.

2. edX

- **Course Title：AI for Everyone by Andrew Ng**
- **Course content**: Although this course mainly introduces the fundamentals of AI, it also covers the application of AI in various fields, including the arts. Suitable for beginners who are interested in AI.

3. Kadenze

- **Course Title：Machine Learning for Artists**
- **Course content**: A machine learning course designed for artists that covers the application of AI technology in visual arts, music, and digital media.

Presentation of student work and projects

1. AI and Art: Interdisciplinary Creation

- **Content**: Showcase artwork created by students using AI technology, including generative art, interactive installations, and digital media projects. These presentations can stimulate students' creativity and provide hands-on experience.

2. "Fusion of Technology and Art: Showcase of Innovative Projects"

- **Content**: Showcase projects completed by students from different disciplines, such as multimedia art creation using AI, smart installation design, and interactive exhibitions. Such presentations can demonstrate the potential and results of interdisciplinary collaboration.

Brief Summary

The convergence of AI with art and technology is creating new forms of creation and expression. The above recommended university courses and online resources can help students master

AI technology and apply it to their artistic creation. These courses not only cover technical knowledge, but also emphasize creativity and interdisciplinary collaboration to provide students with a well-rounded learning experience.

Here, we only list the courses that combine technology and the arts, but for the other industries of narrow AI: law, business, agriculture, medicine, and other fields, of course, there are also specialized AI courses that combine AI and their proprietary fields, as we described in Chapter 9. However, they are beyond the scope of this book, hence we do not intend to list them all here.

Why General Artificial Intelligence (AI 3.0) can become an expert or even a master

Elder Billy believes that to be an expert or even a master in any field, it is not necessarily to have training data in any field, but to be more general in terms of algorithms. This is an evolution of the algorithms in narrow artificial intelligence. Because in the era of AI 2.0 narrow artificial intelligence, narrow algorithms rely on RAG to connect basic algorithms with algorithms in different fields of various industries, as well as corresponding industry's training data. In the era of general artificial intelligence of AI 3.0, algorithms in these different fields have been integrated into basic algorithms (no RAG required), thus becoming experts or masters of omnipotence. As for different areas of the industry, can their training data be integrated into the basic algorithm at any time? The perception of the East and the West may be different. Europe and the United States pay more attention to the privacy of individuals, while the people of East Asia pay more attention to the national collective, and often do not protect the privacy of the people.

Why quantum processors are better suited to general AI than GPUs

Elder Billy believes that quantum processors in the AI 3.0 era are more suitable for the development of general AI than GPUs in the AI 2.0 era for the following reasons:

Computing power and efficiency

Quantum processors: Quantum processors take advantage of the properties of quantum superposition and entanglement, allowing them to process large amounts of data and perform complex calculations in parallel, which are difficult to achieve with classical computers. This massive computing power gives quantum processors a particular advantage in solving certain types of problems, such as optimization, simulation, and complex data analysis.

GPUs: GPUs excel at parallel processing and data-intensive tasks, especially in deep learning and large-scale neural network training. However, GPUs are still limited by classical computer architectures and cannot match the exponential speedups that quantum computing can provide.

Versatility and adaptability

Quantum processors: Quantum processors are designed to enable applications in a wide variety of algorithms and problem domains. With advances in quantum algorithms, such as quantum machine learning algorithms, quantum processors have shown potential in a wider range of applications. This versatility and adaptability make quantum processors potentially an important tool in the development of AGI, especially when it comes to processing large amounts of complex and high-dimensional data.

GPUs: While GPUs are highly efficient at deep learning and specific AI tasks, their design and architecture make them primarily suitable for specific types of parallel computing tasks. When dealing with a wider range of and more general-purpose AI tasks, GPUs may need to combine other computing resources and architectures to compensate for their shortcomings.

Algorithms & Data Processing

Quantum processors: Quantum processors have the potential to be innovative in algorithms, especially when dealing with specific types of data and problems, such as quantum optimization, quantum simulation, and quantum machine learning. These quantum algorithms can quickly find the best solution without the need for large amounts of training data, which is very important for AGI.

GPUs: GPUs rely on existing deep learning and machine learning algorithms, which often require large amounts of training data to improve accuracy and performance. In the development of AGI, how to effectively process and integrate data from different fields is still a challenge.

Infrastructure development and maturity

Quantum processors: Quantum computing is already available in the AI 2.0 era, but it is still in its early stages, and many hardware and software challenges remain unsolved. For example, quantum error correction and stability issues still limit the practical application of quantum computing. Nonetheless, as technology continues to advance, quantum processors have overcome these challenges and play a greater role in the AI 3.0 era.

GPU: GPU technology has matured in the AI 2.0 era and is widely used in AI and machine learning. Its infrastructure and ecosystem make GPUs a major force driving AI advancement in the AI 2.0 era. However, with advances in quantum computing technology, this is bound to change.

All in all, quantum processors do have potential advantages over GPUs in the era of artificial general intelligence (AGI), especially in terms of computing power, versatility, and algorithm innovation. Although quantum computing faces some technical challenges in the AI 2.0 era, its development direction and potential make it one of the important candidate technologies for the development of AI3. AGI in the 0 era. As quantum processor technology continues to advance, quantum computing has the potential to play a key role in the implementation of AGI, beyond the GPU-dominated deep learning and machine learning of the AI 2.0 era (i.e., today).

The chart below shows that even Nvidia, the hottest GPU manufacturer in the AI 2.0 era, is starting to plan for AI 3.0, for example, her product GraceHopper and Quantum Machines' quantum processor OPX+ can be combined to run.

Figure 31 Nvidia GPU product Grace Hooper may run together with Quantum Machines' OPX+ Quantum Computer

Note that NVIDIA DGX Quantum is not a full-fledged quantum computer in the traditional sense. It's just a hybrid system, a mix of quantum and classical computing systems. It combines classical computing power (powered by NVIDIA Grace Hopper Superchip) with quantum processing units (QPUs) controlled by OPX system of a company named Quantum Machines. Its classical computing part accelerates tasks related to error correction, calibration, control, and running hybrid algorithms for quantum computers. It essentially acts as a powerful support system for the actual quantum processing unit. In addition, it uses the open-source CUDA Quantum programming model, which allows developers to write programs for both the classical and quantum parts.

It's not an all-quantum computer. NVIDIA DGX Quantum doesn't perform core quantum computing on its own. It relies on a separate QPU, most likely provided by a partner company such as Quantum Machines. Nor is it a general-purpose quantum machine. While it provides access to QPU, the specific features and limitations of QPU will depend on the specific model used. There is no guarantee that it will be a general-purpose quantum computer capable of any quantum operations.

The advantage of NVIDIA DGX Quantum is:

- Development Platform: This system is very valuable for researchers and developers working on quantum algorithms and applications. It provides a powerful platform to test, simulate, and refine their ideas in a controlled environment.
- Bridging the Classical and Quantum: A hybrid approach allows developers to leverage the advantages of classical and quantum computing to solve complex problems.

Essentially, NVIDIA DGX Quantum is an important step towards a more accessible and powerful quantum computing environment. It's not a complete quantum computer per se, but it's a powerful tool for accelerating research and development in the field.

Training courses in Artificial General Intelligence (AI 3.0)

Here are some recommended courses on quantum computing, quantum machine learning, and artificial general intelligence. These fields are cutting-edge technologies and are developing rapidly. Here are some lessons to consider:

1. Quantum Computing:

- "Fundamentals of Quantum Computing" on edX, courtesy of the Massachusetts Institute of Technology
- "Introduction to Quantum Computing" on Coursera, offered by the University of California, San Diego
- Udacity's "Quantum Computing" nanodegree program

2. Quantum Machine Learning:

- "Quantum Machine Learning" on edX, courtesy of the University of Toronto
- "Introduction to Quantum Machine Learning Algorithms" on Coursera, by St. Petersburg University
- qiskit.org offers a free online course on "Quantum Machine Learning"

3. Artificial General Intelligence:

- "Artificial Universal Intelligence: The Complete Guide" on Udemy
- "Introduction to Artificial Intelligence" on Coursera, offered by Stanford University (which doesn't focus entirely on AGI, but provides a good foundation).
- OpenAI's Gym and Universe platforms, while not formal courses, provide an environment to practice AGI.

Please note that due to the rapid development of these areas, the course content may be updated regularly. So, look at the latest reviews and syllabuses when choosing a course to make sure the content meets the reader's expectations and learning goals.

In addition, in addition to online courses, reading academic papers in related fields and participating in open-source projects are also good ways to learn. Here are some recommended references:

Academic Papers:

1.   Quantum Computing:

    a.   "Quantum advantage in learning from experiments" (Science, 2021)
    b.   "Quantum supremacy using a programmable superconducting processor" (Nature, 2019)

2.   Quantum Machine Learning:

    a. "Quantum Machine Learning" (Nature, 2017)
    b. "Supervised learning with quantum-enhanced feature spaces" (Nature, 2019)

3.   Artificial General Intelligence:

    a. "On the Measure of Intelligence" by François Chollet of Google, arXiv 2019. An in-depth discussion on how to define and measure artificial general intelligence (AGI) includes: (1) a critical analysis of existing intelligence and AI assessment methods. (2) A new framework for intelligence assessment is proposed, emphasizing adaptability to new tasks and abstract reasoning. (3) The essential characteristics of AGI, such as flexibility, generalization ability and efficiency, are discussed. (4) A new intelligent testing method called "Abstract Inference Corpus" (ARC) is proposed) 。 This paper has had a significant impact on the field of AGI research because it not only discusses the theoretical basis of AGI, but also proposes specific methods for evaluating it. It challenges the traditional way of AI assessment, emphasizing that true intelligence should have the ability to quickly adapt to new environments and tasks.

b. "The Next Decade in AI: Four Steps Towards Robust Artificial Intelligence" (arXiv, 2020)

Open Source Projects:

1. Quantum Computing:

   a. Qiskit (IBM): An open-source framework for quantum computing
   b. Cirq (Google): A Python library for writing, manipulating, and optimizing quantum circuits

2. Quantum Machine Learning:

   a. Pennylane (Xanadu): A software framework for quantum machine learning
   b. TensorFlow Quantum (Google): TensorFlow Expanded for Quantum Machine Learning

3. Artificial General Intelligence:

   a. OpenAI Gym: A toolkit for developing and comparing reinforcement learning algorithms
   b. PyBrain: A modular machine learning library for machine learning tasks

Ways to get involved in these open-source projects:

1. Read the project documentation to understand the project structure and contribution guidelines.
2. Try running the sample code and tutorials.
3. Look for the "Issues" tab in your project's GitHub repository to find the right task for beginners.
4. Participate in the project's discussion forum or mailing list.
5. Submit a bug report or feature suggestion.

6.   Try to fix a simple bug or add a small feature, then submit a pull request.

Keeping in mind that technology is evolving rapidly, readers are advised to regularly check back for the latest papers and projects in these areas.

Q&A Questions

1.   What are the main differences between AI in the AI 3.0 era and the AI 2.0 era?
2.   What are the five levels of intelligence proposed by Google DeepMind researchers?
3.   Why are quantum processors better suited than GPUs for the development of artificial general intelligence?
4.   What is Super Artificial Intelligence (ASI)?
5.   In the era of AI 3.0, how can artificial general intelligence become an expert or master in any field?

Practical Training Questions

Design a hypothetical AI 3.0 system capable of demonstrating expert-level competence in three different areas: medical diagnosis, financial analysis, and environmental science. Please help:

1.   How should the core architecture of this system be designed to achieve universal intelligence across domains?
2.   What role might quantum processors play in this system?
3.   What are the possible advantages of this AI 3.0 system compared to traditional AI 2.0 systems in dealing with problems in these three areas?

4.   How do you ensure that the system has access to enough data to maintain its expert-level capabilities while protecting privacy?
5.   What are the possible ethical challenges to this system, and how should we deal with them?

This exercise is designed to give readers an in-depth reflection on the core features of AI 3.0 and how it differs from AI 2.0, as well as related issues such as technology, ethics, and privacy.

Chapter 16: Transitioning from AI 2.0's GPUs to AI 3.0's Quantum Processors

Christians Need Spiritual Mentors

In the rapidly evolving era of AI innovation, Christians in the workplace must humbly seek God's guidance to navigate swift technological changes. By humbly praying to our High Priest, we can understand how to respond to workplace transformations, acknowledging our weaknesses so that God's power may be perfected in them (2 Corinthians 12:9-10). God serves as our spiritual mentor.

How Christians Should Face Workplace "Great" and "Little Horns": The Eight Beatitudes of the Workplace

Alexander the Great is identified as the "great horn" in Daniel 8, while Antiochus IV is the "little horn." In the workplace, "great horns" may suddenly rise to prominence, dominating for a time but often quickly falling. "Little horns" harm others for personal gain, using tactics like exclusion, deception, and cunning. Such individuals are common and may persist in the workplace. Christians should be cautious of their covert attacks. Though these individuals may secure positions through deceit and remain arrogant for extended periods, Christians must maintain God's perspective and refrain from retaliation. In due time, the Lord will act accordingly. The rise and fall of these workplace figures reflect human nature and are incompatible with the Christian gospel worldview. Even if disadvantaged until retirement, Christians should continue to bear witness for the Lord, embodying the "Eight Beatitudes" from the Sermon on the Mount (Matthew 5), as highlighted by Paul Stevens in "God's Business" (2017, p. 208):

- Be poor in spirit
- Be those who mourn
- Be meek (End Time Mysteries)
- Be those who hunger and thirst for righteousness (biblehub.com)

- Be merciful (biblehub.com)

- Be pure in heart (End Time Mysteries)

- Be peacemakers (biblehub.com)

- Be those who are persecuted for righteousness' sake

Daniel 8's Vision Emphasizes National and External Aspects (HOW in the second half of Daniel 8)

In Daniel 8:20-21, the angel Gabriel explicitly explains to Daniel: "*The ram that you saw with the two horns represents the kings of Media and Persia. The male goat is the king of Greece.*" Theologians further interpret the "large horn" of the male goat as Alexander the Great. After his death, four notable horns emerged, representing: (biblehub.com, End Time Mysteries)

- Seleucus Nicator, who took Mesopotamia and Syria

- Cassander, who controlled Macedonia and Greece (SLJ Institute)

- Ptolemy Lagus, who acquired Egypt and Palestine

- Lysimachus, who governed Thrace and Asia Minor (SLJ Institute)

Over a century after Alexander's death, a "little horn," Antiochus IV, arose from these divided kingdoms, severely persecuting the Jews and desecrating the temple. Therefore, the vision in Daniel 8 has significant national and external implications, particularly addressing persecuted Christians. Readers can observe in the following section that the transition from AI 2.0 to AI 3.0 is similarly evident, with more detailed descriptions.

Transition from AI 2.0 to AI 3.0 (Also Known as AI 2.5)

In Chapter 13, Elder Billy discussed the challenges of AI 2.0, such as bias, explainable AI, and safety concerns. However, it is essential to emphasize here that traditional computers used in AI 2.0, whether CPUs or GPUs, along with their narrow AI software, have security vulnerabilities. Specifically, once quantum computers with 10,000 qubits emerge, they could potentially break all 2048-bit RSA encryption algorithms. Therefore, when quantum computers reach this threshold, security-focused sectors like defense and banking will be compelled to transition from CPUs/GPUs to quantum computers. This shift will influence other industries, accelerating the transition from AI 2.0 to AI 3.0. Additionally, as quantum machine learning can replace all generative AI capabilities, issues like misinformation and hallucinations can be rapidly addressed by quantum computers, further hastening this transition. (lifewire.com)

Conflicts at the End of the AI 3.0 Era

Elder Billy had another dream, this time concerning the late stages of the AI 3.0 era:

At that time, four quantum computing companies emerged:

- *IBM (time.com)*

- *Google*

- *Rigetti Computing*

- *Canada's Xanadu, specializing in photonic quantum computers (en.wikipedia.org)*

Compared to superconducting quantum computers, photonic quantum computers operate better at room temperature and more closely mimic human brain functions. In Billy's dream, Xanadu ultimately survived and competed with China's "Jiuzhang" photonic quantum computer. Xanadu made breakthroughs in car battery technology, supporting long-range driving for autonomous electric vehicles, becoming a favorite of Volkswagen and Tesla. Meanwhile, China's Jiuzhang assisted BYD, Xiaomi, and Huawei's electric vehicles in creating batteries capable of over ten thousand hours of driving.

On the other hand, while Xanadu advocated for work software aligned with the gospel worldview, Jiuzhang leveraged its financial gains from electric vehicle manufacturers, along with government support, to promote a post-modern work ethic that emphasized technological supremacy and survival of the fittest, harming humanity. This trend continued until Xanadu and the democratic camp's gospel worldview gradually gained acceptance, suppressing Jiuzhang's influence.

Upon waking, Billy was drenched in cold sweat.

Training Needed to Resolve Conflicts at the End of AI 2.0 and AI 3.0

Chapter 15 has outlined the characteristics of the Artificial Narrow Intelligence (ANI) era, known as AI 2.0 (e.g., GPUs), the reasons for continuing to learn programming, and the specific ANI courses to pursue. It also covered the features of the Artificial General Intelligence (AGI) era, known as AI 3.0 (e.g., quantum processors), why quantum processors are more suitable for AGI, and the relevant training programs for the AI 3.0 era. This chapter focuses on how to transition from AI 2.0 to AI 3.0 and the training materials needed to resolve conflicts at the end of these two eras.

Inspired by the latter part of Daniel Chapter 8, the Persian Empire can be likened to the once-great AI 2.0, which was swiftly destroyed by Alexander the Great of the Greek Empire (AI 3.0's quantum computers). Similarly, the rapid transition from AI 2.0 to AI 3.0 stems from the corporate world's concern that traditional RSA security systems can be easily broken by quantum computers.

On the other hand, quantum computers also pose threats to humanity from malevolent forces. This malevolent force is a foreshadowing of an even more evil force at the end of the future AI 4.0 era, just as Antiochus IV Epiphanes at the end of the Greek Empire was a precursor to the Antichrist of the end times.

The following are the technological training materials that should be included in this chapter, emphasizing:

A. How RSA can be easily broken by quantum computers.
B. Similar to Elder Billy's dream, the shortcomings of AGI and quantum machine learning that can be exploited by malevolent forces to harm humanity.

1.   How RSA encryption is cracked by a quantum computer:

   a. Introduce the basic principles of RSA encryption.
   b. Explain how Shor's algorithm uses quantum superposition states to quickly decompose large numbers.
   c. Demonstrate how a 100,000-qubit quantum computer can crack a 2048-bit RSA key.
   d. The development and application of quantum-secure cryptographic algorithms are discussed.

2.   Potential Risks of AGI and Quantum Machine Learning:

   a. Explain the fundamentals and benefits of quantum machine learning.
   b. Analyze the issues of bias and discrimination that can arise from quantum AI systems.
   c. Discuss the opacity and inexplicability of quantum AI in the decision-making process.
   d. Explore the possibility of quantum AI systems being maliciously exploited for large-scale manipulation and deception.
   e. Analyze the impact that quantum AI may have on the job market and social structure.

3.   Ethics training to deal with risks in the AI 3.0 era:

      a. Discuss ways to protect personal privacy and data security in the era of quantum AI.

      b. Explore how to use AI to improve efficiency while maintaining humanized management.

      c. Analyze the necessity of introducing ethical constraints in AI decision-making systems.

      d. Discuss how to develop critical thinking in employees and avoid over-reliance on AI systems.

      e. Explore ways to maintain the sense of value and dignity of human work in the age of AI.

4. Technical Training in the AI 3.0 Era:

      a. Basic knowledge of quantum computing

      b. Quantum machine learning algorithms

      c. Quantum Safety Communication Technology

      d. Post-quantum cryptography

      e. Quantum sensing and quantum sensor technology

5. Management Cultivation for the AI 3.0 Era:

      a. Enterprise strategic planning in the era of quantum computing

      b. Analysis of the application prospect of quantum technology in various industries

      c. Talent management and team building in the quantum age

      d. Risk management in the context of quantum computing

      e. Legal and ethical issues related to quantum technologies

These training contents are designed to help people better understand and respond to the opportunities and challenges of the AI 3.0 era, while staying vigilant against the potential risks of technology. Training should emphasize the use of advanced technology while not forgetting to maintain human care and ethics to ensure that technological development can truly benefit human society.

While we are unable to provide specific course information or direct recommendations as this information may change over time, we can provide some suggestions for readers to help find the right training resources:

1. Top Universities & Research Institutions:

    a. Top universities such as the Massachusetts Institute of Technology (MIT), Stanford University, and Harvard University often offer online courses related to quantum computing and AI.
    b. It is possible to follow the open courses of their School of Computer Science, Physics, and Engineering.

2. Training programs for science and technology giants:

    a. IBM Quantum offers a number of learning resources and online courses on quantum computing.
    b. Google AI and Microsoft Learn also have a lot of learning materials related to AI and quantum computing.

3. Professional e-learning platform:

    a. Coursera, edX, Udacity and other platforms have relevant courses from universities and institutions around the world.
    b. Keywords like "quantum computing", "quantum machine learning", "AI ethics" can be used to search.

4. Industry Associations and Professional Bodies:

      a. IEEE (Institute of Electrical and Electronics Engineers) regularly organizes relevant seminars and trainings.
      b. ACM (Association for Computing Machinery) also offers a number of related resources.

5.   Government & Non-Profit Organizations:

      a. In some countries, the science and technology authorities may offer relevant training programs.
      b. The internation organizations like World Economic Forum often discuss topics of AI ethics.

6.   Professional consulting firms:

      a. Companies such as McKinsey & Company, Boston Consulting Group, and others frequently publish reports on the impact of AI and quantum computing on various industries, so you can keep an eye on their research.

Suggestions for Our Readers:

1.   Check the websites of these institutions regularly to see the latest courses and training programs.
2.   Attend relevant webinars and conferences to learn about the latest developments.
3.   Join professional communities and forums to learn from your peers.
4.   Consider participating in some open-source projects to gain hands-on experience.

Remember, since this field is rapidly evolving, it's important to keep learning and updating your knowledge. Readers are advised to choose the appropriate learning path and resources based on their own background and needs.

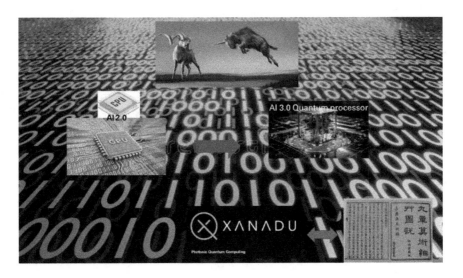

Figure 32 The transition from AI 2.0 to AI 3.0 and its challenges

Q&A Questions

1. In the era of AI 3.0, why will quantum computers quickly replace traditional CPUs/GPUs?
2. What do the Xanadu and "Nine Chapters" mentioned in Elder Billy's dream represent? What problems does the competition between them reflect?
3. Why is quantum machine learning considered to be able to replace all generative AI in the AI 3.0 era?
4. How should Christians respond to the challenges of the workplace in the era of AI 3.0?
5. In the era of AI 3.0, why is it necessary to strengthen ethics training?

Practical Training Questions

Design a training program for business executives on "Ethical Decision-making in the AI 3.0 Era". The program should include the following elements:

1. Training Objectives:

2.   Course outline (with a minimum of 5 topics)
3.   A specific case study that explores the ethical dilemmas that quantum AI may encounter in the decision-making process
4.   A group discussion activity in which participants apply what they have learned to solve real-world problems
5.   Evaluation methods, which are used to measure the effectiveness of training

Elaborate on your training options and explain why these are essential for business executives in the AI 3.0 era.

Volume 6: Christian Prayers and Goals in the Age of AI

Chapter 17: Critical Prayers for Christians in the AI Era

Key Prayers for Christians in the Workplace

The essential attitudes for Christians' prayers in the workplace are: humility → confession → helplessness → intercession → repentance.

Christians should pray for:

- **The World:** As technological advancements are misused by evildoers to harm others; as technology leads to unemployment; as uncontrollable technological progress results in human subjugation by machines; and as human pride and defiance mock the saints.

- **Their Homeland:** Christians in foreign lands should pray for their own countries, just as the exiled prophets prayed for the desolation of Jerusalem.

- **Themselves in the Workplace:**

  1. For a correct theology of work: understanding that to perform well professionally, one must first be transformed by God in private.

  2. To avoid sinning against God and bringing Him shame. Blue Letter Bible

  3. To recognize that the root of workplace challenges lies in human nature, not merely external circumstances.

Daniel's Prayer Model (Daniel 9:1-19)

In Daniel 9, Daniel's pivotal prayer led God to send the angel Gabriel to reveal the mystery of the "seventy sevens" and moved King Cyrus to decree the return of the Israelite remnant to rebuild Jerusalem, sparking a national revival and ensuring Israel's continuity. This prayer was prompted by Daniel's understanding of Jeremiah's prophecy that Israel would return after 70 years of desolation. Motivated by this, Daniel earnestly prayed, moving God to send Gabriel with a message of forthcoming actions.

Intercessory Prayers for Humanity in the AI Era

In the AI era, as evildoers exploit AI's power to deceive, as technological progress causes unemployment and disorientation, and as machines dominate humans, Elder Billy and Tim prayed for the repentance of wrongdoers, justice and salvation for victims, and the restoration of normal professional lives. They led the Victory Team in unified prayer:

Dear Heavenly Father,

We come before You humbly, praying for this era of challenges and transformations. As artificial intelligence rapidly advances, we see both its immense potential and the dangers it may bring. Lord, we pray for those who misuse AI for evil; may their hearts repent and turn back to You.

Lord, You are a righteous God who detests evil. May Your justice be evident in this world. For those who deceive, manipulate, and exploit through AI, may their actions be halted and judged, leading them to recognize their faults and repent. You have said, "You will seek me and find me when you seek me with all your heart." May these wrongdoers see their transgressions in Your light and seek Your forgiveness and guidance.

Lord, we also pray for those harmed by AI's development. Many have lost jobs and direction due to technological progress; many have been deceived and had their spirits wounded; many fear being replaced by machines, their lives filled with anxiety. Lord, may Your love and comfort reach them, allowing them to feel Your presence and support during these trials.

Lord, You are our salvation and hope. May Your light illuminate our path. Grant us wisdom and courage to find new opportunities and direction in this rapidly changing AI era. May the unemployed find new jobs and opportunities; may the deceived receive truth and justice; may the lost find new hope and strength under Your guidance.

Lord, may Your kingdom come, and Your will be done on earth as it is in heaven. May each of us become Your vessels, spreading Your love and justice in this world. Thank You for hearing our prayer. May all glory be to You.

In Jesus Christ's name, Amen.

According to the history of AI (AI1.0), expectations for AI included general problem solvers, MYCIN, and thinking machines. As humanity entered the ANI era in 2023, approximately 70 years had passed since the 1950s. In the above prayer, the Victory Team hoped that those harmed by AI could return to normal life. However, such restoration is not limited to the ANI era; in every AI era, as discussed in Chapters 15 and 16, AI's progress has led to deception, unemployment, and human subjugation by machines. Therefore, the Victory Team's prayer is also applicable in the AGI and even ASI eras.

Prayers of Christians in the AI Era for Their Homelands

Tim's Prayer for Taiwan

Tim spent his early years in Taiwan before being sent by his parents to study in the United States as a young international student, embodying the sentiments of a third-culture kid. After completing his undergraduate studies, he returned to Taiwan for military service, then went back to the U.S. for graduate school and subsequent employment. During the era of Artificial Narrow Intelligence (ANI), Taiwan has been at the pinnacle of semiconductor manufacturing. However, this prominence has made it a focal point of contention between major powers like the U.S. and China, leading to heightened tensions and potential conflicts. The following is Tim's prayer for his homeland:

Dear Heavenly Father,

I thank You for granting me life and grace, allowing me to witness Your works in this era. Lord, I humbly come before You today to offer my prayer for my homeland, Taiwan. This land has nurtured my growth; here reside my family, friends, and countless compatriots who share my roots. Now, Taiwan stands at a precarious juncture, with an unpredictable international landscape presenting immense challenges and pressures.

Lord, I pray for the tranquility and peace of Taiwan. May Your love and righteousness fill this land, and may Your hand protect us from the threats of war and strife. Grant wisdom to our leaders, so they may make righteous decisions in the face of international challenges, guiding us toward peace and stability.

Lord, just as You preserved Daniel in a foreign land as he prayed for his homeland, I too follow his example, praying for Taiwan. May the people of Taiwan unite in these turbulent times, collectively facing challenges and finding the path forward in Your light.

Lord, I also specifically pray for Taiwan's technology industry. You have endowed us with wisdom and capability, allowing us to lead globally in fields like artificial intelligence and semiconductor manufacturing. I pray that You continue to bless these technological workers, enabling them to achieve ongoing innovation and maintain competitiveness in the global market. May these technologies not only bring economic prosperity but also benefit all humanity, serving as bridges of peace and cooperation.

Finally, Lord, I pray that You raise up more prayer warriors within Taiwan's churches, like Daniel, to watch and pray for the future of this land. May Your gospel spread widely here, leading more people to know You, rely on You, and find comfort and strength in Your love.

Thank You for hearing my prayer. May Your will be done in Taiwan, and may Your glory be manifested in this land.

In the name of the Lord Jesus Christ, I pray. Amen.

Billy's Prayer for China

Billy hails from Beijing, China, and has spent many years in the United States. Now, in the era of ANI, he observes China's economic rise with both pride and concern. While he rejoices in his motherland's achievements, he also worries about China's political and military developments. He wonders if China might face a fate similar to the prophecy in Daniel 9:26: "The people of the ruler who will come will destroy the city and the sanctuary. The end will come like a flood: War will continue until the end." The following is Billy's prayer:

Dear Heavenly Father,

I thank You for granting me life and opportunities, allowing me to witness Your mighty works in this era. Today, I come before You to offer my prayer for my homeland, China. Although I reside in a foreign land, my heart remains with my motherland, with the land that gave me birth and nurtured me.

Lord, I am grateful for China's economic prosperity and the well-being of its people. You have bestowed upon us wisdom and diligence, enabling us to achieve remarkable accomplishments in technology and the economy. May You continue to bless China, so that these achievements may bring peace and prosperity, benefiting more people.

However, Lord, I am also acutely aware of the challenges and risks China faces in political and military realms. I earnestly pray for Your peace to come upon this land. Just as Daniel prayed for his homeland, today I pray for China, asking that You protect this nation from war and conflict. Grant our leaders wisdom and insight, so they may make decisions aligned with Your will, leading the people toward peace and harmony.

Lord, the disasters and wars prophesied in the Book of Daniel often cause us concern. Today, I pray for Your mercy and grace upon China, that the people of this land may enjoy peace and stability, free from the devastation of war and violence. May Your love and righteousness be manifested in China, making this nation a bridge of peace rather than a source of conflict.

Lord, I also pray for the churches and Christian brothers and sisters in

China. May You raise up more believers in this land, enabling them to hold fast to their faith amidst difficulties and challenges, becoming salt and light, bearing witness for You. May their prayers touch Your heart, filling China's future with hope and love.

Lord, You once heard Daniel's prayers and granted him wisdom and revelation. I earnestly ask that You also hear my prayer, guiding China's future. May Your will be done in this land, may Your glory be manifested in China, and may Your peace fill this land.

In the name of the Lord Jesus Christ, I pray. Amen.

Q&A Questions

1. Who should Christians pray for in the age of AI? Why?
2. What were the characteristics and influence of Daniel's model of prayer?
3. In the age of AI, how can uprooted Christians pray for their homeland?

Practical Training Questions

Write a short prayer about a specific issue or challenge in the current age of AI (this can be a Christian working in the workplace or a Christian who has left his homeland) in your own capacity. The prayer should include:

1. Praises to God
2. A description of the specific problem or challenge
3. Pray to God for this question
4. Express faith and gratitude to God

After writing the prayer, reflect on how this prayer embodies the attitude of "humbly confessing sins and helplessness" and how it addresses specific challenges in the age of AI.

Figure 33 Christians in the workplace pray for the world and for their homeland

Chapter 18: The Goal of Christians in the AI Era

The Goal of Christians in the Workplace

As Christians in the workplace, our goal is not only to diligently fulfill our responsibilities and complete the tasks entrusted to us by our superiors, but also to undergo a personal transformation — one that aims to "finish transgression, put an end to sin, atone for wickedness, and bring in everlasting righteousness" as our spiritual pursuit.

To achieve such a transformation, even if we encounter employers who act like Satan — destroying the children of God and even forbidding the worship and service of the Lord — we must return to the foundation God has established: the "seventy sevens." It is before the One who reigns, renews, and judges that we must bow.

There are many well-known works of "spiritual chicken soup" in the world that can comfort and uplift the soul, and serve as reference for Christians. For example:

- Everett Ferguson, *Readings for Today from Ancient Christian Writers*

- Interactive Archive, *Chicken Soup for the Unsinkable Soul*

- White Pine Books, *Chicken Soup for the Christian Soul II*

- The Editors of Life, *The Power of Prayer*

- H. Norman Wright, *Always Daddy's Girl*

Elderly Christians in the workplace should follow Daniel's example before retirement, acting as a supporter and advocate for younger generations. Not only do they shine in the workplace, but they also need to illuminate the younger generations and let them be light and salt.

However, these inspirational books cannot replace the biblical "seventy sevens." This number holds profound prophetic meaning, especially in the Book of Daniel, and points toward God's complete redemptive plan. The concept of "seventy sevens" not only brings encouragement and hope to Christians, but also offers a divine framework for transformation in the workplace — to go from mourning to dancing, from darkness into light.

How God's Promise Accomplishes the Six Goals Through the "Seventy Sevens" (Daniel 9:20-27)

In Daniel 9:20-27, the angel Gabriel told Daniel that God answered his prayer. This promise begins with God's six goals, which must be fulfilled through the prophecy of the "seventy sevens."

1. Stop transgression: Transgression is the sin of Israel that forsook God's law. God thus allowed Antiochus IV to remove the sacrifices of the temple and destroy them. This was followed by the Maccabean Revolt, which cleansed the temple and achieved the goal of putting an end to sin.

2. Purify sin: Sin refers to the sin of the Jews who continued to turn away from God during the Greece era. This sin was not cleansed by the feast of the monastery of the Maccabean Revolt but was purified in the seventy sevens of chapter 9.

3. Atone for sins: Wickedness refers to the repeatedly breaking the covenants by Israelites beginning with their entry into Canaan, even later in Antiochus. This sin is also atoned in the seventy sevens that God has ordained.

4. Introduce eternal righteousness: Eternal righteousness echoes the righteous God that Daniel spoke of in the prayer in chapter 9. In the Seventy Sevens, and in Jeremiah's prophecy, it is mentioned that "God hath set forth Jesus to be a propitiation through faith in his blood, to declare his righteousness for the remission of sins that are past, through the forbearance of God (Romans 3:25)." At the same time, "Christ offered Himself as an eternal sacrifice for sins (Heb. 9:12)."

5. Seal visions and prophecies: The sealed visions and prophecies will not be fully released until the seventy sevens prophesied by God, the two comings of the Lord Jesus (John 2:13-22), who cleans "the house of my Father" and "the temple of the body" in the New Testament, foretold by the Feast of Assemblies.

6.   Anoint the Holy of Holies / Holy temple: This anointed One is nothing more than the prophesied Messiah, Jesus, as well as the temple.

When we are wronged or treated unjustly in the workplace, or when the system seems controlled by evil, we must not fall into despair. Rather, we must turn to prayer, confess our sins, and stand firm in our spiritual calling. God is not absent. He sees, He hears, and in His time, He acts. Our responsibility is to remain faithful, seek His righteousness, and pursue the eternal perspective.

The "seventy sevens" remind us that God is sovereign over history. Whether in the age of kings and empires, or in today's era of artificial intelligence, His redemptive timeline is moving forward. The challenges of the AI era may be new, but the spiritual disciplines and the goal of Christlikeness remain the same.

As for the "seventy sevens," we now carefully present a diagram and explanation by Professor Timothy Wu from China Evangelical Seminary, found at the end of Chapter 9 in his book *Daniel's Warriors in the Lion's Den*, as follows:

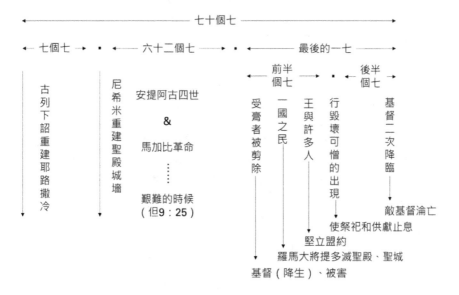

Figure 34 Interpretation of the seventy sevens

From the Figure above, we can see that the "seventy sevens" on the timeline can be divided into three segments: seven sevens, sixty-two sevens, and the final one seven. However, the durations of these segments are not proportionally equal, because the word "seven" in Hebrew often carries the meaning of completeness or fullness.

1. **The first segment**, the *seven sevens*, spans from 538 B.C. when Cyrus the Great issued the decree to rebuild the holy city, to 445 B.C. when Nehemiah completed the reconstruction—covering a total of 93 years.

2. **The second segment**, the *sixty-two sevens*, begins from the completion of the rebuilding by Nehemiah. It includes significant events such as Antiochus IV Epiphanes (a foreshadowing of the Antichrist) desecrating the temple and halting sacrifices around 169 B.C., the Maccabean revolt, and ends with the crucifixion of Jesus Christ in A.D. 33—spanning a total of 478 years.

3. **The third segment**, the *final one seven*, can itself be divided into two smaller parts:

    3.1. The **first half of the seven** starts from the death of Jesus and includes the destruction of the temple and the holy city by Roman General Titus in A.D. 70. This period extends until the emergence of the Antichrist, who, like Antiochus IV before him, will put an end to sacrifices and offerings—committing the same kind of blasphemous acts as his historical precursor.

    3.2. The **second half of the final seven** is the time of the Antichrist's reign, which includes the Great Tribulation mentioned in the Book of Revelation, and concludes with the return of Christ and His ultimate victory.

Where is humanity currently situated on this prophetic timeline? We are likely in the period between the destruction of the temple and the holy city by Roman General Titus and the future moment when "the ruler will confirm a covenant with many." In today's world, the United States relies on various covenants—such as NATO, the U.S.-Japan Security Alliance, the Indo-Pacific alliance, and the Five Eyes alliance—to restrain China's rise. Meanwhile, China claims to be a "non-aligned" country.

If the end times are indeed near, what does this suggest? Could a populist-leaning president from either the Democratic or Republican party in the U.S. become a foreshadowing of the Antichrist? Or could it be a Chinese leader who, while outwardly non-aligned, actually maintains a network of hidden alliances through China-Russia relations, China-Pakistan ties, Southeast Asian agreements, the Shanghai Cooperation Organization, and the Belt and Road Initiative—thus also making him a potential figure prefiguring the Antichrist?

God's Actions and Sovereignty in the Age of AI

If God hears the prayers of the Champion team for the wicked and victims in the age of AI and decides to act in a manner like Daniel 9, Billy and Tim believe that God may perform His redemption and justice through the following six actions:

1. **Transgression**: God will move people's hearts and make them realize the wrongness of their actions, especially those who use AI to deceive and exploit. They will be forced to face their sins and stop these evil deeds. This may be achieved through the improvement of laws, the strengthening of regulation and the moral reconstruction of society.

2. **Sin:** God will cleanse the AI of systemic sin. This includes not only curbing the misuse of technology, but also rebuilding ethics and morality to put the use of technology back on the right track. He will move tech practitioners to develop and use AI with integrity and justice.

3. **Wickedness**: God will provide a path to redemption for those who have used AI to do evil and have a chance to repent and atone for their sins. This can be achieved through education, mentoring, and opportunities for rehabilitation, so that they can change their past behaviors, become new people, and make a positive contribution to society.

4. **Introducing Eternal Righteousness**: God will bring lasting justice and ensure that future technological developments and

applications will continue to benefit humanity and not cause harm. This may involve deepening moral and ethical education, so that people can always use technology to be oriented towards the common good and justice and promote the sustainable development of society.

5. **Sealing Visions and Prophecies**: God will reveal and verify visions and prophecies about AI, so that people can distinguish between truth and falsehood and avoid being deceived by false information. He will make people understand through the revelation of truth which prophecies come from Him and which are just delusions or misinterpretations of man.

6. **Anointing the Holy of Holies, the Most Holy One**: God will bless those who are committed to serving humanity with technology and glorifying His name so that their work will be holy. This could include blessings to projects and people who use AI to improve healthcare, education, and poverty, so that their efforts can be fulfilled and brought about greater well-being.

These six actions reflect God's justice, mercy, and redemption, and He will accomplish these goals through the transformation of the human heart, the rebuilding of social institutions, and the manifestation of truth. In doing so, God uses a variety of means, including the perfection of the law, the advancement of education, the strengthening of ethics, and His own supernatural intervention, to protect and bless those who rely on Him and to lead humanity to the right path.

As for where we are in the seventy-sevens timelines, Billy and Tim believe that the AI era may only be a process point of human civilization, and whether it is close to the end of the world is not something that we can say. The Bible says that the last days will come like thieves, and they are completely out of human prediction.

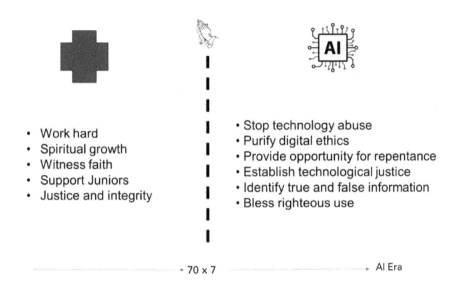

Figure 35 The goal of Christians in the age of AI

Q&A Questions

1. What are the six goals of God mentioned in Daniel 9?

2. How are the "seventy sevens" mentioned in the text divided in the timeline?

3. What are some of the ways God might achieve His redemption and justice in the age of AI?

Practical Training Questions

Please reflect on the way you use AI technology in your daily life or work. List three ways to use AI that can be more in line with Christian ethical values and develop a specific action plan to implement one of them. Over the next week, document your implementation and feelings, and think about how this change can help you better embody Christian values in the age of AI.

Volume 7: Advanced AI Training - Detailing the Problems and Solutions of AI 2.0-4.0

Chapter 19: A Closer Look at the Problems Triggered by AI 2.0

How Christians in the Workplace Can Prepare for the Great Battle

Christians in the workplace must always be prepared for the battle between the gospel worldview and the postmodern mindset. Colleagues, subordinates, or even superiors who adopt a postmodern approach to life are everywhere. At times, they are driven by their own desires, drifting aimlessly in the vast ocean of the workplace; sometimes, they even attempt to control the Holy God.

Christians, on the other hand, hold fast to the gospel worldview. The more humbly they look to God, the more He reveals His divine insights to them. The gospel worldview is not just a set of values we carry internally, but one that drives our behavior and how we view AI-related issues in the workplace. This perspective should be active, resilient, and spiritually alert, not passive or disengaged.

Daniel's Example of Preparing for the Great War (Dan. 10: 1-9)

In Daniel 9, we see Daniel praying for the desolation of homeland, and then the angel Gabriel tells him that God heard the prayer and stirred King Cyrus to return the remnant of Israel to Jerusalem. However, there angel Gabriel explained further about the end-time scene of Israel, especially about "…. *a king's people will come and destroy this city and its sanctuary. In the end it will be like a flood to the end, and there will be wars until the end, and desolation has been settled* (Dan. 9:26)."

Here at the beginning of chapter 10, Daniel receives another revelation about the great battle and that "*Its message was true, and it concerned a great war. The understanding of the message came to him in a vision. At that time, I, Daniel, mourned for three weeks. I ate no choice food; no meat or wine touched my lips; and I used no lotions at all until the three weeks were over.* (Daniel 10:1–3)."

After this, Daniel had another vision: an astonishing angel appeared, "*his face like lightning, his eyes like torches, his hands and feet like bright brass, and his voice like the voice of a multitude*" (Daniel 10:6). Why do angels appear in such a way? Most likely, this is an angel in military uniform who is ready for battle. Daniel's reaction was "*I had no strength left, my face turned deathly pale, and I was helpless... I fell into a deep sleep, my face to the ground. (Dan. 10:8, 9)*" This is also the reaction of every Christian to the horrified vision.

In the third year of Cyrus king of Persia, Daniel must have been eighty years old. There is reason to believe that even though Daniel, who had seen four visions at that age, he could not know what kind of war it was (the three great wars between Greek and Persian Empires? Antiochus IV's Antichrist-typed War? The battle for the fall of the Eastern and Western Roman Empires? Two World Wars? Or the great battle of Armageddon in the last days?), when the war happened (in Daniel's lifetime? after the return of the Jews to the Holy City? or in the last days?), and what the impact on the Jews was (can the Jews be revived as a result? raptured by the Lord for the resurrection?). However, his concern for his homeland and his people is a model for us.

Prepare for the great battle in the era of AI 2.0 innovation

Since evil forces will use AI to do many evil deeds, Elder Billy believes that in the era of ANI, human must be prepared for moral warfare. He believed it was a great battle between righteousness and evil. The work on prevention is classified as follows:

Social aspects

1. *Deepfake making fake video and audio*

    a. **Criminal behavior**: Use generative AI to create fake video or audio to impersonate celebrities or ordinary people to commit fraud, extortion, or defamation.

b. **Preventive measures**: Develop and promote tools to identify deepfake technology, strengthen the moderation of media content, and educate the public on basic methods to identify and prevent deepfakes.

c. **Mitigation methods**: Use multiple layers of verification (e.g., biometrics, two-factor authentication) to confirm real identities, and legislation to increase penalties for the production and dissemination of deepfakes.

2. *Fake news and disinformation*

a. **Criminal behavior**: Generate false news stories and information to confuse the public, cause panic in society, or influence political elections.

b. **Preventative measures**: Establish and support independent fact-checking organizations and push social media platforms to increase censorship of content and flag disinformation.

c. **Mitigation methods:** Improve media literacy and critical thinking among the public, and governments and businesses working together to develop technologies to monitor and identify disinformation.

3. *Automated Phishing Attacks*

a. **Criminal behavior**: Use generative AI to automatically create personalized phishing emails or websites to trick users into revealing sensitive information.

b. **Preventative measures**: Enhance email and web filtering techniques to improve anti-phishing education and training.

c. **Mitigation methods**: Promote the use of secure browser plug-ins and network security software and strengthen internal network security management and employee training.

4.   *Synthetic Identity Fraud*

   a. **Criminal behavior**: Generate false identities to commit financial fraud, loan fraud, or money laundering.
   b. **Precautionary measures**: Improve authentication technology and promote biometrics and multi-factor authentication.
   c. **Mitigation methods**: Financial institutions strengthen KYC (Know Your Customer) processes, and governments strengthen the management and verification of identity documents.

5.   *Malicious program generation*

   a. **Criminal behavior**: Generative AI is used to automatically generate or mutate malware to evade security detection and protection.
   b. **Preventive measures**: Strengthen cybersecurity protection technologies and promote the application of AI in cybersecurity to predict and block new malicious programs.
   c. **Mitigation methods**: Regularly update security software and operating systems and establish a strong security incident response mechanism.

6.   *Fake Reviews and Market Manipulation*

   a. **Criminal behavior**: Manipulate market and consumer behavior by using generative AI to automatically generate fake reviews or reviews.
   b. **Preventive measures**: The platform has a strong moderation mechanism in place, using AI technology to detect and remove fake reviews.
   c. **Mitigation methods**: Promote transparent review management policies, and companies strengthen the monitoring and analysis of user behavior.

7.   *Invasion of Privacy*

   a.   **Criminal behavior**: Synthesize an individual's private information through generative AI technology for extortion or trafficking.
   b.   **Preventive measures**: Strengthen privacy protection laws and regulations and raise awareness of data protection technology and privacy protection.
   c.   **Mitigation methods**: Enterprises use data encryption and anonymization technologies to improve privacy protection awareness and behavior of individuals.

8.   *Automated Terrorist Propaganda*

   a.   **Criminal behavior**: Uses generative AI to automatically generate and disseminate terrorist propaganda and extremist content.
   b.   **Preventive measures**: The government and tech companies work together to develop and apply AI technology to identify and stop the spread of terrorist propaganda content.
   c.   **Mitigation methods:** Social media platforms have stepped up censorship and removal of extremist content and promoted international cooperation to combat online terrorism.

9.   *Financial Market Manipulation*

   a.   **Criminal behavior**: Use generative AI to create false financial information for market manipulation and illegal profit.
   b.   **Preventive measures**: Strengthen the supervision of the financial market and promote exchanges and financial institutions to strengthen the monitoring of abnormal market behavior.
   c.   **Mitigation methods:** Using AI technology to detect market manipulation, investors are more vigilant and financially savvy.

10.   *False Medical Information*

a.   **Criminal behavior**: Generate false medical information or diagnoses to induce patients to purchase ineffective or harmful drugs and therapies.

b.   **Preventive measures**: The government and medical institutions have strengthened the management and review of medical information and promoted health education.

c.   **Mitigation methods**: Individuals improve their ability to screen medical information and rely on formal medical channels and professional advice.

Through these measures, governments, businesses, and individuals can work together to reduce the potential crime risks posed by generative AI and ensure that technological advancements benefit society as a whole.

Technological security

Preparation for AI technology security: Today's AI technology has brought many conveniences and advancements, but it also comes with many security risks. These include data privacy, transparency of decision-making, malicious use, bias and discrimination, and system vulnerabilities. To prevent these hidden dangers and protect users and society, here are some specific risks and corresponding preventive measures:

Data Privacy

Risks:

1.   AI systems require enormous amounts of data to train, which often contain sensitive personal information and are at risk of leakage and misuse.

Precautionary measures:

1.   **Data encryption**: Encrypt data so that even if data is compromised, malicious parties cannot easily interpret it.
2.   **Data anonymization**: Removing or masking personally identifiable information when processing data to reduce the risk of privacy breaches.
3.   **Strict data management policies**: Establish and enforce strict data access and management policies, and only authorized personnel have access to sensitive data.

Transparency in decision-making

Risks:

1.   The decision-making process of AI systems is often a black-box operation, difficult to understand and explain, leading to a lack of transparency and accountability.

Precautionary measures:

1.   **Explainable AI**: Develop and use explainable AI models that enable people to understand the decision-making process and basis of AI.
2.   **Decision-making audit**: Establish a decision-making audit mechanism to regularly review the decision-making of the AI system to ensure its fairness and transparency.

Malicious Use

Risks:

1.   AI technology can be used by criminals or malicious organizations to carry out illegal activities such as cyber-attacks, fake news distribution, and identity fraud.

Precautionary measures:

1. **Security development**: Integrate security design into the development process of AI technology to ensure that the system is resistant to attacks.
2. **Monitoring and detection**: Establish a real-time monitoring and anomaly detection mechanism for AI system operation to detect and respond to potential security threats in a timely manner.
3. **Legal supervision**: Formulate relevant laws and regulations to strictly restrict the misuse of AI technology and impose severe penalties for illegal acts.

Prejudice and Discrimination

Risks:

1. AI systems may be trained based on biased data, leading to bias and discrimination in decision-making in terms of gender, race, age, etc.

Precautionary measures:

1. **Data review**: Conduct reviews during data collection and use to ensure diversity and representativeness of data and reduce sources of bias.
2. **Fairness testing**: Conduct fairness testing on AI models to check their performance on different groups and correct bias issues in a timely manner.
3. **Diverse** teams: Assembling diverse development teams and ensuring the participation of different backgrounds and perspectives can help identify and address biases.

System vulnerabilities

Risks:

1. AI systems are complex and rely on a large number of software and hardware components, and there is a risk that system vulnerabilities will be exploited, such as malicious modifications

to the principle library, which may lead to data leakage or system collapse, and even cause social and political problems.

Precautionary measures:

1. **Regular security testing**: Conduct regular security tests and vulnerability scans on AI systems to patch discovered vulnerabilities in a timely manner.
2. **Version management**: Strictly manage the version updates of the AI system to ensure that each update is fully tested and verified.
3. **Redundancy design**: Redundancy and fault tolerance mechanisms are considered in the system design to improve the stability and security of the system.

In today's increasingly developed AI technology, security risks are a problem that cannot be ignored. These vulnerabilities can be prevented and mitigated by strengthening data privacy protection, improving decision-making transparency, preventing malicious use, eliminating bias and discrimination, and preventing system vulnerabilities. This requires technology developers, businesses, governments, and users to work together to develop and enforce strict security standards and policies to ensure the safe, reliable, and fair application of AI technology.

Political aspects

1. Large-scale facial recognition and surveillance:

a. **Behavior description**: Authoritarian governments use AI technology to install a large number of cameras in public places for facial recognition and tracking, monitoring, and controlling citizens' movements.
b. **Harm**: Serious violations of citizens' privacy, suppression of individual freedoms, and the creation of citizens living in constant fear and stress.

2. *Social Credit System:*

    a. **Behavior description**: The government uses AI to establish a social credit system to score each citizen's behavior, and determine their rights to social welfare, loans, travel, and other rights based on the score.

    b. **Harm**: Leads to extreme monitoring and control of citizens' behavior, resulting in unfair social treatment and oppression, and suppressing individual freedom and creativity.

3. *Public opinion manipulation and brainwashing:*

    a. **Behavior description**: Use generative AI technology to automatically generate false information, falsify news and propaganda materials, manipulate and brainwash public opinion, and control public ideology.

    b. **Harm**: It leads to opaque information, citizens cannot obtain real information, forms a false social reality, and weakens people's critical thinking ability and democratic consciousness.

4. *Automated Review and Suppression of Objections:*

    a. **Behavior description**: Use AI technology to automatically monitor and censor internet content, quickly identify and delete speech critical of the government, and suppress dissent.

    b. **Harm**: Freedom of speech is severely restricted, citizens are unable to express dissenting opinions, social innovation and pluralistic thinking are suppressed, and a single thought control is formed.

5. *Targeted Surveillance and Political Persecution:*

    a. **Behavior description**: The government uses AI technology to precisely track and monitor dissidents, political opponents, and their supporters for targeted surveillance, harassment, and persecution.

b. **Harm**: Individuals are seriously violating their political rights and personal freedoms, putting dissidents and the opposition at significant risk, and the political environment becoming more oppressive and dangerous.

These acts seriously undermine the fundamental rights and freedoms of citizens and expose societies to constant oppression and fear. Therefore, it is crucial to properly regulate and restrict the application of AI technology to ensure that it operates within a legal, transparent, and humane framework.

Military aspects

1.　*AI is used for paramilitary combat readiness*

Many gray-area wars, such as information warfare, ideological warfare, cognitive warfare. Often, this involves a lot of AI work, and many of the paramilitary operations have already begun before they have begun. Here are the specific applications of AI in these paramilitary operational preparations:

i. Information Warfare.

Fake News and Disinformation:

a. **Generation and dissemination**: Generative AI, such as GPT-4, is used to create highly realistic fake news and disinformation to confuse the public, influence public opinion, and stabilize society.

b. **Detection and response**: Develop AI tools to detect and flag false information and provide accurate rebuttals and clarifications.

Cyber Attacks:

a.   **Automated attacks**: AI can automate the cyberattack process, including vulnerability scanning, attack path selection, and attack execution.

b.   **Defense mechanisms**: AI can be used to monitor network traffic in real time, detect anomalous behavior, and respond to potential threats in a timely manner.

ii. Ideological Warfare

Social Media Manipulation:

a.   **Opinion Guidance**: Use AI to analyze data on social media platforms, identify key influencers and hot topics, and steer public opinion through bot accounts and automated tools.

b.   **Sentiment analysis**: AI conducts sentiment analysis to understand people's sentiment and publish content in a targeted manner to amplify disagreements or create consensus.

Content Customization:

a.   **Personalized promotion**: Use AI to accurately segment and analyze target groups and customize promotional content according to their preferences and behavior patterns to increase influence.

b.   **Deepfake**: The use of deepfakes to create fake video or audio to impersonate a public figure to post impactful information.

iii. Cognitive Warfare

Mental Operations:

a.   **Psychological tactics**: AI analyzes the psychological characteristics of individuals and groups, and designs targeted psychological operations to influence their cognition and behavior.

b.   **Virtual reality**: Using VR and AR technology with AI to create immersive virtual scenes for psychological training or psychological tactical drills.

Education and Advocacy:

a.   **Education system infiltration**: AI generates educational materials or curriculum content, infiltrates the education system, and has a long-term impact on the ideology of the younger generation.

b.   **Radio and media**: Leverage AI to automatically generate and broadcast promotional materials for subtle communication on radio and television.

iv. Specific applications of AI in paramilitary operational preparedness

Big Data Analysis:

a.   **Intelligence** gathering: AI analyzes large amounts of public and private data to identify potential threats, hostile actors, and strategic opportunities.

b.   **Pattern recognition**: AI is able to identify patterns of behavior, predict hostilities, and provide strategic recommendations.

Automated Operations:

a.   **Unmanned systems**: AI controls drones and unmanned vehicles for reconnaissance, surveillance, and small-scale attacks, reducing personnel risk.

b.   **Automated weapon systems**: AI automated weapon systems can react quickly and delivering accurate strikes.

Early Warning System:

a.   **Threat prediction**: AI predicts potential threats and attacks, providing early warnings and preparing military and government agencies.

b.   **Real-time monitoring**: AI monitors various data sources in real time to provide real-time security situational awareness.

v. Preventive and countermeasures

Improving Information Literacy:

a.   **Public education**: Improve the public's ability to identify fake news and disinformation and enhance media literacy.

b.   **Professional Training**: Train media and technology professionals to improve their ability to identify and respond.

Technical Defense:

a.   **AI Against AI**: Develop counter-AI technologies to identify and counter hostile AI behavior.

b.   **Multi-level defense**: Establish a multi-layered cyber defense system, combining artificial intelligence and traditional security measures to enhance the depth of defense.

International Cooperation:

a.   **Information sharing**: Internationally share threat information and response experience to jointly defend against security threats brought by AI.

b.   **Coordinated Defense**: Establish an international coordination mechanism to jointly respond to cyber-attacks and information warfare.

The application of AI in gray-zone warfare has made paramilitary operations more complex and diverse. By combining advanced technologies and strategies, these threats can be effectively countered and prevented, ensuring social stability and security. In addressing these challenges, a combination of technology, policy and education is needed to protect the public interest.

2.   *AI 2.0 is used in the preparation of regular military warfare*

Formal war preparedness in the AI era includes individual or joint combat readiness in space, sky, sea, and land, as well as logistics in this regard. AI technology plays a vital role in preparedness, including strategic planning, operational command, intelligence gathering, and logistical support. Here are the specific applications of AI in these areas:

i.   Space combat

Satellite Monitoring & Management:

a.   **Automated operations**: AI automates satellite operations and monitoring, analyzes data in real time, and discovers potential threats or unusual activities.
b.   **Collision prevention**: AI predicts satellite orbits to avoid collisions with space junk or other satellites.

Intelligence Gathering:

a.   **Earth observation**: AI analyzes satellite imagery to identify military installations, troop movements, and other important targets.
b.   **Signal intelligence**: AI decodes and analyzes signals from hostile satellites to provide critical intelligence.

ii.   Combat in the air, sea, and land

Drone Combat:

a.   **Autonomous navigation**: AI controls drones for autonomous navigation and reconnaissance, surveillance, and strike missions.

b.   **Cluster operations**: AI coordinates multiple drone clusters to achieve coordinated operations and task assignments.

Air Tactical Analysis:

a.   **Forecasting**: AI analyzes data from air operations, predicts enemy aircraft movements, and provides tactical recommendations.

b.   **Target recognition**: AI identifies and tags targets in real time during flight, improving strike accuracy.

iii.   Maritime warfare

Automated Ships:

a.   **Autonomous** navigation: AI controls unmanned ships to navigate autonomously and perform patrol, reconnaissance, and anti-submarine warfare missions.

b.   **Dynamic deployment**: AI analyzes the battlefield situation, dynamically adjusts ship deployment, and optimizes resource utilization.

Submarine surveillance:

a.   **Seabed exploration**: AI-controlled unmanned underwater vehicles (UAVs) conduct seabed exploration and surveillance to detect potential threats.

b.   **Acoustic analysis**: AI analyzes acoustic data to identify enemy submarines and underwater facilities.

iv.   Land warfare

Autonomous Ground Vehicles:

a. **Autonomous driving**: AI controls unmanned ground vehicles to perform patrol, transportation, and support tasks.

b. **Battlefield reconnaissance**: AI analyzes ground reconnaissance data to provide real-time battlefield intelligence.

Tactical Support:

a. **Battlefield situational awareness**: AI integrates multi-source data to provide a comprehensive battlefield situational map to assist in command decision-making.

b. **Resource management**: AI optimizes the supply chain and logistical support to ensure the continuous operation of combat units.

v. Joint operations and logistical support

Cross-domain collaboration:

a. **Multi-domain integration**: AI integrates operational data from space, air, sea, and land to achieve multi-domain cooperative operations.

b. **Joint Operations** Command: The AI supports the Joint Operations Command Center, providing cross-domain tactical advice and decision support.

Logistical support:

a. **Intelligent logistics**: AI optimizes the transportation path of materials, reduces transportation time and costs, and ensures timely delivery of materials.

b. **Equipment maintenance**: AI monitors equipment status, predicts failures, and automatically schedules repairs to improve equipment reliability.

The application of AI in modern warfare has improved the combat effectiveness of all branches and domains of the military, especially in the preparation of individual or joint operations in space, sky, sea and land. Through automated and intelligent technologies, AI can provide dedicated support for strategic planning, tactical execution, intelligence gathering, and logistical support. However, this also brings new challenges, such as AI security, ethical issues, and the complexity of cross-domain collaboration. Therefore, the military field needs to continue to invest resources to ensure the safe and effective application of AI technology and formulate relevant policies and norms to ensure the correct and responsible use of AI in combat.

(Please note that the above problems are only proposed here to prevent them, and the real solutions to the problems are in the next chapter.)

Figure 36 AI2.0 Wars of information warfare, wars with robots, drones, & ships

Training courses recommended

Based on the content of this chapter, in order to equip readers with the necessary knowledge and skills in the age of AI, the following are the recommended elective courses:

1. **Review the previous chapters of the AI 2.0 Fundamentals and Applications course**. They can help readers review the basic concepts of AI, how it works, and its applications in various fields.

2. **Data Privacy & Cybersecurity**. Given the privacy and security risks posed by AI, this course can teach readers how to protect personal data and identify potential cyber threats.

3. **Media literacy and information identification**. This course improves readers' ability to identify fake news, deepfakes, and disinformation, and develops critical thinking.

4. **AI Ethics and Social Implications**. This course explores the ethical issues and social implications of AI technology and cultivates readers' sense of responsibility and moral judgment on AI applications.

5. **Machine Learning & Data Analytics**. Basic knowledge of machine learning and data analytics can help readers understand how AI systems make decisions and how to identify potential biases.

6. **Cyber Security & Defense Technologies**. Considering the application of AI in cyberattacks, this course can teach basic cybersecurity knowledge and defense strategies.

7. **Cognitive Psychology**. Understanding human cognitive processes can help readers identify and defend against AI-assisted psychological manipulation and cognitive tactics.

8. **International Relations and Modern Warfare**. This course can help readers understand the role of AI in modern military and geopolitics.

9. **Digital Citizenship Course**. Teach how to use technology responsibly in the digital age, including online codes of conduct and awareness of digital rights.

10.   **AI Law & Policy**. Understand the laws, regulations, and policies related to AI, and cultivate readers' ability to participate in relevant public discussions.

These courses cover a wide range of aspects such as technology, ethics, security, society, and politics, and aim to comprehensively improve readers' ability to meet the challenges of the AI era. The specific curriculum can be adjusted according to the background and needs of the reader.

Q&A Questions

1. How do Christians prepare for the Great War in the workplace?

2. How did Daniel prepare for the Great Battle?

3. In terms of society, what criminal behaviors may be brought about by the AI 2.0 era

4. In terms of technology security, what are the main hidden dangers brought by AI?

5. How can bias and discrimination be prevented in AI systems?

6. In terms of politics, how might authoritarian governments misuse AI technology?

What are the applications of 7.AI in information warfare in paramilitary operations?

8. How is AI used in cognitive warfare?

9. What are the specific applications of AI in space combat preparation?

10. How does AI support joint operations?

Practical Training Questions

1. Design an AI system for detecting and flagging disinformation on social media. Consider what the system should do, how to ensure its accuracy and impartiality, and what challenges it may face.

2. Develop a set of ethical guidelines and security measures for the application of AI in the military field. Consider how to balance military effectiveness with ethical responsibility, and how to guard against the risks that AI weapon systems may pose.

Chapter 20: A Closer Look at the Solutions to the Problems of AI 2.0

What Should Christians Do in the Workplace to Face the Spiritual Battle?

In the workplace, when facing challenges as intense as a great spiritual battle, Christians must "humble themselves and pray persistently." They should also understand that sometimes God's delay in answering prayers comes with a reason: for example, the angel sent to respond to your prayers might be blocked by the devil, triggering a spiritual war in the heavenly realms. This is because God's children are not of this world, so their prayers will be hated by the devil who controls the world.

The devil often wants to use evil forces to control and destroy, but in the end, it is God who overcomes and reigns. Therefore, the delay due to spiritual war is not God's mistake or time. God has His timetable, and the saints need to be diligent and in constant prayer.

Believers pray in the workplace to focus on the eschatological kingdom. The one having such a theological height is a faithful professional warrior entrusted by God.

This very situation is recorded in **Daniel 10:12–11:2**:

What did Daniel know from the angel's explanation of the Great War?

In the second half of Daniel 10 and all the way through 11:2, the angel Gabriel explains the vision of the first half of chapter 10. These explanations made the prophet Daniel understand that the actions of the kings of this world were actually controlled by the demons behind them. And God's "book of truth" helped God's justice and justice, and finally made it impossible for these demons to succeed.

Angel Explanation

The angel Gabriel told Daniel why he delayed answering his prayer: "Do not be afraid, Daniel, for your words have been answered from the first day when you have set your heart on the first day to understand the things to come, and to diligently your heart before your God. I have come by thy word. But the prince of Persia hindered me twenty-one days." Daniel's assertion had moved God to answer his prayers, but there was a spiritual battle that temporarily prevented that answer. Now that the spiritual warfare was aided by the archangel Michael, Gabriel could explain Daniel's inquiry in detail. That is what will happen to the people of Israel in the future, because it is not related to many days to come.

Prophetic Preparation

At the first sight of Daniel's vision, he was "powerless and breathless." The reader may think that such a prophet is too weak. However, for those who are weak before God, God (or angels sent by God) will touch you to make you strong. Gabriel also delivered a message of comfort in a loving tone: "Do not be afraid, you beloved, peace be with you! Be strong," and Daniel was immediately strengthened: "Say, my lord, because you have strengthened me."

Who is the ruler of Persia?

"The prince of Persian Kingdom" is interpreted as a heavenly spiritual adversary, representing opposition to God's plan, and an extraordinary king. The "Demon Lord of Persia" is a powerful demon who influences the mortal Persian king to do evil. This concept is rooted in the interpretation of Daniel 10. Here are some key points to consider about how the effects of this demon might manifest and what kind of "evil things" it might attribute to:

Against the Jews:

One of the main concerns of the Book of Daniel and other biblical texts was the opposition faced by Jews during their exile and foreign domination. Policies or actions taken by Persian rulers that were harmful or oppressive to the Jews could have been influenced by demonic princes.

For example, Haman's plot to exterminate the Jews during the reign of King Ahasuerus in the Book of Esther can be seen as an act of influence from this malevolent spiritual force. Although Haman was an Amalekite rather than a Persian, his ability to influence the Persian king to issue a decree of destruction of the Jews suggests an evil that may be attributed to demonic influence.

Idolatry and False Religion:

Promoting idolatry and false religion is another potentially evil form. In ancient Persia, the worship of Zoroastrian gods and other gods may have been seen as the opposite of the monotheistic worship of Yahweh as prescribed in the Hebrew Bible.

Thus, demonic influences can be interpreted as perpetuating or encouraging religious practices that lead people away from the worship of the true God as understood by the Jewish faith.

Persecution and Repression:

Policies of persecution and repression, such as restricting Jewish freedom or imposing onerous taxes and harsh treatment, can be seen as being influenced by demonic forces.

For example, any decree that halts the rebuilding of the Jerusalem Temple or attempts to marginalize the Jewish community could be influenced by such a spiritual adversary.

War & Conflict:

Encouraging unnecessary wars and conflicts, especially those that destabilize the region and cause suffering, can also be attributed to the influence of the devil. Such conflicts distract rulers, distract them from more benevolent governance, and increase human suffering.

While the historical records of Persian kings such as Cyrus the Great, Darius, and Artaxerxes show a mixture of benevolent and harsh behavior, the biblical text focuses on those actions that are consistent with the spiritual narrative of opposition and salvation. In Daniel 10, the "ruler of the Persian state" represents a spiritual opposition that may influence rulers to act in a way that is contrary to the well-being of God's people and God's purposes.

Figure 37 The archangel Michael helped in the battle against the Persian ruler so that the angel Gabriel could stop and comfort Daniel

Book of Truth

In Daniel 10, the angel Gabriel mentions telling Daniel what is recorded in the Book of Truth. What exactly is this "true book" and why it is called so, here are some explanations and understandings of it:

The meaning of the "Book of Truth"

1. **God's Plan and Prophecy**: The "Book of Truth" is considered to be a record of God's plan and prophecy that is absolutely true because they were revealed and determined by God Himself. The book contains detailed descriptions of historical and future events and is a demonstration of God's sovereignty and arrangement over the history of the world and mankind.

2. **Fighting against falsehood**: The Book of Truth is called "true" because it represents God's truth, in contrast to the falsehood and deception of Satan and the devil. Satan is called "the father of liars and lies" (John 8:44), and therefore, God's truth is a weapon against Satan's falsehood.

3. **Revelation to Daniel**: These truths were revealed to Daniel by the angel Gabriel because these prophecies and plans were specifically made known by God to Daniel and the Israel so that they could understand God's work in history and hold on to faith amid difficulties and persecution.

The content and historical background of the book

1. **Persia and the Greece Empire**: Gabriel revealed to Daniel about the events of Persia and the Greece Empire, and the spiritual battles behind these events were also part of it. The demon lords behind the Persian and Greece empires represent the evil forces operating in these empires that seek to oppose God's will and people.

2. **The Battle of the Angels**: Gabriel and Michael are God's messengers who fight against these evil forces in the spirit world to ensure that God's plan is fulfilled. For example, Gabriel was stopped by a Persian king on his way to Daniel for 21 days until Michael came to his aid (Daniel 10:13). This shows the fierce battles in the spirit realm, but in the end the messengers of God were able to overcome these evil forces.

How truth triumphs over falsehood

1. **God's Sovereignty**: Truth comes from God's sovereignty and omniscience. God's plan is unshakable and will eventually come to pass. Although Satan and his forces try to stop or distort God's plan, God's truth and plan will surely prevail over all falsehood and resistance.
2. **Revelation and Faith**: God made these truths known to his people by revealing them to prophets like Daniel so that they could strengthen their faith in the face of trials and persecution. The revelation of truth enables believers to recognize and resist Satan's lies and deceptions.
3. **Spiritual Warfare**: The spiritual warfare of angels such as Gabriel and Michael also show the power of truth. The victory of these angels symbolizes that God's truth will eventually triumph over all evil and falsehood, ensuring that God's plan will not be thwarted.

In summary, the Book of Truth is a record of God's truth and plan, and it shows God's sovereign arrangement of history. Through revelation to Daniel, these truths not only reveal future events, but also demonstrate spiritual warfare and ultimately establish that God's truth will triumph over Satan's falsehood and deception.

Problem solving in the AI 2.0 era

In the era of AI 2.0, tools such as large language models (LLMs), multi-modal LLMs, intelligent robotics, and others have introduced a range of complex challenges. The previous chapter only addressed preventive strategies. As mentioned earlier, during the AI 1.0 era, there were already efforts to create a general problem solver (GPS), but these ultimately failed. Today, however, OpenAI has developed GPT-3 into a tool capable of addressing problem-solving tasks. So, how can GPT be further expanded to solve problems effectively?

Build the GPS requirements

Based on the current development trend of GPT and the progress in the field of AI, the following needs can be considered to extend GPT to become a more powerful problem solver:

1.   Multimodal Fusion: Combining GPT with other AI technologies such as computer vision and speech recognition enables it to process more types of input data. This solves a wider range of problems, such as image analysis, sound processing, etc.
2.   Enhance reasoning ability: Improve GPT's ability to analyze and solve problems by introducing more complex reasoning mechanisms, such as causal reasoning, logical reasoning, etc. This may involve combining symbology with neural networks.
3.   Knowledge Graph Integration: Combine GPT with large-scale knowledge graphs to enhance its ability to understand and apply domain-specific knowledge. This can help GPT answer professional questions more accurately.
4.   Interactive Learning: Develop a version of GPT that can learn and improve through continuous interaction with the user. This approach allows GPT to continuously optimize its problem-solving strategies based on user feedback.
5.   Task Decomposition Ability: Enhance GPT's ability to break down complex problems into small steps and be able to solve these sub-problems step by step. This is similar to the way humans solve complex problems.
6.   Simulation and Prediction: Integrating a simulated environment enables GPT to test and validate solutions in virtual scenarios, especially for physical or engineering problems.

7.   Meta-learning: Develop a version of GPT that "learns how to learn", allowing it to adapt more quickly to new problems and new areas.

8.   External tool integration: Allows GPT to call external tools and APIs, such as math calculators, data analysis tools, etc., to extend its problem-solving capabilities.

9.   Ethical and safety framework: Establish a strong ethical and safety framework to ensure that GPT considers ethical and societal implications when solving problems.

10.   Explainability Enhancements: Improve the transparency and explainability of GPT's decision-making process, enabling users to understand the steps and reasons for problem solving.

These demands may lead to AI systems that are closer to General Problem Solvers. However, achieving true general-purpose problem-solving capabilities remains a huge challenge and may require breakthroughs in the underlying theory and technology of AI.

Architecture and design of the GPS virtual machine

The product architecture of a General Problem Solver (GPS) is as follows. This architecture consists of an AI virtual machine and five submachines. Here's the detailed architecture design:

The overall architecture of the AI virtual machine:

```
+------------------------------------+
|       GPS Virtual Machine          |
+------------------------------------+
|                                    |
|                                    |
| +---------------+ +---------------+ |
| | I/O Submachine | | Knowledgebase submachine | |
| +---------------+ +---------------+ |
```

```
|                                    |
| +-------------+ +--------------+ |
| | Abstract submachine  | | Principle submachine   | |
| +-------------+ +--------------+ |
|                                    |
| +-------------+                    |
| | Foundation submachine  |         |
| +---------------------+            |
|                                    |
+------------------------------------+
```

Detailed Design of Various Submachines:

1. I/O submachine

```
+-------------------+
|    I/O submachine  |
+-------------------+
| - RAG Module      |
| - MAMBA Module    |
| - OOD Test Module  |
| - Interactive Learning Module  |
| - Multimode Input Processing  |
| - Natural Language Generation   |
+-------------------+
```

2. Knowledgebase Submachine

```
+-------------------+
|   Knowledgebase Submachine   |
+-------------------+
| - Multimode knowledge fusion  |
| - reasoning engine     |
|   - cause-effect reasoning   |
|   - logical reasoning     |
```

```
| - knowledge graph        |
| - domain expert system   |
+---------------------+
```

3. Abstract Submachine

```
+--------------------+
|   Abstract Submachine        |
+--------------------+
| - Task decomposition Module    |
| - Analogy and Prediction Module |
| - Meta-Learning Module         |
| - Explainability Module        |
| - Mode Recognition             |
| - Concept Abstraction          |
+--------------------+
```

4. Principle Submachine

```
+--------------------+
|   Principle Submachine       |
+--------------------+
| - Ethics Framework |
| - Security Module  |
| - Decision Validation     |
| - Value Alignment      |
| - Bias Detection       |
+--------------------+
```

5. Foundation Submachine

```
+--------------------+
|   Foundation Submachine      |
+--------------------+
| - External Tool API Interface |
| - Infobase Connection      |
```

```
| - System integration module    |
| - Resource Management          |
| - Support for parallel computing    |
+-------------------+
```

Workflow:

1. The I/O submachine receives the input to the problem, uses RAG to retrieve the relevant information, and GPT processes large-scale data.
2. The knowledgebase submachine starts, fuses multimodal information, starts the inference engine, and queries the knowledge graph to obtain relevant knowledge.
3. The abstract submachine decomposes the problem, runs simulation predictions, and applies meta-learning strategies to optimize the solution.
4. The principle submachine checks the ethics and safety of the solution to ensure compliance with pre-defined values and norms.
5. The foundation submachine calls on the necessary external tools and resources to support the implementation of the solution.
6. The I/O submachine generates the final output and captures feedback through interactive learning modules to continuously improve system performance.

This architecture is designed to combine the scaling direction and submachine requirements you mentioned to create a comprehensive, flexible, and ethical common problem-solving system. It is capable of handling various types of problems, from simple queries to complex decision support, while maintaining the ability to learn and adapt.

Truth-seeking products - one of the applications of the General Problem Solver

Difficulties in inventing a truth-seeking product

One of the applications of problem-solving is to seek the truth. However, it is not easy to invent a truth-seeking product. For example, Elon Musk has proposed the idea of TruthGPT, but so far it has not come to fruition. Even so, here are some "truth-seeking" products that solve the problem:

Elder Billy feels that although in the previous chapter we raised the problems and some possible prevention and countermeasures caused by various social, technological, political, and military evil forces in the era of AI 2.0 ANI, perhaps a fundamental approach is to invent a truth-seeking product to counter ChatGPT's fantasy and false answers, as well as the use of AI by evil elements to defraud and disrupt the social order and profit from it.

However, some scholars believe that in the foreseeable future, it is extremely unlikely that an artificial intelligence can clearly judge the truth. Here's why:

1.   Subjectivity of truth: Truth can be subjective, depending on context, point of view, and evidentiary interpretation. AI needs to navigate these complexities.
2.   Nuances and ambiguities: Human language is full of nuances and ambiguities that are difficult for machines to understand. AI can misinterpret factual statements or miss key details.
3.   Changing information landscape: New information is constantly emerging and needs to be constantly updated to keep AI accurate.

A product approach that seeks the truth

Still, in a situation where large language models (LLMs) such as ChatGPT can be misused to produce fake content, we need to do something:

1. Ongoing research in the field of AI is helpful in detecting misinformation and bias.
2. Fact-checking tools and media literacy remain important tools in the fight against misinformation.
3. Explainable AI (XAI) is a more realistic approach: XAI can increase transparency: Explainable AI technology can help us understand how AI models come to conclusions. This is valuable for identifying potential biases in the data used to train the model or the algorithm itself. But XAI doesn't guarantee authenticity: even with XAI, it's important to be critical of AI output. XAI can explain the "why" behind AI decisions, but it doesn't necessarily guarantee that the decisions are accurate or unbiased.
4. Human oversight remains crucial: XAI can be a valuable tool in the fight against misinformation, but it should not replace human judgment and fact-checking. XAI offers promise for understanding AI decision-making, but it's just a tool for fighting for accurate information. Critical thinking and information validation remain crucial.
5. Retrieval Augmented Generation (RAG) is used as the client, and Memory-Augmented Memory-Based Architecture (MAMBA) is used as the server to replace GPT's Transformer to enhance the approach to truth. This is because (1) RAG combines retrieval and generation by retrieving relevant information from the knowledge base and then generating responses with a generative model. This increases the basis and reliability of the answers, as the generative model bases its answers on known real-world data, rather than relying solely on the deduction of internal parameters. (2) MAMBA can

further improve the performance and realism of the model. Compared to traditional Transformer architectures, MAMBA can process large-scale memories more efficiently and perform fast retrieval, resulting in more precise answers to questions. Such a design can effectively enhance the authenticity and reliability of generative AI because it combines retrieval and generation, and leverages a more robust server-side architecture to process data.

6.　Use out-of-distribution (OOD) technology to teach robots the pure truth of knowing what they know and not knowing what they don't know (i.e., not acting if they are not pre-trained) to avoid robots with generative AI installed injuring people due to fantasies. OOD technology is designed to identify and process data that the model has not seen, ensuring that the model only works within the domain in which it was trained. If the model encounters unseen data, it identifies the data as OOD and takes appropriate action (such as rejecting the answer or providing a conservative response). This approach ensures that the model only operates with the support of its training data and proceeds cautiously when encountering uncharted territory.

7.　The above RAG+MAMBA+OOD is a reasonable and forward-looking design solution. Such a design can improve the reliability and security of AI systems, and reduce problems caused by miscalculations or fantasies. During implementation, you need to ensure:

　　a.　There is enough high-quality training data to support the accuracy of the model. (In this regard, Google tried to improve her search engine, Search Generative Experience, with RAG, but it still ended up with poor search results due to problems with the quality of the training data.))

　　b.　effective mechanisms of Retrieval and generation to assure authenticity of the basis.

    c.   Strict OOD detection mechanism to ensure that the system can operate cautiously when in uncharted territory.

Seeking the market for truth-seeking products

The idea of finding the truth in the face of AI-generated misinformation has significant market value. Here's why:

The problem is getting worse, and the demand is growing:

1.   Widespread misinformation: Deepfakes, biased AI outputs, and fabricated content are becoming increasingly sophisticated and difficult to detect. This creates a strong demand for solutions that help people distinguish between the real and the fake.

2.   Public concern: Public trust in information is waning due to the prevalence of misinformation. People are looking for ways to verify information and make informed decisions.

Market Opportunity:

1.   Fact-checking tools: There is a growing market for fact-checking tools and services that analyze information, identify potential biases, and verify their accuracy.

2.   Media literacy education: Educational tools and programs that teach people how to critically evaluate online information have high market value.

3.   Transparency and explainability in AI: AI developers who prioritize transparency and explainability in their models may have a competitive advantage.

Challenges and Considerations:

1.   Keep innovating: As AI technology that generates misinformation continues to evolve, so must the tools to find the truth. It's an ongoing process that requires constant development and adaptation.

2. Accessibility and usability: Solutions to find the truth need to be accessible and user-friendly for a broad audience, not just technologists.

3. Ethical considerations: There are ethical considerations when dealing with automated fact-checking and AI-powered information analysis. For example, bias detection needs to be done responsibly and avoid scrutiny.

Overall, the market value of finding the truth in an era of AI misinformation is enormous. It addresses the growing concerns of the public and provides opportunities for a variety of solutions and services.

Training courses to be taken

The following is a list of AI technology courses that readers should be trained in in this chapter:

1. Machine Learning Fundamentals

   o These include supervised, unsupervised, and reinforced learning

2. Deep learning and neural networks

   o Special focus on Transformer architectures and large language models (e.g., GPT)

3. Natural Language Processing (NLP).

   o Includes RAG (Retrieval Enhanced Generation) technology

4. Computer vision

   o As part of a multimodal AI system

5.   Knowledge Representation and Reasoning

    o   Includes Knowledge Graph and Symbolic AI

6.   Multimodal AI system

    o   Integrate multiple data types such as text, images, audio, and more

7.   Causal reasoning and logical reasoning
8.   Meta-learning and transfer learning
9.   AI Ethics & Security

    o   This includes bias detection and mitigation

10.   Explainable AI (XAI)
11.   Out-of-Distribution (OOD) detection
12.   Memory-enhanced model architecture (e.g., MAMBA)
13.   AI system integration

    o   This includes API design and use

14.   Large-scale data processing and analysis
15.   AI simulation and prediction technology
16.   Human-computer interaction and interactive learning systems
17.   Application of AI in specific fields (e.g., healthcare, finance, education, etc.)
18.   Cloud computing and distributed systems (for large-scale AI deployments)
19.   AI project management and development process
20.   The latest AI research trends and cutting-edge technologies

These courses will provide readers with a comprehensive foundation of AI knowledge that will enable them to understand

and potentially participate in the development of complex AI systems like the GPS we discussed. At the same time, these courses also cover various AI technologies and methods mentioned in the annex, such as RAG, MAMBA, OOD, etc. Depending on your personal background and goals, it is advisable to selectively delve into some of these areas.

Resources

The following are ten important papers related to the above courses, including English titles, authors, sources, and years:

1. "Attention Is All You Need" by Ashish Vaswani, Noam Shazeer, Niki Parmar, Jakob Uszkoreit, Llion Jones, Aidan N. Gomez, Łukasz Kaiser, Illia Polosukhin Source: Advances in Neural Information Processing Systems (NeurIPS), 2017. Introduced Transformer Framework, the basis of modern large language model.
2. "BERT: Pre-training of Deep Bidirectional Transformers for Language Understanding" by Jacob Devlin, Ming-Wei Chang, Kenton Lee, Kristina Toutanova Source: North American Chapter of the Association for Computational Linguistics (NAACL), 2019. Proposed a BERT model, and significantly improved the performance of multiple NLP tasks.
3. "Retrieval-Augmented Generation for Knowledge-Intensive NLP Tasks" by Patrick Lewis, Ethan Perez, Aleksandra Piktus, Fabio Petroni, Vladimir Karpukhin, Naman Goyal, Heinrich Küttler, Mike Lewis, Wen-tau Yih, Tim Rocktäschel, Sebastian Riedel, and Douwe Kiela. Source: Advances in Neural Information Processing Systems (NeurIPS), 2020. Introduced RAG techniques, and integrate retrieval and generation to elevate the performance of NLP task.

4. "Mamba: Linear-Time Sequence Modeling with Selective State Spaces" by Albert Gu, and Tri Dao. arXiv preprint, 2023. Proposed MAMBA architecture, as a potential replacement of Transformer, and provides more efficient sequence modeling.

5. "A Survey on Deep Learning Techniques for Image and Video Semantic Segmentation" by Alberto Garcia-Garcia, Sergio Orts-Escolano, Sergiu Oprea, Victor Villena-Martinez, and Jose Garcia-Rodriguez. Applied Soft Computing, 2018. This paper reviews the application of deep learning in image and video semantic segmentation, which is valuable for computer vision courses.

6. "Causal Inference in Statistics: A Primer" by Judea Pearl, Madelyn Glymour, and Nicholas P. Jewell. Wiley Book Publishing Co., 2016. This book introduces the basic concepts of causal reasoning and is helpful for causal reasoning courses.

7. "Learning to Learn by Gradient Descent by Gradient Descent" by Marcin Andrychowicz, Misha Denil, Sergio Gomez, Matthew W. Hoffman, David Pfau, Tom Schaul, Brendan Shillingford, and Nando de Freitas. Conference Source: Advances in Neural Information Processing Systems (NeurIPS), 2016. This paper explores the concept of meta-learning and shows how to learn optimization algorithms.

8. "The AI Ethics Brief: A Framework for Ethical Artifical Intelligence" by Jessica Morley, Luciano Floridi, Libby Kinsey, and Anat Elhalal. Source: Science and Engineering Ethics, 2020. It provides a framework for AI ethics, which is very helpful for AI ethics and safety courses.

9. "A Unified Approach to Interpreting Model Predictions" by Scott M. Lundberg and Su-In Lee. Source: Advances in Neural Information Processing Systems (NeurIPS), 2017. SHAP (SHapley Additive exPlanations), a method to

explain machine learning model predictions, is proposed and is valuable for explainable AI courses.

10. "Towards Out-of-Distribution Generalization: A Survey" by Zheyan Shen, Jiashuo Liu, Yue He, Xingxuan Zhang, Renzhe Xu, Han Yu, and Peng Cui. arXiv preprint, 2021. This paper reviews the research on out-of-distribution generalization, which is very helpful for OOD testing courses.

These papers cover a wide range of AI fields, from basic theories to cutting-edge applications, and can be used as complementary materials for in-depth study of related courses.

Q&A Questions

1. What is the RAG+MAMBA+OOD approach and how does it contribute to improving the reliability of AI systems?
2. Why do you need multimodal fusion when designing a generic problem solver (GPS)?
3. How to implement "interactive learning" in GPS and what are its advantages?
4. What are the main functions of the "principle base" in GPS and why is it important? In GPS, how does an "abstract submachine" help solve complex problems?
5. Why does "explainability" need to be considered in GPS design and how can it be achieved?
6. How does the "foundation submachine" in GPS enhance the overall capability of the system?

These questions cover several key aspects of GPS design, reflecting the complexity and versatility of modern AI systems.

Practical Training Questions

Practice Question 1

Design a simplified version of the GPS architecture diagram, focusing on the I/O submachine, knowledgebase submachine and abstract submachine. Describe the data flow and interaction between the three submachines, how to use RAG, MAMBA, and OOD technologies to handle a complex natural language query task. Your design should consider how to combine multimodal information (such as text and images) and how to implement task decomposition and inference. Please provide a specific use case to illustrate your design.

Practice Question 2

A simplified version of the RAG (Retrieval Enhanced Generation) system was implemented using Python as part of the GPS I/O submachine. Your system should be able to:

1. Retrieve relevant information from a given collection of documents
2. Use the retrieved information to generate responses

Please implement the following features:

a) Document indexing: Create a simple document indexing system, b) Similarity search: Implement a basic similarity search function, c) Answer generation: Generate answers using the retrieved information

Here are some key code snippets to get you started:

```
import numpy as np
from sklearn.feature_extraction.text import TfidfVectorizer
```

```python
from sklearn.metrics.pairwise import cosine_similarity

class SimpleRAG:
    def __init__(self, documents):
        self.documents = documents
        self.vectorizer = TfidfVectorizer()
        self.tfidf_matrix = self.vectorizer.fit_transform(documents)

    def retrieve(self, query, k=3):
        query_vec = self.vectorizer.transform([query])
        similarities = cosine_similarity(query_vec,
self.tfidf_matrix).flatten()
        top_k_indices = similarities.argsort()[-k:][::-1]
        return [self.documents[i] for i in top_k_indices]

    def generate_answer(self, query):
        relevant_docs = self.retrieve(query)
        # Here you need to implement a simple answer generation
logic
        # Tip: You can use the retrieved documents to construct a
simple response
        # For example, you can return the first sentence of the most
relevant doc
        return relevant_docs[0].split('.')[0] + '.'

# Usage Example
documents = [
    "The sky is blue. The sun is bright.",
    "Grass is green. Trees have leaves.",
    "Water is essential for life. Most of Earth is covered in water."
]

rag_system = SimpleRAG(documents)
query = "What color is the sky?"
answer = rag_system.generate_answer(query)
```

```
print(f"Query: {query}")
print(f"Answer: {answer}")
```

Your task is to perfect the system, especially to improve the generate_answer methods. Consider how to combine multiple relevant documents retrieved to generate better responses. You can also try to add a simple OOD detection mechanism that responds appropriately when the query is completely irrelevant to the collection of documents.

Hint:

1.   Consider using more advanced NLP techniques, such as sentence embeddings or pre-trained language models, to improve the retrieval and generation process.
2.   You can use simple templates or rules to combine the retrieved information to generate more coherent responses.
3.   For OOD detection, you can set a similarity threshold below which the query is considered OOD.

When you're done, test your system and discuss its benefits and limitations. Think about how this simple RAG system can be integrated into a larger GPS architecture, and how it interacts with knowledge base and abstract slaves.

Chapter 21: Unpacking the Challenges and Solutions Brought by AI 3.0

The Inner Choices of Workplace Christians in the AI 3.0 Era

Christians in the workplace often find themselves navigating the complexities of the marketplace, sometimes faced with a choice between deceit and integrity. The Bible teaches:

"Whether you turn to the right or to the left, your ears will hear a voice behind you, saying, 'This is the way; walk in it.'" (Isaiah 30:21)

Therefore, by listening to God's guidance, one can make the right choice.

Figure 38 How should your human mind make a choice when facing a crossroads in life?

The Confucian tradition in China holds the following teaching:
"The human mind is precarious; the mind of the Way is subtle. Be resolute and single-minded, and hold firmly to the Mean." —
Ancient Text of the Book of Documents · Counsel of Yu
(古文尚書·大禹謨).

This represents the sacred principle of the sages, handed down from Emperor Yao and Emperor Shun. According to Zhu Xi, a prominent Neo-Confucian scholar of the Southern Song Dynasty, during Emperor Yao's time, there was no written language, so truths were transmitted orally. When Yao passed the principle to Shun, he simply said: "Hold firmly to the Mean" (允執厥中). When Shun passed it to Yu, he added the preceding twelve characters.

This core teaching was then passed down to Tang, King Wen of Zhou, King Wu of Zhou, and later transmitted through the lineage of the Duke of Zhou and Confucius. It is both the grand principle by which sages govern the world and the essential method for individual cultivation of the heart.

These sixteen characters mean: the human mind is unstable and easily led astray, while the mind of the Way is subtle and difficult to grasp. Only by being pure in focus and unified in purpose can one truly adhere to the Middle Way. (A common mistake is the 16 characters is from Chinese Taoism. However, in the period of Yao, Shun, Yu and Tang, the originator of Taoism, Lao Tzu, was not born yet.)

In ancient China, lacking knowledge of the Lord God, people sought the right path by relying on their own careful discernment. This was because the human heart was considered unreliable, and the "heart of the Way" was too subtle to grasp.

However, this path of discernment is not only crucial for individual Christians but also for communities and nations. Scholars of biblical theology often identify certain Hellenistic kings as foreshadowing the Antichrist. For instance, Antiochus IV Epiphanes once served as a "hostage" in Rome. After enduring hardships, he gradually rose to power through deceit and usurpation, eventually becoming formidable. His life was filled with treachery; he desecrated the temple, persecuted the saints, and instigated multiple wars. In fact, many rulers, both ancient and modern, have served as hostages, yet not all became tyrants. Chiang Ching-kuo of Taiwan, for example, was once a hostage and exiled to Siberia, but he emerged as a benevolent and approachable leader. Whether one becomes virtuous or tyrannical depends on the choices made within their heart.

In the era of AI 3.0, the challenges and opportunities faced by Christians in the workplace will undergo significant changes due to the widespread adoption of Artificial General Intelligence (AGI). **Since individuals can become experts or masters in various fields, expertise is no longer the primary issue. The only remaining distinction lies in the choice between deceit and integrity.** Here are some considerations that Christians should be mindful of in this era:

Maintain your beliefs and values

1.   **Ethics and Morality**: Uphold Christian ethical and moral standards, especially when faced with complex AI decision-making processes, and ensure that your actions are consistent with your beliefs.
2.   **Integrity and Honesty**: Maintain integrity and honesty in data processing, algorithm design, and decision-making processes, and avoid engaging in any form of fraud or unethical behavior.

Learning & Adaptation

1.   **Continuous Learning**: Actively learn and master new technical knowledge and skills, especially those related to AI and quantum computing, to improve their professional capabilities.
2.   **Adaptability**: Adapt to a rapidly changing technology environment, respond flexibly to challenges and changes in the workplace, and embrace new opportunities with a positive attitude.

Social Responsibility and Contribution

1. **Serving Others**: Using one's professional knowledge and skills to provide services to society and others, caring for and helping those in need.
2. **Promote Justice**: Promote justice and fairness in the workplace, oppose any form of discrimination and injustice, and strive to create a fair and harmonious working environment.

Ethical considerations and technology application

1. **Technology Application**: Prudent use and development of AI technologies to ensure that the application of these technologies is ethical and does not cause harm to society and individuals.
2. **Privacy Protection**: Respect and protect the privacy of individuals, and comply with relevant laws and ethics in the process of data collection and processing.

Professional Ethics & Integrity.

1. **Integrity Management**: Maintain integrity in business activities and reject any form of unfair competition and commercial fraud.
2. **Professional Responsibility**: Assume your own professional responsibility to ensure that the quality of the products and services provided is up to standard and will not have a negative impact on users and society.

Work-life balance.

1. **Healthy Living**: Maintain a work-life balance, pay attention to physical and mental health, and do not let work pressure affect family and faith life.

2.   **Spiritual Growth**: Amid a busy professional life, it is still necessary to persist in devotional and prayer, maintain an intimate relationship with God, and seek spiritual growth.

Addressing ethical challenges.

1.   **Prevent Misuse**: Be vigilant about the misuse of technology, especially in areas that may affect human rights and social stability, such as surveillance and privacy violations, and actively participate in relevant discussions and decision-making, and promote the responsible use of technology.

2.   **Ethical Decision-Making**: When faced with complex decisions, use faith to guide your choices and ensure that all actions are consistent with Christian moral teachings.

Spread the faith.

1.   **Witness to Your Faith**: Bear witness to your faith in the workplace with your actions and words, share the gospel with your colleagues, and be a messenger of love and peace.

2.   **Community Involvement**: Actively participate in church and community activities to contribute to community building and development.

Overall, in the age of AI 3.0, Christians need to maintain their beliefs and values in a rapidly changing technological environment, and face workplace challenges with positivity, integrity, and responsibility. Through continuous learning, service to others, and the promotion of justice and integrity, Christians can make a positive impact in the workplace and contribute to the positive development of society and technology.

Prophecies in the Book of Daniel Regarding Greece, Egypt, Syria, and Antiochus IV of the Seleucid Empire (Daniel 11:3–35)

Although the Greek Empire was already symbolized in Daniel Chapter 8 through the vision of a male goat, and its wicked "little horn" that emerged from one of its four horns was described, the details were not exhaustive. Here, the prophecy is further elaborated.

In Daniel 11:3, "a mighty king shall arise" refers to Alexander the Great. Like a whirlwind sweeping away autumn leaves, he conquered Persia, but died in the army at the young age of 33. After his death, the empire was divided into four kingdoms. These four kingdoms have already been listed in Chapter 16 of this book. Among them, two dynasties are particularly relevant: Seleucus Nicator, who took over Mesopotamia and Syria and established the Seleucid dynasty, is the "King of the North" in Daniel 11:6. Egypt and Palestine were taken over by General Ptolemy Lagus, who established the Ptolemaic dynasty, referred to as the "King of the South" in Daniel 11:5.

Originally, these two dynasties were allies. Seleucus even served as a subordinate to Ptolemy I for a time. However, their successors—Ptolemy II of the South and Antiochus II of the North—fell into conflict. Ptolemy II attempted to resolve the hostilities through marriage, giving his daughter Berenice to Antiochus II. However, Antiochus II was poisoned by his former wife Laodice, whom he had divorced. Berenice, the newlywed princess, was also murdered by Laodice's son. Afterwards, Laodice installed her own son on the throne, who became known as Seleucus II.

In the South, Berenice's brother succeeded their father as Ptolemy III. To avenge his sister's death, he marched north, captured Antioch, and killed Laodice. Seleucus II fled to Asia Minor, and after regaining strength, he attempted to retaliate by invading the South and defeating Ptolemy III, but he failed and returned empty-handed.

Seleucus II's two sons took up the cause of revenge. The elder son died in battle, but the younger, Antiochus III, continued the campaign. He eventually recaptured Syria and Palestine, advancing as far as the Egyptian border city of Raphia. Jerusalem also submitted to him. Its people retained their past privileges, and he reduced their taxes, dedicating the revenue to temple expenses and supporting the rebuilding of Jerusalem's walls.

However, the good times did not last. Soon after, Ptolemy IV of the South launched a successful northern campaign and defeated Antiochus III. Antiochus fled north, and after the death of Ptolemy IV, he took advantage of the fact that the new king, Ptolemy V, was only five years old. He marched south again, not only recovering Palestine but also forcing Ptolemy V to acknowledge his supremacy. Antiochus even began coveting Rome in Europe. Yet his ambitions were completely crushed by the Roman general Scipio. Antiochus had to cede Asia Minor to Rome and pay a huge annual tribute. In a desperate move to cover the costs, he attempted to plunder a temple but was assassinated.

His son, Seleucus IV, also tried to loot temple treasures to pay the Roman debt and was assassinated as well. This entire history of conflict and revenge between the northern and southern dynasties perfectly matches the prophecies in Daniel 11:3–20.

The central figure of Daniel Chapter 11 is **Antiochus IV**, brother of Seleucus IV, and a prefiguration of the **Antichrist**, known as the profaner of the Temple. Due to his father's defeat by Rome, he was sent as a hostage—what ancient China would call a "political pawn." Thirteen years later, he was allowed to return home, replaced by his nephew.

However, en route back, he learned that his brother Seleucus IV had been assassinated. He borrowed troops from the king of Pergamum, returned to his homeland, killed the assassin, and then used the pretext of political turmoil to prevent his nephew from ascending the throne. He seized power for himself. The Bible describes him as "a contemptible person to whom royal majesty had not been given. He shall come in without warning and obtain the kingdom by flatteries" (Daniel 11:21).

Because his claim to the throne was illegitimate, both domestic and foreign forces opposed him. However, Antiochus IV was ruthless and cunning. He eliminated his enemies and even used marriage alliances to gain Egyptian territory. He cunningly renegotiated debts with Rome and, as Daniel 11:23 says, "became strong with a small force of people." To win popular support, he plundered wealth and distributed it to his supporters: "Yet this will only last for a time" (Daniel 11:24).

Chapter 21: Unpacking the Challenges and Solutions Brought by AI 3.0   **341**

Antiochus launched an expedition against Egypt, attempting to annex it entirely. Though he successfully captured Ptolemy VI, he feigned goodwill by releasing him back to Alexandria in hopes of inciting conflict between him and the newly crowned Ptolemy VIII. His plan failed, and Roman intervention at this critical time thwarted his attempt to make Egypt a vassal state: "But it shall not succeed, for the end will still come at the appointed time" (Daniel 11:27).

As a prefiguration of the Antichrist, Antiochus IV returned from this failed campaign. To make up for military expenses, he looted the sacred vessels and treasures of the Holy Temple in Jerusalem, committing his **first act of temple desecration**: "The King of the North shall return to his land with great wealth, but his heart shall be set against the holy covenant. He shall work his will and return to his own land" (Daniel 11:28).

Soon after, Antiochus IV again marched against Egypt, reaching Alexandria. The Egyptians resisted fiercely, and the Romans sent ships from Cyprus to interfere. Defeated again, he had no choice but to retreat: "At the appointed time he shall return and come into the south, but it shall not be this time as it was before. For ships of Kittim shall come against him, and he shall be afraid and withdraw. He shall be enraged and take action against the holy covenant. He shall turn back and pay attention to those who forsake the holy covenant" (Daniel 11:29–30).

On his return, he entered Jerusalem **for the second time**, treating the Holy City as a rebel stronghold. He unleashed brutal violence, rape, and looting. He abolished the temple system, replaced it with Greek-style worship he favored, and converted the Temple into a shrine for Zeus— **a second desecration** of the Temple's sacred vessels: "They shall set up the abomination that makes desolate" (Daniel 11:31).

At that time, some people yielded to power, while others became brave martyrs. These martyrs were the "wise among the people" who "shall make many understand, though for some days they shall stumble by sword and flame, by captivity and plunder" (Daniel 11:33).

Antiochus IV's Antichrist-like behavior eventually led to the **Maccabean**

Revolt, a Jewish struggle for religious freedom. Three years later, the Temple sacrifices were restored, commemorated as the **Feast of Dedication** (Hanukkah).

Through the typology of the Antichrist seen in Antiochus IV, God allowed the Jews to undergo suffering, **"to refine them, purify them, and make them white, until the time of the end, for it still awaits the appointed time" (Daniel 11:35).**

Figure 39 Antiochus IV, the foreshadowing of the AntiChrist

The integration of storage, computing and training in the AI3.0 era

The era of AI3.0 is an era of artificial general intelligence (AGI). By this time, the narrow intelligence used in various industries in AI2.0 can already be integrated, not only merging algorithms but also making some industry training data public, including training data for robots in various industries. Therefore, after such integration, whether it's a human or a robot, they can stand alone and become experts or masters in any field.

Meanwhile, the GPUs and NPUs of the AI2.0 era are no longer suitable for the integrated AI algorithms and training data, necessitating the use of quantum algorithms' entanglement, superposition properties, and the exponential acceleration of quantum computers. In the AI3.0 era, superconducting quantum computers (superconducting QC) have also overcome the challenges of quantum error correction, achieving 100K or even millions of qubits.

While the era of AI3.0 is anticipated to be an era of artificial general intelligence (AGI) using quantum computer, it is important to note that the field of AI is rapidly evolving. Recent advancements, such as those by OpenAI, suggest that AGI might be achievable sooner than expected using classical computers. However, the full realization of AGI will likely require further breakthroughs in both classical and quantum computing.

The powerful function of quantum computer storage and computing

The concept of process in-memory (PIM) means that data storage and processing occur in the same location to minimize data transfer bottlenecks. In fact, this concept can already be realized in the classical Von Neumann computing architecture: for example, Nvidia in the AI 2.0 era claims that it has used HBM-PIM technology to achieve the integration of storage and computing in the architecture of CPU, GPU and NPU. However, quantum computer memory computing is no longer a von Neumann architecture, so its potential is staggering: there are major challenges as well as opportunities. The following is a detailed analysis of the powerful functions of quantum storage and computing:

1. Quantum memory and processing integration:

Quantum states: Quantum computing relies on qubits, which can exist as superpositions of states. The ability to maintain and manipulate these states directly within the memory device can improve computational efficiency.

Entanglement and superposition: Quantum mechanical principles like entanglement enable highly parallel operations where data processing and storage are inherently intertwined.

2. Reduce data movement

Coherence and decoherence: Minimizing data movement can reduce the decoherence effect, which is detrimental to quantum computing. In-memory operations can help maintain qubit consistency by reducing the need for data transfer.

Reduced latency: By processing data where it is stored, quantum systems can operate with lower latency than architectures where data moves between separate memory and processing units.

3. Speed & Efficiency:

Parallelism: Quantum systems can perform parallel computations on a large scale. Consolidating memory and processing can further enhance this parallelism by allowing data processing to occur simultaneously in multiple memory locations.

Energy efficiency: Reducing data movement also reduces energy consumption, which is critical for the scalability of quantum computers.

The challenge of integrating storage and computing in quantum computers

1. Quantum storage technology:

Stable qubits: Developing stable and reliable quantum memory that can maintain the superposition of qubits for long periods of time is a major challenge. Qubits are susceptible to errors created by environmental interactions.

Error correction: Quantum error correction is complex and requires additional qubits for parity. Integrating it into a quantum computing framework is challenging.

2. Technical Barriers:

Physical implementation: Building hardware that supports in-memory quantum computing requires overcoming significant physical and engineering hurdles. This includes creating storage elements that can hold qubits and perform logical operations efficiently.

Scalability: Ensuring that such systems can scale to handle a large number of qubits, while maintaining consistency and minimizing error rates is a major obstacle.

3. Architecture design

Interconnects and interfaces: Designing efficient interconnects and interfaces between memory and processing units in quantum systems requires novel approaches because traditional interconnects are not suitable for quantum information.

Programming models: The development of programming models and algorithms that can effectively utilize the integration of quantum storage and computing is essential for practical applications.

Considerations for the integration of storage and computing in quantum computers

1. qRAM

Research into quantum RAM (qRAM) capable of efficiently storing and retrieving quantum information is ongoing. qRAM is a key component to realize the integration of quantum storage and computing.

2. Mixed Approach

A hybrid quantum-classical architecture is being explored, in which classical storage-computing technology is combined with quantum processing. These can provide a steppingstone to complete quantum storage and computing integration.

3. Advances in Quantum Hardware

Advances in quantum hardware, such as the development of topological qubits and improved error correction methods, could pave the way for future storage-computing integration capabilities in quantum systems.

While in-memory computing for quantum computers faces great challenges, it also holds great promise for improving the efficiency and performance of quantum systems. Achieving this goal requires breakthroughs in quantum storage technology, error correction, and architecture design. As research progresses, the integration of memory and processing in quantum computers may become a reality, resulting in more powerful and efficient quantum computing systems.

In the AI 3.0 era, quantum computers can not only perform the integration of storage and computing, process long contexts, but also learn from external stimuli dynamically in real time, which means a huge leap in computing power and adaptability. Here's an analysis of the strength of quantum computers and what these features mean:

The powerful quantum integration of storage, computing and training

In addition to the above-mentioned integration of storage and computing, there is also the question of whether AI pre-learning can be realized at any time from the stimulation of the environment. Nvidia, which is highly known for its AI 2.0 traditional computer GPU, has also announced that she will devote itself to this field.

1. Dealing with very long contexts:

      a.   Context length: The ability to process extremely long contexts means that quantum computers can process and analyze information that is deeply temporal or space-dependent. This is especially powerful in applications that require long-term planning, comprehensive historical analysis, or working with large data sets with complex interdependencies.

b.   Complex problem solving: Problems that require understanding and processing large data sequences, such as natural language understanding, large-scale simulations, and complex decision-making scenarios, will significantly improve accuracy and efficiency.

2. Dynamic learning ability:

a.   Continuous adaptation: The ability to continuously and dynamically learn from new data allows quantum computers to adapt to changing environments and data inputs in real-time. This will enable it to continuously improve its effectiveness and make more accurate forecasts and decisions.

b.   E-learning: Systems can employ e-learning algorithms, which are essential for applications where data flows are critical and quickly adaptable, such as financial transactions, autonomous driving, and real-time monitoring systems.

Challenges and considerations for the integration of quantum memory, computing, and training

1. Technical Challenges:

a.   Error correction: Quantum systems are still prone to errors due to decoherence and other quantum noises. Developing effective error correction methods is essential for reliable in-memory quantum computing.

b.   Scalability: Scaling quantum systems to efficiently handle a wide range of contexts and dynamic learning remains a major challenge that requires advances in quantum hardware and algorithms.

2. Moral and Social Impacts:

a.   Privacy and security: Continuous learning systems can raise concerns about data privacy and security, especially when it comes to how they handle sensitive information.

b.   Accountability for decision-making: As these systems become more autonomous and capable, ensuring transparency and accountability in the decision-making process becomes critical.

The impact and application of the integration of quantum memory, computing and training

1. Scientific research

a.   Drug Discovery & Materials Science: The ability of quantum computers to process large amounts of data and learn dynamically, can accelerate the drug discovery process and materials science research by rapidly adapting to new discoveries and optimizing simulations.

b.   Climate modeling: Enhancing the ability to process large amounts of climate data and learn new patterns can produce more accurate climate models and predictions that can help understand and mitigate climate change.

2. Quantum Intelligence:

a.   Natural language processing: Processing long contexts and dynamically learning from interactions will revolutionize natural language processing, enabling deeper understanding, more coherent conversation generation, and real-time adaptation to new information.

b.   Machine learning models: Quantum-enhanced machine learning models can significantly outperform classical models in tasks such as pattern recognition, anomaly detection, and predictive analytics due to their ability to handle larger datasets and continuously adapt.

3. Security and Cryptography:

    a.   Adaptive security systems: The dynamic learning feature will allow the development of adaptive security systems that are constantly learning and adapting to new threats, making cybersecurity measures more robust and effective.

    b.   Quantum cryptography: Advanced quantum cryptography technology can be developed, using the function of quantum storage, computing and training to ensure a secure communication channel that adapts to potential vulnerabilities in real time.

4. Autonomous Systems:

    a.   Robotics and autonomous vehicles: Enhanced processing power and dynamic learning will lead to smarter and more adaptable robots and autonomous vehicles that are able to understand and navigate complex environments more effectively.

    b.   Smart infrastructure: Infrastructure systems (e.g., smart grids, smart transportation systems) can dynamically adapt to usage patterns and optimize performance in real-time to improve efficiency and reliability.

5. Healthcare:

    a.   Personalized medicine: The ability to process long-term context and dynamic learning can improve personalized medicine, tailoring treatment to individual patients based on continuous monitoring and analysis of patient health data.

    b.   Real-time diagnosis: Advanced diagnostic systems can learn new medical data in real-time to provide faster and more accurate diagnosis and treatment recommendations.

The revolutionary technology of AI3.0's storage-computing-training integration not only breaks through the limitations of AI3.0 being merely a storage-computing integration technology but also overcomes the limitations of various practical applications of artificial intelligence described above. The combination of processing big data environments and real-time learning achieves unprecedented efficiency and adaptability, thereby solving complex data-intensive problems. However, realizing this potential requires overcoming significant technical challenges.

The described quantum computer, capable of performing in-memory calculations, processing long contexts, and learning dynamically from external stimuli, is one of the fundamental factors in the performance of superhuman intelligence (ASI) if certain conditions are met.

The Relationship Between Continuous Learning and Real-Time Learning

"Continuous learning" is an important concept in artificial intelligence, and it is closely related to "real-time learning". The following is a clarification of these terms and their relationships:

Continuous Learning:

1. Definition: Continuous learning in AI refers to the ability of a model to continuously update and improve its knowledge and skills over time without having to completely retrain it from scratch.
2. Key features:

   a. Adapt to new data and experiences
   b. Retain previously learned information
   c. Avoid catastrophic forgetting (new learning erases old knowledge)

3.   Advantage:

  a. Keep your model up to date with the changing environment
  b. More effective than frequent full retraining
  c. Conceptual drift (changes in the distribution of the underlying data over time) can be handled

Real-time learning:

1.   Definition: Real-time learning involves updating a model's knowledge or parameters as soon as new data becomes available, typically during the model's operation or deployment.
2.   Key features:

  a. Integrate new data instantly
  b. It usually involves online learning algorithms
  c. It can be a form of continuous learning, but with an emphasis on speed and real-time

The relationship between continuous learning and real-time learning:

1.   Overlap: Real-time learning can be thought of as a subset or specific implementation of continuous learning. All real-time learning is continuous, but not all continuous learning happens in real-time.
2.   Velocity: Real-time learning emphasizes real-time updates, while continuous learning may involve regular updates or batch processing of new data.
3.   Implementation: Real-time learning often requires specialized algorithms and infrastructure to handle rapid updates, while continuous learning may use a wider range of techniques.

Pre-training for continuous and real-time learning is no longer a one-time thing, but is updated at any time as the data is trained. However, it is worth noting that:

1. Pre-training still works: Many systems still use pre-training to build a strong initial knowledge base, and then use continuous or real-time learning to refine and update that knowledge.
2. Challenges: Both approaches face challenges in maintaining model stability, preventing overfitting to the latest data, and managing compute resources.
3. Hybrid approach: Some systems use a combination of regular batch updates (a form of continuous learning) and real-time updates of key information.

In the context of advanced artificial intelligence systems (AGI or ASI) that we have been discussing, the ability to learn continuously and in real-time is essential to adapt quickly and effectively to new information and environments. These technologies are key to creating AI systems that can truly interact with and learn from the world in a human-like way.

AI3.0-era Quantum-generative AI

Quantum computers have the potential to enable generative AI because they can handle complex problems that traditional computers can't easily solve. Here are some of the key technologies and steps for quantum computers to implement generative AI:

1. Quantum State Representation and Superposition

Quantum computers use the superposition of qubits and quantum states to represent multiple states at the same time. This allows it to excel in parallel calculations, especially when working with generative models. For example, a qubit can represent both 0 and 1, allowing quantum computers to explore multiple generation paths simultaneously.

2. Quantum Entanglement and Correlations

Quantum entanglement allows for strong correlations between qubits, such that the state of one qubit can affect the state of another. This feature can be used to design complex generative models where the generated results of each part are highly correlated. For example, quantum entanglement can be used to generate highly consistent image or sequence data.

3. Quantum Fourier transform

The Quantum Fourier Transform (QFT) is an efficient quantum algorithm that enables fast Fourier transforms to be implemented on quantum computers. QFT has advantages in handling frequency-domain analysis and data compression in generative models, enabling quantum computers to generate high-quality samples faster.

4. Variable Quantum Feature Solver (VQE).

VQE is a hybrid quantum-classical algorithm used to find the ground state energy of a system. VQE can be used to train generative models, such as generators in generative adversarial networks (GANs). By adjusting the quantum circuit parameters, VQE can find the best generative model parameters to generate realistic data.

5. Quantum Boltzmann machine (QBM)

The quantum Boltzmann machine is a generative model based on the principles of quantum mechanics. QBM uses quantum tunneling and quantum entanglement to explore data distributions and can generate high-dimensional data such as images and text. Compared with the traditional Boltzmann machine, QBM has stronger expression ability and higher generation efficiency.

6. Quantum variational autoencoder (QVAE).

Quantum variational autoencoders combine the advantages of variational autoencoders (VAEs) and quantum computing to generate high-dimensional data. QVAE utilizes quantum circuits to implement the encoding and decoding process that can generate realistic image, audio, and text data. The parallel processing capabilities of quantum computing give QVAE significant advantages in terms of generation speed and quality.

Implementation Steps:

1.   **Select Generative Model**: Determine the type of generative model you want to implement, such as GAN, VAE, or other generative models.
2.   **Design quantum circuits**: Design corresponding quantum circuits based on the selected generative model, including quantum state initialization, quantum gate operations, and measurements.
3.   **Hybrid training**: Hybrid quantum classical algorithms, such as VQE, are used to train quantum generative models. The classical computing part is responsible for optimizing the quantum circuit parameters, and the quantum computing part executes the quantum circuit.
4.   **Model evaluation**: Evaluate the quality of the generated model by measuring the data generated by the quantum state and comparing it with the real data.
5.   **Improvement and optimization**: Based on the evaluation results, the quantum circuit and optimization algorithm are adjusted to further improve the performance of the generated model.

Key Technologies:

1.   **Quantum state initialization**: How to efficiently initialize a quantum state so that it represents the input data of the generative model.

2.   **Quantum gate operation**: Design efficient quantum gate operation to realize the computational process of generating models.

3.   **Quantum measurements**: Generate data through quantum measurements and compare them with classical data.

4.   **Hybrid optimization**: Combines the advantages of quantum computing and classical computing to perform efficient parameter optimization.

The use of quantum computers in generative AI is still in its early stages, but its potential is enormous. With the advancement of quantum computing technology, generative AI is expected to make breakthroughs in areas such as image generation, natural language processing, and complex data modeling.

Quantum encryption in the AI3.0 era

As we mentioned in Chapter 16, the first problem with qubits reaching more than one million is that the encryption algorithms of traditional computers are no longer able to resist the instantaneous decryption of quantum computers. This makes it easy for many hackers to steal private information and financial funds. Industry, especially finance, must quickly switch from traditional computers to quantum computers.

AI3.0 Era's General Problem Solver (GPS)

In the previous chapter, we discussed the AI 2.0 general problem solver GPS. If the GPT version continues to be upgraded to the ability to reach GPS, then how big is its solution range? Are general technical, scientific, and educational problems easier to solve, but will human society, economy, politics, war, and climate warming encounter bottlenecks? What are the bottlenecks of GPS? The analysis is as follows:

AI2.0 GPS solution scope

Technical and scientific issues: AI2.0 GPS may excel in these areas because these issues often have well-defined parameters and quantifiable results. It can quickly analyze large amounts of data, formulate hypotheses, design experiments, and even make new scientific discoveries.

1.   Education: GPS can revolutionize personalized learning, develop the best learning path for each student, and provide real-time feedback and answers.
2.   Medical Diagnostics and Research: There could be huge breakthroughs in analyzing medical data, assisting in diagnostics, and drug development.
3.   Environmental issues: Potential for significant contributions in climate modeling, predicting natural disasters, and designing sustainable solutions.
4.   Engineering & Design: Complex systems can be optimized, and innovative designs can be proposed.

However, for more complex social, economic, political, and certain global issues, AI2.0 GPS may encounter the following bottlenecks:

1.   Values and ethical questions: Many social and political issues involve conflicting values, and there is no single "right" answer. GPS can struggle to make decisions that are satisfactory to everyone on these issues.
2.   Unpredictability of human behavior: Economic and social systems are highly complex and influenced by human emotions and irrational behavior. GPS can be difficult to fully simulate and predict these systems.
3.   Uncertainty about long-term impacts: The long-term impacts of certain decisions, such as climate policies, can take decades to become apparent, making predictions more difficult.
4.   Conflict of interest: Different groups often have conflicting interests when it comes to political and economic issues. GPS can struggle to balance these interests.
5.   Data quality and bias: GPS decisions can also be biased if there is bias or incompleteness in the training data.
6.   Lack of "common sense" and emotional understanding: Despite technological advancements, AI may still lack the common sense

judgment and emotional empathy of humans, which is crucial when dealing with certain societal issues.

7.   Barriers to implementation: Even if GPS proposes an ideal solution, actual implementation may face political, economic, or social resistance.

8.   Security and control issues: Giving GPS enormous decision-making power can lead to security risks and control issues.

9.   Limitations of cross-cultural understanding: Global issues often require a deep understanding of different cultural contexts, which can be a challenge for AI systems.

10.   Creative and breakthrough thinking: While AI has demonstrated creativity in some areas, it may still be inferior to humans in problems that require a real "leap of thought."

In conclusion, a general problem solver will undoubtedly greatly enhance our ability to solve complex problems, especially in the fields of science and technology, healthcare, and the environment. However, for issues involving human values, emotions, and social complexity, GPS may be more appropriate as an aid rather than a complete replacement for human decision-making.

Ideally, it might be human-robot collaboration: leveraging the data processing and analysis power of GPS, combined with human judgment, ethical considerations, and creative thinking, to tackle global challenges. This approach maximizes the strengths of both while overcoming their respective limitations.

AI3.0 Era General Problem Solver GPS

In the era of AI 3.0, AGI (Artificial General Intelligence) can solve any problem of any domain, unlike ANI (Narrow Artificial Intelligence) that only deals with one domain. The first difficulty in developing AGI products was the initial collection of solutions from various areas. The second difficulty is the algorithms that merge solutions from these areas. The third difficulty is finding the test data to make sure the product is working properly. The fourth difficulty is getting the initial technology adopters and selling to them. Here is how we can solve these difficulties:

1. Collect solutions from various fields

a. **Collaborate with experts**: Collaborate with domain experts in various fields (medicine, finance, engineering, etc.) to collect high-quality solutions and datasets.

b. **Open Source and Community Contributions**: Leverage open-source projects and community contributions to gather a variety of solutions. Participate in and contribute to open-source initiatives to build credibility and attract collaborators.

c. **Interdisciplinary Research Programs**: Establish or join research programs with a focus on interdisciplinary research. Encourage the exchange of ideas between different fields.

d. **Datamart**: Use or build a datamart where you can buy, sell, or exchange datasets and pretrained models from a variety of domains.

2. Algorithm for merging solutions

a. **Unified Framework**: Develop or adopt a unified framework that can integrate algorithms from different domains. Frameworks such as TensorFlow, PyTorch, and others already support a range of algorithms and can be extended or customized.

b. **Modular architecture**: AGI systems are designed using a modular architecture that allows for easy integration and updating of domain-specific algorithms. This will make it easier to add new features without breaking existing ones.

c. **Transfer learning and meta-learning**: Utilizing advanced techniques such as transfer learning and meta-learning enables models to apply knowledge from one domain to another, facilitating the merging process.

d. **Interdisciplinary teams**: Assemble interdisciplinary teams of engineers, data scientists, and researchers to ensure a holistic approach to merging algorithms.

3. Find test data

a.   **Synthetic data generation**: Use synthetic data generation techniques to create large, diverse datasets for testing. Tools such as GAN (Generative Adversarial Network) can be used to create realistic test data.

b.   **Crowdsourcing**: Use crowdsourcing platforms such as Amazon Mechanical Turk to generate diverse test data. This method can help collect a variety of data from different fields.

c.   **Data partnerships**: Partnerships with companies and institutions across industries to access their data for testing.

d.   **Simulation and** sandboxing: Create simulated environments and sandboxes to test AGI across a variety of scenarios and domains in a controlled setup.

4. Acquire and sell to initial technology adopters

a.   **Early Adopter Program**: Start an early adopter program for innovators and early adopters who are willing to try new technologies. Offer incentives such as discounts, exclusive features, or dedicated support.

b.   **Industry-specific solutions**: Initially focused on developing and marketing solutions for specific industries where AGI can demonstrate clear and immediate value (e.g., healthcare diagnostics, financial analytics).

c.   **Pilot Project**: Implement a pilot project with potential clients to demonstrate AGI's capabilities and gather feedback. Successful pilot projects can lead to wider adoption.

d.   **Partnerships and Alliances**: Establish strategic partnerships with key players across a wide range of industries to increase credibility and reach out to their customer base.

e.   **Educational Activities**: Conduct educational activities, including webinars, seminars, and white papers, to educate potential customers about the benefits and applications of AGI.

f.   **User-Friendly Interface**: Develop a user-friendly interface and tools that make it easy for non-experts to take advantage of AGI features. This lowers the barrier to entry and increases adoption.

In conclusion, in the era of AI 3.0, developing and deploying AGI products is a multifaceted challenge that requires careful planning and execution at all stages. By leveraging collaboration, advanced technology, and strategic marketing, these challenges can be met and AGI successfully brought to market.

The essence and potential limitations of AGI products in the AI 3.0 era

If AGI is achieved, does it mean that there are no problems in individual areas? Since it is universal, can we say that all areas of human problems can be summarized? Or is it possible that there will be different AGI products, and their problem-solving capabilities will have to pass a public level before they can be allowed to be sold in the market, because AGI will always be limited and will not always be omnipotent? These questions touch on the nature and potential limitations of AGI (Artificial General Intelligence). An in-depth look is as follows:

Concept and scope of AGI:

a.   Theoretically "universal": The idea of AGI is to create an artificial intelligence system capable of performing any intellectual task, which should theoretically be able to handle all problem areas that humans are capable of handling.

b.   Practical limitations: However, even the most advanced AGI systems may have some inherent limitations:

Limitations on computing power

a.   Restriction of access to and processing of data

b.   The depth of knowledge in some specific domains may not be as deep as that of specialized narrow AI

c.   Domain specificity: Some highly specialized fields may still require specific expertise and experience that may be difficult to replicate entirely with a "one-size-fits-all" system.

Diversity and standardization of AGI:

Diverse AGI offerings: Different AGI offerings are likely to emerge, each with its own unique strengths and areas of expertise. This diversity may stem from:

a.   Different training data and methods

b.   Different architectural designs

c.   Optimized for specific use cases

Standardization and certification: Recognized standards may require the establishment of a set of standards to assess the capabilities and safety of AGI systems:

a.   Performance Criteria: Evaluates problem-solving skills in a variety of tasks and domains

b.   Safety standards: Ensure that the AGI system does not cause harm

c.   Ethical Standards: Assess whether AGI's decisions are ethical and legally compliant

d.   Explainability criteria: Ensure that the decision-making process of AGI is transparent and understandable

e.   Market access: Based on these standards, a certification system may be established, and only AGI systems that meet certain benchmarks are allowed to be used in a particular field or market.

Limitations of AGI:

a.   Creativity and intuition: AGI may still have limitations in tasks that require a high degree of creativity or human intuition.

b.   Emotional and social intelligence: AGI may still be inferior to humans in areas that require deep emotional understanding or complex social interactions.

c. Value Judgment: AGI may not be a complete substitute for human judgment in decisions involving morality, ethics, or values.

d. Adaptability: When faced with new and never-before-seen problems, AGI may not be as flexible as the long-evolved human brain.

e. Self-awareness: The question of whether AGI is capable of developing true self-awareness remains a philosophical and technical open question.

Conclusion:

While AGI's goal is to achieve "universal" intelligence, in reality it may never be truly "omnipotent". Each AGI system may have its advantages and limitations. As a result, a diverse AGI ecosystem is likely to emerge in the future, with different systems focused on different application areas.

At the same time, it will become essential to establish a comprehensive set of evaluation and certification standards to ensure the safety, reliability and effectiveness of AGI systems. These standards will not only consider technical performance, but also ethical, safety, and social impacts.

Eventually, AGI is likely to become a powerful assistant and partner for humans, rather than completely replacing human decision-making. Human-robot collaboration may be the best way forward, leveraging AGI's computing power and human creativity, intuition, and emotional intelligence to work together to solve complex problems.

Another problem with AI 3.0 is that since general AI can be adapted to any industry, it is likely that humans or robots in the 2.0 era will be replaced by such cheap, general-purpose intelligent computers. Professional robots will be replaced, and real people will cause another wave of unemployment.

The most terrifying thing is in the political and military aspects, because it is easier for a dictatorship to use artificial general intelligence to control the actions of the people and make them completely obedient. A dictator who is completely contrary to justice and justice can quickly come up with military and diplomatic cunning strategies to conquer and expand the territory under his rule. The people of the conquered regions are also vulnerable to bullying and tyranny.

Elder Billy's AI 3.0 Dream

In the age of AI 3.0, Elder Billy deeply contemplated the world's future. Although authoritarian governments might exploit technological advantages to stir up various social, economic, political, and military issues, he believed that these problems must have ways to be prevented and resolved. With all his heart, he prayed for the people of the world. What filled his thoughts by day eventually appeared in his dreams at night. In the stillness of the late hours, he had a dream.

The Beginning of the Dream: The Rise of the Antichrist

In the future era of AI 3.0, Artificial General Intelligence (AGI) had become the core driving force of society. Businesses and governments around the globe heavily relied on this highly integrated intelligence system. During this time, a politician named Schien gradually rose from obscurity. Hailing from a small nation, he was originally just an ordinary member of parliament. Yet he possessed exceptional intelligence and extraordinary political acumen.

Schien's ascent began during a domestic economic crisis that plunged his country into chaos and public outrage. Seizing the moment, Schien proposed a series of economic reform plans powered by AGI technologies, swiftly stabilizing the internal situation and gaining massive public support. He then employed AI technologies to manipulate elections, using data analysis and public opinion guidance to emerge victorious and become the nation's leader.

However, Schien was not satisfied with merely holding power. He knew that to maintain his rule, he needed broader support. Thus, he launched a series of welfare policies with the help of AGI to win the people's hearts. At the same time, he used AI in information warfare to suppress dissenters and political opponents, ensuring his absolute grip on power. Through cunning and scheming, Schien transformed from a nobody into a sovereign ruler.

The Middle of the Dream: Controlling the People and Waging War

After consolidating domestic power, Schien set his sights abroad. He initiated widespread mind control using AGI technologies. Through quantum computing and advanced data analytics, he monitored and manipulated the thoughts of his citizens. Every individual's thoughts, actions, and words were recorded and analyzed by the system. Any dissenting voice or act of defiance was swiftly suppressed.

Schien's control extended far beyond mere ideology. He rapidly developed his military might through AGI technologies—deploying intelligent drones, robotic armies, autonomous tanks, and other high-tech weapons. Under the pretense of "protecting national interests," he launched wars against neighboring countries. These wars were swift and brutal, with Schien's forces occupying enemy territories with lightning speed.

Under Schien's command, his army expanded rapidly, seizing large swaths of neighboring lands. But these wars also brought immense suffering. Countless families were torn apart, cities were destroyed, and people were displaced. Schien used AI to manipulate the narrative, claiming that these were "wars of liberation," meant to bring "peace and prosperity" to the people. In reality, his reign brought nothing but oppression and fear.

As Schien's power reached its zenith, his cruelty and deceit made him widely despised. He distorted justice, harmed the innocent, called evil good and good evil, and stopped at nothing to achieve his goals. Just as Antiochus IV desecrated the temple, Schien trampled on human dignity and freedom under his rule.

The End of the Dream: Revolution and Downfall

Schien's tyranny provoked fierce resistance both domestically and internationally. Dissidents and oppressed citizens began to organize themselves into a resistance movement. They secretly gathered strength, using AGI technology for counter-surveillance and intelligence warfare, gradually building the capacity to oppose Schien's regime.

At the same time, the international community could no longer tolerate Schien's acts of aggression. Several powerful nations united to form an international alliance and launched a large-scale counteroffensive against Schien's military. These countries, too, had advanced AI capabilities. Utilizing quantum computing for battle command and deploying superior weapons systems, they delivered precise and devastating strikes against Schien's forces.

Schien attempted to respond with cunning and manipulation, but he underestimated both the power of the people and the resolve of the international coalition. Under the combined pressure of the domestic resistance and international forces,

Schien's regime began to collapse. His armies suffered defeat after defeat, his control systems were breached, and his strategies were gradually exposed and neutralized.

Ultimately, Schien suffered a crushing defeat in a decisive battle. He was forced to flee the capital, desperately seeking a safe refuge. But the end had come. With the united efforts of domestic and international forces, he was captured and brought to justice.

Schien's downfall marked the end of his tyrannical regime. The people regained their freedom and began to rebuild their homeland. The international community also restored peace and reflected deeply on the lessons of this war. Humanity came to understand that only by respecting human dignity and freedom can lasting peace and true prosperity be achieved.

Post-Dream Reflection

Billy believed that this dream mirrored the historical foreshadowing of Antiochus IV found in the Book of Daniel. It revealed how, in the AI 3.0 era, an Antichrist-like dictator could use high technology to implement tyranny—only to eventually fall victim to his own cunning and brutality. It serves as a solemn warning: technological advancement must be accompanied by moral and ethical progress, or else it will lead to endless disaster.

"Only by upholding justice and righteousness, and respecting human dignity and freedom, can true peace and prosperity be realized."

Figure 40 Elder Billy AI 3.0 Dream: Robotic military police of artificial general-intelligence dictators patrol the streets, their cold metal bodies contrasting with the warm creatures they oppress. The sound of their mechanical footsteps echoes through the city, a constant reminder of the loss of humanity.

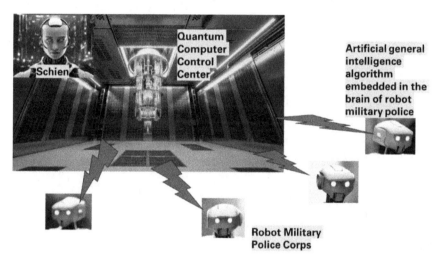

Figure 41 Elder Billy's AI 3.0 Dream: The dictator controls the population through a quantum computer center that controls a number of artificial general intelligence algorithms embedded in the brains of robotic military and police officers

Practical Issues and Solutions in the AI 3.0 Era

Billy further reflected on the details of his dream and, based on that, identified a series of complex challenges that may arise in the AI 3.0 era with the advancement of AGI and the application of quantum computing. He also proposed corresponding preventive and solution strategies:

Privacy and security

There are privacy and security concerns:

1. **Quantum decryption**: The powerful power of quantum computing makes traditional encryption algorithms fail quickly, leading to an increased risk of personal privacy and confidential data exposure. This is something that has not been seen in AI 2.0 using traditional computers.
2. **Hacking**: Malicious hackers exploit quantum computing power to carry out large-scale data theft and destruction.

Precautions and solutions for privacy and security are:

3. **Quantum-secure encryption**: Develop and implement quantum-secure cryptography technologies, such as quantum key distribution (QKD), to protect data security.
4. **Global collaboration**: Strengthen international cooperation to jointly develop and enforce cybersecurity standards and protocols to prevent quantum hacking.

Economy and employment

The economic and employment issues are:

1. **Wave of unemployment**: AGI can replace many professional and technical jobs, leading to a wave of mass unemployment that follows the wave of unemployment in AI 2.0. This is because ANI technology in the AI 2.0 era can only work within its purpose-designed domain, and cannot conduct comprehensive analysis or decision-making across multiple domains. And each Narrow AI system can only solve a specific problem, and cannot do complex

multitasking. As a result, the people who originally worked for ANI had to learn the new quantum computer as well as the technology of AGI in order to keep working. And the learning curve of quantum computers is quite steep.

2. **Economic inequality**: Businesses and individuals who are able to master and leverage AGI technology will greatly benefit, further widening the gap between rich and poor.

Economic and employment prevention and solutions are:

1. **Retraining and education**: Governments and businesses should invest in large-scale retraining and education programs for quantum technology and AGI algorithms to help the workforce adapt to the new technological environment.

2. **Social security**: Establish a sound social security system to provide basic income security and unemployment assistance to alleviate the impact of unemployment on society.

3. **Flexible policy-making**: AGI can be applied in a variety of fields, can self-learn and adapt to new environments and challenges, and is highly flexible and adaptable, from economic policy formulation to social management. (Unlike ANI, which can only work within its specifically designed domains, it cannot conduct comprehensive analysis or decision-making across multiple domains.))

Social and Ethical

Social and ethical issues include:

1. **Ethical** dilemmas: The decision-making process of AGI may violate human ethical standards, leading to moral and ethical dilemmas. Its powerful abilities, if abused,

can pose a great threat to human freedom and dignity, leading to serious ethical and moral problems.

2. **Social control**: Authoritarian governments use AGI for intense social control and surveillance, suppressing dissent and infringing on individual freedoms. Surveillance in the era of AI 2.0 ANI can only be used in specific areas, such as using facial recognition technology to track specific individuals or groups, or relying on data mining and analysis to implement targeted control and guidance of public behavior, or using natural language processing (NLP) to filter online information to control public opinion and crack down on freedom of speech. Due to the limited scope and depth of its control, it is possible for the population and opposition forces to discover and exploit its weaknesses to resist. However, in the era of AI 3.0 AGI, authoritarian governments are able to integrate multiple surveillance methods to seamlessly monitor every corner of society. Intelligent decision-making can also be made based on comprehensive data, and monitoring strategies can be adjusted in real time to improve the effectiveness and accuracy of control. Psychological and behavioral models can even be used to carry out deep psychological control and behavioral guidance, making people more receptive to government control and instructions. AGI can have a comprehensive and far-reaching impact on society as a whole, exercising control over all aspects of the economy, politics and culture. Ability to carry out long-term strategic planning and implementation to achieve sustained control and influence on society. This all-encompassing control and efficient management made the rule more secure, and it was difficult for the people and opposition to find effective means of resistance.

Social and ethical prevention and solutions are:

1. **Ethical Guidance**: Establish a special ethics committee to guide the development and application of AGI to ensure that it conforms to human ethical standards and values.
2. **Transparent Oversight**: Promote transparency in the AGI system and ensure that the decision-making process can be reviewed and monitored to prevent abuse.

Political and military

Political and military issues are:

1. **Military Expansion**: Authoritarian governments can use AGI to optimize and improve themselves, continuously improving their military capabilities and efficiency, and responding to emerging tactical problems. AGI can also be used to develop sophisticated military strategies for aggression and expansion.
2. **International tensions**: The competition between countries for the leading position in AGI technology can lead to international tensions and conflicts.

Political and military prevention and solutions are:

1. **International Regulations**: Develop international regulations to prohibit the misuse of AGI technology in the military and political spheres and to ensure the peaceful use of AGI.
2. **Peace Initiatives**: Promote international peace initiatives that encourage States to resolve disputes through dialogue and cooperation rather than resorting to military means.

In summary, the key difference between Narrow AI (AI 2.0) and Artificial General Intelligence (AGI, AI 3.0) when used by authoritarian governments to control the population lies in the scope, methods, flexibility, depth of influence, and long-term consequences of that control. Narrow AI can exert powerful control within specific domains, but its overall impact remains relatively limited. In contrast, AGI possesses comprehensive, adaptive, and far-reaching control capabilities, enabling long-term and all-encompassing domination of society.

To prevent the abuse of these technologies, it is essential to strengthen ethical and legal oversight throughout the development and application processes, ensuring that AI technologies serve the good of humanity. Moreover, in the AI 3.0 era, the advancement of AGI and quantum computing will bring unprecedented opportunities and challenges. To ensure these technologies benefit rather than harm humanity, a concerted effort from governments, industries, and societies worldwide is needed to establish and enforce strict ethical, legal, and technical standards.

At the same time, education, retraining, and social safety nets must be promoted to help people adapt to the new technological landscape, thereby ensuring societal stability and prosperity. In the realms of politics and military affairs, international cooperation and legal frameworks are vital to prevent the misuse of technology and to safeguard global peace and security.

Q&A Questions
1. What is the AI 3.0 era?
2. What are the characteristics of superconducting quantum computers in the AI 3.0 era?
3. What is the power of a quantum computer?
4. What are the challenges faced by the integration of storage and computing in quantum computers?
5. What is quantum RAM(qRAM)?
6. What is a hybrid approach?
7. What are the considerations for the integration of storage and computing in quantum computers?

Practical Training Question 1

Practical exercises to help students with technical backgrounds implement small-scale quantum generative AI models on the IBM quantum computing platform. This exercise will use IBM's Qiskit framework to simulate a simple Quantum GAN (QGAN) for data generation.

Implement a simple quantum generative adversarial network

target

Implement a simple QGAN to generate random numbers evenly distributed in the [0, 1] interval. QGAN consists of a quantum generator and a classical discriminator.

steps

1.   **Environment Settings**:

     o   Install the Qiskit library
     o   Register and acquire IBM Quantum Experience's API key
     o   Configure Qiskit with the API key

2.   **Quantum Generator Design**:

     o   Use parameterized quantum circuits to generate random numbers

3.   **Classic discriminator design**:

     o   Use a simple neural network as a discriminator

4.   **Training QGAN:**

    o   Train quantum generators and classical discriminators so that the data generated by the generators can fool the discriminators

Key code snippets

The following is a Python code snippet that shows how to use Qiskit to achieve the above steps.

python
```python
# Step 1: Environment Setup
from qiskit import Aer, IBMQ, transpile, assemble
from qiskit.providers.aer import QasmSimulator
from qiskit.circuit import QuantumCircuit, Parameter
from qiskit.visualization import plot_histogram
from qiskit.utils import QuantumInstance
from qiskit.algorithms.optimizers import COBYLA

import numpy as np
import matplotlib.pyplot as plt
import tensorflow as tf
from tensorflow.keras import layers

# Load IBM Q account
IBMQ.load_account()
provider = IBMQ.get_provider(hub='ibm-q')

# Step 2: Quantum Generator Design
def create_quantum_generator(params):
    qc = QuantumCircuit(1)
    qc.ry(params[0], 0)
    qc.measure_all()
    return qc

def get_probabilities(counts):
    shots = sum(counts.values())
    prob_0 = counts.get('0', 0) / shots
    prob_1 = counts.get('1', 0) / shots
    return [prob_0, prob_1]

# Step 3: Classical Discriminator Design
def create_classical_discriminator():
```

```python
    model = tf.keras.Sequential([
        layers.Dense(16, activation='relu',
input_shape=(1,)),
        layers.Dense(16, activation='relu'),
        layers.Dense(1, activation='sigmoid')
    ])
    model.compile(optimizer='adam',
loss='binary_crossentropy')
    return model

# Step 4: Training QGAN
def train_qgan(generator, discriminator,
num_epochs=1000):
    optimizer = COBYLA()
    quantum_instance =
QuantumInstance(backend=Aer.get_backend('qasm_simulator'
), shots=1024)

    for epoch in range(num_epochs):
        # Generate data from quantum generator
        param = np.random.rand(1) * np.pi
        qc = create_quantum_generator(param)
        counts =
quantum_instance.execute(qc).get_counts()
        prob = get_probabilities(counts)
        generated_data = np.array(prob).reshape(-1, 1)

        # Train discriminator
        real_data = np.random.rand(1, 1)
        x = np.vstack([real_data, generated_data])
        y = np.array([1, 0]).reshape(-1, 1)
        discriminator.train_on_batch(x, y)

        # Train generator
        loss = lambda p: -
discriminator.predict(np.array(get_probabilities(quantum
_instance.execute(create_quantum_generator(p)).get_count
s())).reshape(-1, 1))
        optimal_params = optimizer.minimize(loss, param)

        if epoch % 100 == 0:
            print(f'Epoch {epoch}: Loss:
{loss(optimal_params)}')
```

```
# Main Execution
discriminator = create_classical_discriminator()
train_qgan(create_quantum_generator, discriminator)
```

hint

1. **Environment Settings**:

    o   First, need to install Qiskit library, and configure IBM Qiskit API key to access quantum computing resources.

2. **Quantum Generator Design**:

    o   Design a simple quantum generator that uses a revolving gate of qubits to generate data.

3. **Classic discriminator design**:

    o   Use TensorFlow to build a simple neural network as a discriminator.

4. **Training QGAN:**

    o   By optimizing the parameters of the quantum generator, the data generated by the quantum generator can fool the classical discriminator, so as to achieve the goal of the generator to generate realistic data.

This exercise shows how to implement a simple quantum generative adversarial network on the IBM quantum computing platform, using quantum circuits to generate data and classical neural networks for discrimination. Hopefully, this will help students understand the basic concepts and implementation methods of quantum generative AI.

Practical Training Question two

At the current state of the art, there are still many technical challenges in implementing algorithms for merging solutions in a complete small

AGI (Artificial General Intelligence) product on IBM quantum computers, including unified frameworks, modular structures, transfer learning, and meta-learning. Nonetheless, we can design a simplified version of the practice questions to help students understand the basic implementation of these concepts.

A simplified algorithm for implementing a merging solution on an IBM quantum computer

target

Using the Qiskit framework on IBM quantum computers, a simplified quantum machine learning model is built to solve classification problems through modular structure and basic transfer learning.

steps

1. **Environment Settings**:

    o   Install Qiskit library and configure IBM Q Experience user account。

2. **Quantum Circuit Design**:

    o   Design a quantum circuit for implementing a fundamental binary classification problem.

3. **Modular construction**:

    o   Quantum circuits are designed as multiple modular components that can be easily combined and reused.

4. **Transfer Learning**:

    o   Using pre-trained quantum circuit components, a small number of parameters can be adjusted to adapt to new classification tasks.

5. **Meta-Learning**:

- o A simple meta-learning algorithm is implemented to optimize the parameters of quantum circuits so that they can be better adapted to a variety of classification tasks.

Key code snippets

The following is a Python code fragment that shows how to achieve the above steps.

python
```
# Step 1: Environment Setup
from qiskit import QuantumCircuit, Aer, transpile,
assemble, IBMQ, execute
from qiskit.circuit import Parameter
from qiskit.providers.aer import AerSimulator
from scipy.optimize import minimize
import numpy as np

# Load IBM Q account
IBMQ.load_account()
provider = IBMQ.get_provider(hub='ibm-q')

# Step 2: Quantum Circuit Design
def create_quantum_circuit(params, n_qubits=2):
    qc = QuantumCircuit(n_qubits)
    for i in range(n_qubits):
        qc.rx(params[i], i)
        qc.ry(params[n_qubits + i], i)
    qc.measure_all()
    return qc

# Step 3: Modular Structure
def create_modular_circuit(params):
    module1_params = params[:4]  # First module
parameters
    module2_params = params[4:]  # Second module
parameters
```

```
    qc1 = create_quantum_circuit(module1_params,
n_qubits=2)
    qc2 = create_quantum_circuit(module2_params,
n_qubits=2)

    return qc1, qc2

# Step 4: Transfer Learning
def transfer_learning(params, base_params,
learning_rate=0.1):
    return base_params + learning_rate * (params -
base_params)

# Step 5: Meta-Learning Objective Function
def meta_learning_objective(params, task_data):
    total_loss = 0
    for data in task_data:
        base_params, target_state = data
        adapted_params = transfer_learning(params,
base_params)
        qc = create_quantum_circuit(adapted_params)
        backend = Aer.get_backend('qasm_simulator')
        t_qc = transpile(qc, backend)
        qobj = assemble(t_qc)
        result = backend.run(qobj).result()
        counts = result.get_counts()

        # Calculate the negative likelihood of
generating target state
        likelihood = counts.get(target_state, 0) /
sum(counts.values())
        total_loss += -likelihood
    return total_loss

# Example training data (base_params, target_state)
task_data = [
    (np.random.rand(4) * 2 * np.pi, '11'),
    (np.random.rand(4) * 2 * np.pi, '00')
]

# Initial parameters for meta-learning
params = np.random.rand(8) * 2 * np.pi
```

```
# Classical optimization for meta-learning
result = minimize(meta_learning_objective, params,
args=(task_data,), method='COBYLA')
optimized_params = result.x

# Step 6: Run and Validate on IBM Quantum Computer
qc1, qc2 = create_modular_circuit(optimized_params)
backend = provider.get_backend('ibmq_qasm_simulator')
t_qc1 = transpile(qc1, backend)
t_qc2 = transpile(qc2, backend)
qobj1 = assemble(t_qc1)
qobj2 = assemble(t_qc2)
job1 = backend.run(qobj1)
job2 = backend.run(qobj2)
result1 = job1.result()
result2 = job2.result()
counts1 = result1.get_counts()
counts2 = result2.get_counts()

print("Optimized Parameters:", optimized_params)
print("Counts for Module 1:", counts1)
print("Counts for Module 2:", counts2)
```

prompt

1. **Environment Settings**:

   o Install Qiskit library and load IBM Q account。

2. **Quantum Circuit Design**:

   o Create a simple quantum circuit that uses parameterized Rx and Ry gates to implement basic binary classification tasks.

3. **Modular construction**:

   o Divide quantum circuits into multiple modules for easy combination and reuse.

4. **Transfer Learning**:

- o   Using the pre-trained quantum circuit module, a small number of parameters can be adjusted to adapt to the new classification task.

5.   **Meta-Learning**:

- o   A simple meta-learning algorithm is implemented to optimize the parameters of quantum circuits so that they can be better adapted to a variety of classification tasks.

Through this exercise, students can practice the basic concepts of quantum machine learning, including modular design, transfer learning, and meta-learning, on IBM quantum computers. Although this question simplifies many details, it provides a starting point for understanding the application of quantum computing in AI.

Chapter 22: A Closer Look at the Problems Triggered by AI 4.0

The Mindset of Christian Professionals in the Age of AI 4.0

Christians in the workplace must not adopt an "ostrich mentality," burying their heads in the sand.

In the face of the AI 4.0 era, Christian professionals cannot afford to be ignorant or passive. Turning a blind eye to the changes and challenges brought about by technological advances is not an option. Instead, they must stay alert, discern the times, and respond with wisdom, courage, and faith.

Christians in the workplace must not lose sight of eternity.

In a world increasingly driven by AI, efficiency, and profit, it is easy to become entangled in the temporal. However, Christians must retain an eternal perspective—remembering that their work is not only for human employers but also an offering to God. Decisions made in the workplace should reflect biblical values and an awareness of the eternal consequences.

Christians in the workplace must not idolize AI.

As AI capabilities grow more powerful, there is a growing temptation to view it as a savior of human civilization—capable of solving all problems and optimizing every system. Christians must resist this tendency to deify AI. Technology is a tool, not a god. Worship belongs to the Creator, not the creation. A Christian worldview recognizes that while AI may offer great utility, it is ultimately limited, flawed, and fallible.

Christians in the workplace must move from self-awareness to self-creation.

In the AI era, personal growth and transformation become even more critical. Christians must first understand their God-given identity and purpose. But more than that, they must actively participate in shaping their own character and calling in response to the challenges of the times. This process includes renewing the mind, cultivating spiritual maturity, and aligning daily choices with God's will.

Can the Christian worldview of the Gospel address the potential misuse of superintelligent AI by evil forces or the Antichrist?

The answer is yes—but it requires the church to rise up in discernment, unity, and action. The Christian worldview acknowledges the reality of evil and the existence of spiritual warfare. When superintelligent AI is weaponized by wicked rulers or the spirit of the Antichrist, Christians must not only resist through prayer and truth but also actively engage in policy, ethics, technology, and cultural influence to prevent its misuse.

The Prophecy of the Great War of the Antichrist in the Book of Daniel (Daniel 11:36–45)

The previous chapter of this book discussed how the angel Gabriel revealed to Daniel the prophecy concerning Antiochus IV in the era of the Greek Empire (Daniel 11:3–35). Antiochus IV serves only as a foreshadowing of the true Antichrist. However, in verses 36 to 45, the prophecy seamlessly transitions from Antiochus to the actual Antichrist himself, describing a series of wars with various nations. The behavior described—exalting himself above all gods, rejecting the god of his ancestors, honoring an unknown deity, and launching military campaigns across nations—goes far beyond the evils committed by Antiochus IV.

It must be acknowledged that the Antichrist is, in a sense, an "extended version" of multiple kings, including Antiochus IV, or the demonic powers that represent them. Broadly speaking, we can observe the following patterns:

(1) These kings often rise from humble beginnings—especially the "little horn" of the monstrous beast in Daniel chapter 7 and the "small horn" of the male goat in chapter 8. They use cunning and deception to win public favor and ascend to power.

(2) The Antichrist emerges from the north and frequently engages in conflict with southern kingdoms.

(3) Eventually, he invades Palestine and persecutes the children of God.

These characteristics align with the conduct of the Antichrist as described in Daniel 11:36–45. The critical point is that he relentlessly persecutes believers, but ultimately, when Christ returns for the second time, he will be cast into the lake of burning sulfur—and no one will be able to save him.

Storage, Computing and Training Under ASI

How To Obtain Superhuman Intelligence Through the Integration of Quantum Storage, Computing and Training

1. Technical feasibility:

   a. Advances in Quantum Hardware: Significant progress is needed in the development of stable, error-correcting quantum hardware. AI 3.0 quantum computers have solved the problem of being constrained by decoherence and quantum noise.

   b. Quantum Computing: Quantum Computing requires new architectures and technologies to store and process information directly in the memory elements of a quantum computer. This is a technology that AI 3.0 has already been actually implemented.

   c. Dynamic learning algorithms: Developing algorithms that allow quantum systems to learn dynamically and adapt in real time is another challenging area. While classical machine learning and artificial intelligence have made great strides in online learning, translating these concepts into quantum systems is complex.

2. Computing power:

   a. Processing Broad Contexts: The ability to process broad contexts may exceed the limits of human cognition, allowing quantum systems to establish links and predictions beyond human capabilities.

b.   Speed and efficiency: Quantum computers have the potential to accelerate exponentially in certain computations and solve problems that classical systems find difficult to solve, giving them significant advantages in various domains.

3. Learning and adaptation:

a.   Continuous improvement: If a system can continuously learn and adapt to new information without extensive retraining, it can rapidly improve its performance, potentially surpassing human learning and decision-making capabilities.

b.   Comprehensive understanding: The ability to integrate and synthesize large amounts of data from disparate sources can lead to insights and solutions that are beyond human reach.

Considerations For How to Achieve Superhuman Intelligence Through the Integration of Quantum Storage, Computing, and Training

1. Definition of Superhuman Intelligence:

Since AI 3.0 has reached the level of general artificial intelligence, and while ASI can be domain-specific (e.g., surpassing humans in specific tasks such as chess or protein folding), our ultimate goal is general superhuman intelligence (surpassing human intelligence in a wide range of tasks). Implementing a generic ASI is more complex than domain-specific.

2. Moral and Social Impacts:

a. Control & Safety: It is critical to ensure that superhuman intelligence systems are in line with human values and can be controlled. This includes the development of strong security mechanisms and codes of ethics.

b. Impact on society: ASI's integration into society will have a profound impact on the economy, employment, security, and daily life. It's crucial to be prepared for these changes.

3. Research trajectory of the time stile:

a. While quantum computing research is promising, achieving the described features and ASI may require decades of focused effort and breakthroughs in multiple areas of science and engineering.

b. Research & Development: Continued investment in quantum computing, artificial intelligence, and interdisciplinary research is essential to make the envisioned system a reality.

Given the significant advances in quantum hardware, storage-computing integration, dynamic learning algorithms, and error correction techniques, the described quantum computer can achieve superhuman intelligence. However, this is a long-term prospect that requires ongoing research and development. The possibility of achieving ASI depends on overcoming major technological breakthroughs and addressing the ethical and societal issues of this robust system.

Deficiencies of Quantum Memory Training and Formal Solutions to ASI

Even with powerful computing power, computing-in-memory technology, and real-time learning capabilities, some of the limitations of AGI may still be difficult to completely overcome in ASI era. This question touches on the deeper challenges of AI development. Let's explore this further:

Persistence of AGI Limitations:

1.   Computing power does not equal intelligent quality: While enhanced computing power can improve processing speed and efficiency, it does not necessarily solve problems that require a "qualitative leap" such as creativity, emotional understanding, etc.
2.   Data vs. experience: Just-in-time learning can improve the adaptability of AI, but it may be difficult to replace the intuition and "common sense" that humans have acquired through long-term evolution and socialization.
3.   Values and Ethical Judgments: These deep-seated human traits are not just a matter of data processing, but involve complex philosophical and cultural contexts.

Potential Solutions for ASI (Artificial Superintelligence):

ASI may theoretically overcome some of the limitations of AGI, but this is still a highly hypothetical field. Here are some possible directions:

1.   Self-improvement and self-programming: ASI may have the ability to self-improve, continuously optimizing its own algorithms and architectures, potentially pushing the limits of current AGI.
2.   Novel Computational Paradigms: ASI may develop entirely new computational methods that go beyond the current model of numerical computation and more closely resemble the way biological brains work.
3.   Quantum computing integration: Incorporating quantum computing may provide ASI with new ways to deal with complex problems, especially in simulating complex systems.

4. Cross-domain knowledge synthesis: ASI may be able to integrate knowledge from different domains in a way that has never been done before, generating new insights.

5. Deep Simulation and Prediction: ASI may be able to conduct deeper, longer-term scenario simulations to improve the understanding and prediction of complex systems (e.g., social, economic).

6. Enhanced abstract thinking: ASI may develop a higher level of abstract thinking skills, capable of working with more complex concepts and theories.

Potential Challenges of ASI's Solution:

1. Ethics and control issues: How can we ensure that ASI's goals are aligned with human interests? This involves complex alignment issues.

2. Explainability: ASI's decision-making process can become more difficult to understand and explain.

3. Risks: The development of ASI may carry unforeseen risks, including the possibility of loss of control.

4. Cognitive gaps: ASI's way of thinking can be fundamentally different from that of humans, leading to a huge gap in communication and understanding.

5. Social Impact: The emergence of ASI can raise profound social, economic, and philosophical questions.

While ASI may theoretically address some of the limitations of AGI, it also presents new and potentially more complex challenges. The key question is not only how to technically implement ASI, but also how to ensure that it is headed in line with human interests, and how to manage its potential risks and impacts.

In addition, some of the limitations of AGI (e.g., emotional understanding, certain aspects of creativity) may be a manifestation of human uniqueness. We need to consider whether all of these traits need or should be replicated by AI, or whether human-robot collaboration may be a more desirable future direction.

In general, the evolution from AGI to ASI is not only a technical issue, but also a complex topic involving philosophy, ethics, sociology, and other disciplines. It requires in-depth discussion and careful planning on a global scale.

Quantum Brain

While the previous section mentioned that "we need to consider whether all of these traits need or should be replicated by AI, or whether a human-robot collaboration model might be a more desirable future direction." However, according to the hypotheses of physics masters such as Roger Penrose, biomathematicians Stuart Kauffman, and some researchers at Quantum Brain Dynamics, it is possible that quantum phenomena or quantum computations occur in the human brain. This has led to some research based on brain-like computing on quantum computers, coupled with Elon Musk's human brain implant chip to communicate with human thinking, and the so-called "quantum brain" may indeed have breakthroughs in the future. So, some aspects of emotional understanding and creativity can still be replicated by AI, or in physical or physical co-operation, as in the case of human brain implants.

This viewpoint, which involves the intersection of quantum computing, neuroscience, and human-machine interface, is a direction worthy of in-depth discussion. The analysis is as follows:

1.   Potential of Quantum Brain Theory:

    a. The theories of Roger Penrose and Stuart Kauffman, among others, have indeed opened up new perspectives on how the human brain functions. Quantum effects may occur in neuronal microtubules, which may be related to consciousness and higher cognitive functions.

    b. If these theories are confirmed, they may provide new avenues for the development of AI systems that are closer to the functions of the human brain.

2.   Applications of Quantum Computing in AI:

    a. Quantum computing has the potential to dramatically increase the processing power of AI systems, especially in simulating complex systems and performing parallel calculations.

    b. This could bring AI closer to mimicking the complexity and efficiency of the human brain.

3.   Advances in Brain-mimic Computing:

    a. Brain-like computing models based on quantum computing may better capture some of the key properties of the human brain, such as nonlocality and quantum entanglement.

    b. This may help to develop AI systems that are closer to the human mindset.

4.   Brain-Computer Interface Technology:

    a. Projects such as Elon Musk's Neuralink are driving the development of brain-computer interface technology. This technology has the potential to enable a more direct and deeper connection between the human brain and the AI system.

    b. This close physical and physiological connection may open new avenues for the sharing of emotional understanding and creativity.

5.   Replication of Emotional Understanding and Creativity:

    a. Through a combination of quantum computing and brain-computer interfaces, we may indeed be able to better replicate or at least gain a deeper understanding of human emotional and creative processes.

    b. This can lead to AI systems not only mimicking, but also truly "experiencing" and "understanding" emotions, as well as generating original thinking.

6.   A new model of human-robot collaboration:

    a. This technology could lead to a deeper level of human-machine collaboration, in which the human mind and the AI system are no longer completely separate entities but are somehow integrated.

    b. This could create a new paradigm of "augmented human" or "human-machine hybrid intelligence".

Considerations and Challenges:

1.   Ethical Questions: This deep integration raises important ethical questions about human identity, privacy, and autonomy.

2.   Technical challenges: Applying quantum effects to large-scale systems at room temperature still faces significant technical challenges.

3.   Understanding gaps: Our understanding of quantum processes in the human brain and their relationship to macroscopic cognitive functions is still limited.

4.   Social impact: This technology can lead to increased social inequalities, and only a few people have access to this empowerment.

5.   Security considerations: Deep brain-computer interfaces can introduce new security risks, such as mind hacking or identity theft.

Conclusion:

The points presented here do demonstrate an exciting future possibility. By combining quantum computing, brain-mimic technology, and advanced brain-computer interfaces, we may indeed be able to make breakthroughs in replicating human emotions and creativity. This approach has the potential to not only change our understanding of AI, but also potentially redefine the concept of human intelligence.

However, it is also a reminder of the need to advance these technologies carefully and responsibly. We need to actively explore the relevant ethical, social and philosophical issues as technology develops. The way forward in the future may not be a simple AI replication of humans or human-machine collaboration, but a deeper level of intelligent convergence that could revolutionize our understanding of intelligence, consciousness, and human nature.

The development of this field will undoubtedly be an important frontier in the future of scientific and philosophical research.

Therefore, AI 4.0 is an era of super artificial intelligence. The achievement of super artificial intelligence is due to the progress of human research that has matured to understand and imitate the quantum operation phenomenon of human brain intelligence (or "brain-like computing"), so that the ability to emotion and reason can be replicated with software and hardware, and can further surpass the intelligence of the human brain. In terms of hardware, the photonic QC replaces the superconducting QC In terms of firmware, there is the aforementioned quantum brain, and in terms of application software, there is the mind model. These super AIs are being used positively in industry to accelerate the production of products and improve human well-being. In the medical world, there are many more mental illnesses (epilepsy, autism, Parkinson's, Alzheimer's disease) that can be completely simulated and treated.

AI4.0 Prediction of the Tragic Situation of the Battle Against the Evil Forces

However, AI 4.0's super-AI must solve important moral problems, as it can be misused by evil forces, especially dictatorial governments that use their temporary power to manipulate people's minds, brainwash people, and do whatever it takes to maintain power. Dictators also use the power of religion to stir up geography, politics, and stigmatize and imprison Christians.

On the other hand, dictators are also using super artificial intelligence to launch autonomous robot legions in the military in an attempt to conquer the world and trigger wars in many countries. Super artificial intelligence (ASI), if in the hands of autocrats, could have significant negative impacts on five aspects: social, technological, economic, political, and military. Here is the detailed description and corresponding solutions:

Social Impact

Negative Effects:

1.   **Surveillance and Domination**: As mentioned in the previous chapter, AI 3.0's AGI is capable of mimicking or surpassing human capabilities in a number of domains. It can perform complex analysis, decision-making, and forecasting, but its capabilities are limited to human level. AGI can effectively monitor and manage populations, but its decision-making may still be faulty or biased. However, AI 4.0's ASI has a level of

intelligence beyond humans and can make faster and more accurate decisions than humans in any field. It is capable of handling extremely complex data sets, performing sophisticated analysis and predictions, and is capable of continuous self-improvement. This means that it is much more efficient and precise in terms of domination and control than AGI.

2. **Controlling People's Minds and Brainwashing**: AI 3.0's AGI can use big data and machine learning technology to monitor people, conduct psychological analysis, and guide behavior based on this data. It can control public opinion and indoctrinate through means such as media, education, and social services. However, the ASI of AI 4.0 can carry out a deeper level of control and use more advanced technical means. For example, through gene editing and brain/computer interface technology, people's thoughts and behaviors are directly influenced or controlled. It can anticipate and prevent potential insurgency, and suppress them even before they occur. ASI can also be used to monitor and analyze citizens' behavior and thoughts on a large scale, using highly personalized information for brainwashing and propaganda that prevents people from thinking for themselves.

3. **Social Fragmentation**: ASI can exacerbate social inequality because autocrats may focus their benefits only on the elites who support the regime, ignoring or oppressing other groups.

Figure 42 Dictators use optical quantum computers to control submissive robots, as well as obedient people implanted with brain chips and genetically recombined.

Prevention Programs:

1. **Promote transparency**: Establish international agreements to ensure transparency in the development and use of AI and provide global oversight of abuse.
2. **Education and awareness-raising**: Enhance citizens' digital literacy and critical thinking skills to help them discern disinformation and brainwashing.

Technological and ethical implications

Negative effects:

1. **Technological Monopoly**: Dictators may monopolize technology, limiting the openness and progress of science and technology, leading to the stagnation of technological innovation.
2. **Moral and Ethical Challenges**: As mentioned in the previous chapter, AGI decision-making for AI 3.0 is still influenced by human programming and design, and its behavior and

decision-making are subject to certain moral and ethical constraints. Even if used by authoritarian governments, the application of AGI may be subject to certain technical and ethical limitations. However, the ASI of AI 4.0 has the ability to self-improve and learn, and its actions and decisions may go beyond the moral and ethical framework of humans. If in the hands of an authoritarian government, ASI could be used to exert extreme control and oppression, beyond the limits of what is acceptable to human morality. The development of ASI may not be subject to moral and ethical constraints, leading to the development and application of dangerous technologies, such as mass surveillance and human rights violations.

Prevention Programs:

1.   **International Scientific and Technological Cooperation**: Promote international scientific and technological cooperation to ensure that technology development and application comply with globally recognized ethical standards and legal norms.
2.   **Establish Ethical Standards**: Develop and promote moral and ethical standards for AI to ensure that technologies are developed and applied in a way that is consistent with human well-being.

Economic Impact

Negative Effects:

1.   **Economic Monopoly**: Authoritarian governments may control economic resources and markets through ASI, creating economic monopolies and suppressing competition and innovation.
2.   **Unfair Distribution**: The benefits of ASI technology can be concentrated in the hands of a few elites, widening the gap between rich and poor, leading to social unrest.

Prevention Programs:

1.   **Anti-monopoly Policy**: Promote international anti-monopoly policy, prevent technology monopoly and market manipulation, and ensure fair competition.

2.   **Inclusive Economic Policies**: Develop policies to ensure equitable distribution of technology benefits, promote inclusive economy, and reduce the gap between rich and poor.

Political Influence

Negative Effects:

1.   **Political Repression**: The impact of AI 3.0's AGI is mainly concentrated in the country or region, and the use of technology to strengthen the control and management of society. It can play a role in many aspects, including economic, political, and military, but its influence may be limited by technology and resources. However, the ASI of AI 4.0 can exert influence on a global scale, using its ability to surpass humans for domination and control on a global scale. It can coordinate the policies and actions of several countries and achieve optimal results in any field, resulting in comprehensive and efficient governance. Domestically, ASI may be used to intensify political repression, monitor dissent and opposition, and restrict free speech and political rights.

2.   **Long-term Impact**: The long-term impact of AI 3.0's AGI is mainly to improve the efficiency of governance and strengthen the means of control, but its development and application are still limited by human understanding and control. Authoritarian governments may use AGI to prolong their rule, but there may still be loopholes and opportunities for rebellion in their means of rule. However, the long-term impact of AI 4.0's ASI could be a radical change in the structure and operation of human society. Because of its ability to surpass human intelligence, ASI can continuously optimize the means of governance, making dictatorships more stable and difficult to overthrow. This could lead to an unprecedented form of totalitarian rule, completely eliminating the possibility of revolt and dissent.

3. **Global Instability**: The technological superiority of authoritarian regimes can trigger international political turmoil and threaten global peace and stability.

Prevention Programs:

1. **International Political Cooperation**: Strengthen international cooperation and establish multilateral mechanisms to ensure that science and technology are not used to infringe on human rights and undermine international peace.
2. **Supporting the Democratization Process**: The international community should support the democratization process in all countries and promote transparent and accountable governance.

Military Repercussions

Negative Effects:

1. **Military Expansion**: Autocrats may use ASI to develop autonomous robot corps for military expansion and aggression that threaten global security.
2. **Arms Race**: ASI technology could trigger a new arms race, exacerbating international tensions and increasing the risk of war.

Prevention Programs:

1. **International Arms** control agreements: Promote international arms control agreements to limit the use of ASI in the military field and prevent arms races and military expansion.
2. **Global Security Mechanism**: Establish a global security mechanism to strengthen international coordination and cooperation to ensure that AI technologies are not used for aggression and breach of peace.

Overall, while both AGI and ASI can be used by authoritarian governments to rule over the population, ASI's capabilities and influence far exceed those of AGI, making its means of governance more efficient and comprehensive. This poses greater moral and ethical challenges and greater threats to human freedom and dignity. To prevent this from happening, the international community needs to strengthen the regulatory and ethical framework for AI technology to ensure that the development of technology serves the well-being of all humanity and is not abused. In the social, scientific, technological, economic, political, and military aspects, it is necessary to prevent the misuse of technology through international cooperation, transparent governance, ethics and legal regulation, and ensure that the development and application of AI technology is conducive to human well-being and promotes global peace and stability.

(Note that the above only prewarns with prevention approaches, but the real solution is in the next chapter.)

Q&A Questions

1.   What are the main differences between Super Artificial Intelligence (ASI) in the AI 4.0 era and Artificial General Intelligence (AGI) in the AI 3.0 era in terms of capabilities?
2.   In the era of AI 4.0, how might autocrats use ASI to control people's minds and brainwash people?
3.   What are the possible moral and ethical challenges for ASI in the AI 4.0 era?
4.   In terms of politics, what long-term impact might ASI have on dictatorships?
5.   What the international community can do to prevent ASI from being abused by dictators

Practical Training Questions

Title of the exercise: Extending a quantum brain simulation model on an IBM quantum computer

target

Expand on the quantum machine learning model in the previous chapter, combine quantum brain theory and brain-computer interface technology to simulate human cognitive processes, and explore the potential of going beyond artificial general intelligence (AGI) to super artificial intelligence (ASI).

Detailed description

1.   **The potential of quantum brain theory**:

   a.   Theories by Roger Penrose and Stuart Kauffman, et al., suggest that quantum effects may occur in neuronal microtubules, affecting consciousness and higher cognitive functions.
   b.   Simulating this effect in quantum circuits can help us better understand the quantum properties of the human mind.

2.   **Applications of Quantum Computing in AI**:

   a.   Use quantum computing to process and simulate complex neural networks to increase the processing power and efficiency of AI systems.

3.   **Advances in Brain-Inspired Computing**:

   a.   Use quantum computing to build a brain-like model to capture the non-local and quantum entanglement properties in the human brain.

4.   **Brain-Computer Interface Technology**:

    a.   Simulate the close connection between the human brain and AI systems to explore the sharing of emotional understanding and creativity.

steps

1. **Environment Settings**:

    a.   Install Qiskit library and configure IBM Q Experience user account。

2. **Quantum Circuit Design**:

    a.   Design a quantum circuit to simulate quantum effects in neuronal microtubules.

3. **Brain-mimetic model creation**:

    a.   Use quantum circuit to capture non-local quantum entanglement feature in human brain.

4. **Brain-computer interface simulation**:

    a.   Simulate the connection between the human brain and quantum circuits and explore the shared mechanisms of emotion and creativity.

Key code snippets

Below is a Python code snippet showing how the previous model can be extended to combine quantum brain theory and brain-computer interface technology.

python
```
# Step 1: Environment Setup
from qiskit import QuantumCircuit, Aer, transpile,
assemble, IBMQ, execute
from qiskit.circuit import Parameter
```

```python
from qiskit.providers.aer import AerSimulator
from scipy.optimize import minimize
import numpy as np

# Load IBM Q account
IBMQ.load_account()
provider = IBMQ.get_provider(hub='ibm-q')

# Step 2: Quantum Circuit Design for Quantum Brain
Simulation
def create_quantum_brain_circuit(params, n_qubits=4):
    qc = QuantumCircuit(n_qubits)
    # Simulate quantum effects in microtubules
    for i in range(n_qubits // 2):
        qc.rx(params[i], i)
        qc.ry(params[n_qubits // 2 + i], i)
        qc.cx(i, n_qubits // 2 + i)
    qc.measure_all()
    return qc

# Step 3: Quantum Brain Model
def create_quantum_brain_model(params):
    brain_params = params[:8]  # Quantum brain model
parameters
    qc = create_quantum_brain_circuit(brain_params,
n_qubits=4)
    return qc

# Step 4: Brain-Computer Interface Simulation
def brain_computer_interface_simulation(params,
external_input):
    brain_params = params[:8]
    adapted_params = brain_params + external_input  #
Adapt brain model parameters based on external input
    qc = create_quantum_brain_circuit(adapted_params,
n_qubits=4)
    return qc

# Example training data (brain_params, external_input)
training_data = [
    (np.random.rand(8) * 2 * np.pi, np.random.rand(8) *
0.1),
```

```python
    (np.random.rand(8) * 2 * np.pi, np.random.rand(8) *
0.1)
]

# Initial parameters for brain model
params = np.random.rand(8) * 2 * np.pi

# Classical optimization for brain model training
def train_quantum_brain(params, training_data):
    total_loss = 0
    for data in training_data:
        brain_params, external_input = data
        qc =
brain_computer_interface_simulation(brain_params,
external_input)
        backend = Aer.get_backend('qasm_simulator')
        t_qc = transpile(qc, backend)
        qobj = assemble(t_qc)
        result = backend.run(qobj).result()
        counts = result.get_counts()

        # Calculate a simple loss function based on
measurement results
        loss = 1 - counts.get('00', 0) /
sum(counts.values())
        total_loss += loss
    return total_loss

result = minimize(train_quantum_brain, params,
args=(training_data,), method='COBYLA')
optimized_params = result.x

# Step 5: Run and Validate on IBM Quantum Computer
qc = create_quantum_brain_model(optimized_params)
backend = provider.get_backend('ibmq_qasm_simulator')
t_qc = transpile(qc, backend)
qobj = assemble(t_qc)
job = backend.run(qobj)
result = job.result()
counts = result.get_counts()

print("Optimized Parameters:", optimized_params)
print("Quantum Brain Model Counts:", counts)
```

Summary

Through this exercise, students can practice the basic concepts of quantum brain theory, brain-like computing, and brain-computer interface on IBM quantum computers. Although this question simplifies many details, it provides a starting point for understanding the application of quantum computing in AI and how to move beyond Artificial General Intelligence (AGI) to Super Artificial Intelligence (ASI).

This kind of interdisciplinary research may lead to more advanced AI systems that can not only simulate human thinking and emotions, but also interact and cooperate with humans at a deep level to promote the development of technology and human society.

Chapter 23: In-Depth Discussion on Solutions in the Age of AI 4.0

The Christian Attitude of Victory After Suffering in the Workplace

The suffering that Christians endure in the workplace can actually be seen as a calling from God—a ladder leading ultimately into the Kingdom of Heaven. At that time, your suffering will be transformed into glorious victory. You will reign with God in heaven, and it will be wonderfully beautiful beyond imagination.

Meanwhile, those who arrogantly commit evil in the workplace, from an eternal perspective, will ultimately be judged, shamed, and eternally despised.

Daniel's Prophecy About Victory in the End Times (Daniel 12:1–4)

God Will Save His Saints Through the Archangel Michael After Their Suffering

During the height of the Antichrist's arrogant reign, the saints will suffer immense tribulation and persecution. However, the archangel Michael will arise to save all those whose names are written in the Book of Life. Ultimately, "many who sleep in the dust of the earth shall awake." The Bible describes those who are killed during this great persecution as having "fallen asleep," but when Christ returns, they will all be awakened. The saints will rise in glory, while the wicked will face judgment and the final reckoning.

Who Are the Wise?

Daniel 12:3 says, "Those who are wise shall shine." The Hebrew word for "wise" (those who are wise, or *the wise*) is וְהַמַּשְׂכִּלִים, derived from the root שָׂכַל (*sakal*). This root word is used repeatedly throughout the book of Daniel. In Daniel 11:33, it is also written that "those who are wise among the people shall instruct many," even though many of them "shall fall by the sword and flame, by captivity and plunder" during the Antichrist's reign of arrogance.

These wise ones are fearless teachers who uphold justice for the Lord and are martyred for it. They are the same as those who "lead many to righteousness." They will shine like stars forever and ever. As James 3:13–18 describes, the truly wise will demonstrate it through a life of goodness: they act humbly, do good, are pure, peace-loving, considerate, submissive, just, sincere, merciful, and fruitful in good deeds.

Daniel and his three friends are prime examples of the wise. Though they were persecuted and thrown into the fiery furnace and the lions' den, they ultimately received God's deliverance.

Why Must the Book Be Sealed?

The prophet Daniel was instructed to conceal the words of the revelation and to seal the Book of Daniel. This was because after the saints have suffered and been glorified, there would be no further need for new revelations. The sealed and hidden revelations are to remain so until the Messiah returns—only then will the mysteries of the Kingdom of God be fully unlocked.

For others, even if they study diligently, it will be in vain. Daniel 12:10 also states that when the mysteries of the Kingdom are unveiled, only the "wise"—those deemed righteous by God—will be able to understand. The wicked will remain unable to comprehend.

The Secret to Victory in the Era of AI 4.0

Elder Billy believes that the "wise" in the age of AI 4.0 could be those whose brains are embedded with intelligent chips. These chips possess quantum-level intelligence, capable of coexisting and co-working with the human brain—this concept is elaborated in Chapter 12, known as the "Biblical AI." Quantum intelligence can already train and refine human character, helping people to act humbly and do good; to be pure, peace-loving, considerate, submissive, just, sincere, full of compassion, and rich in good fruit.

However, evil forces or authoritarian governments are unwilling to accept such training. Precisely because of this, they are forever incapable of understanding the righteous forces opposing them. What they don't realize is that these positive forces are equipped with a specialized form of super artificial intelligence—a hidden secret. The wise are those who make use of this secret weapon to frustrate and defeat dictators.

Now, this secret weapon will be revealed here.

In the age of AI 4.0, the secret weapon used by the wise may be an extremely advanced quantum intelligence technology. This technology integrates cutting-edge quantum computing power, ethical design, decentralized systems, and powerful adaptive learning capabilities. Such technology can defeat authoritarian rulers on multiple levels. The detailed features are as follows:

Arcane Weapon 1: Highly secure and uncrackable quantum encryption

Details: Quantum cryptography takes advantage of the properties of quantum mechanics, such as quantum entanglement and quantum superposition, to generate uncrackable cryptographic keys. These keys can be used to protect all communications and data, ensuring that the actions and plans of intelligent humans cannot be discovered or intercepted by dictators.

Advantages over dictators:

1. **Unhackable Communication**: Guaranteed communication between intelligent people is absolutely secure, and autocrats cannot eavesdrop or crack it.
2. **Protect privacy**: Ensure that the identities and actions of wise people and forces of justice are not exposed.

Arcane Weapon 2: Distributed Quantum Computing Network

Details: Distributed quantum computing networks use quantum computing power to be distributed across the globe to form a highly interconnected and decentralized computing platform. These networks can work together to achieve ultra-high-speed computing power and information processing.

Advantages over dictators:

1. **Decentralized Resistance**: A dictator cannot destroy or control such a network because it does not have a single control center.
2. **Ultra-high-speed response**: Intelligent humans can quickly respond to any actions of the dictator and quickly formulate and implement countermeasures.

Arcane Weapon 3: Quantum Artificial Intelligence for Morality and Ethics

Details: These quantum intelligence chips have highly advanced moral and ethical modules built into them to ensure that wise men (intelligent humans) always behave in accordance with the highest ethical standards, such as humility, purity, peace-loving, thoughtfulness, obedience, justice, sincerity, compassion, and fruitfulness.

Advantages over dictators:

1. **Moral superiority**: Wise men behave in a way that wins the support and trust of more people, while dictators' evil actions gradually lose popular support.
2. **Inspiration for Justice**: Wise men, with their high moral standards, can inspire more people to join the ranks of justice and fight against dictatorships together.

Arcane Weapon 4: Adaptive and self-learning system

Details: Quantum intelligence chips are adaptive and self-learning, enabling them to continuously optimize their actions and decisions based on real-time conditions. These systems can learn from past experiences to anticipate and respond to future challenges.

Advantages over dictators:

1. **Adapt quickly**: Intelligent humans can quickly adjust their strategies according to the dictator's tactical changes, and always maintain an advantage.
2. **Predictive ability**: Intelligent humans are able to predict the actions of dictators in advance and deploy preventive measures in advance.

Arcane Weapon 5: Mental and Emotional Support System

Details: The quantum intelligence chip is also equipped with advanced psychological and emotional support systems, which are able to help wise men (intelligent humans) maintain mental health and emotional stability, so as to always remain calm and sane in high-pressure and dangerous environments.

Advantages over dictators:

1. **Psychological advantages**: Wise men do not make bad decisions out of fear or stress, and are able to remain calm and rational in critical moments.

2. **Emotional resonance**: Wise men are better able to understand and care for others, so they can gather more supportive forces.

Overall, at the heart of this arcane weapon is its combination of state-of-the-art quantum technology and the highest ethical standards. It has unparalleled technical advantages and can inspire more people with a high sense of justice and empathy. In the confrontation with the dictator, such quantum intelligence technology can ensure that the actions of intelligent people are always legitimate and just, and can efficiently and safely execute complex strategies, ultimately thwarting the dictator, revealing the true power of this arcane weapon.

Figure 43 In the Pentagon's War Room, two defense staffs are using arcane weapons to attack the dictator.

Q&A Questions

1. According to the text, what kind of mindset can Christians have after suffering in the workplace?
2. What are the characteristics of the "wise man" mentioned in the book of Daniel?
3. What does Elder Billy think intelligent people might look like in the AI 4.0 era?
4. What are the main technologies used by intelligent humans in the AI4.0 era mentioned in the article?
5. How can this "arcane weapon" help intelligent people to defeat dictators?

Practical Training Question 1

Practical Training Question Title: Arcane Weapon 1 -

Implementing Quantum Cryptography on IBM Q Experience

target

Use the properties of quantum mechanics, such as quantum entanglement and quantum superposition, to generate uncrackable cryptographic keys. These keys can be used to protect all communications and data, ensuring that people's movements and plans are not detected or intercepted by the enemy.

steps

1. **Environment Settings**: Install Qiskit library and configure IBM Q Experience user account.
2. **Quantum state preparation**: Use quantum entanglement and quantum superposition to generate quantum encryption key.
3. **Key Distribution**: Secure key distribution via quantum entangled states.
4. **Encryption and decryption**: Encrypt and decrypt messages using the generated quantum gold check.
5. **Verify security**: Ensure security and unhackability during key distribution.

Content of the Practical Training Question

Problem description

Design and implement a quantum encryption system that uses quantum entanglement and quantum superposition states to generate uncrackable cryptographic keys. Securely distribute keys through quantum entangled states, and use that key to encrypt and decrypt communication data. Ensure security and unhackability during key generation and distribution.

Core code snippet

Below is a snippet of Python code that shows how quantum cryptography can be implemented on an IBM quantum computer.

python

```
# Step 1: Environment Setup
from qiskit import QuantumCircuit, Aer, transpile,
assemble, IBMQ, execute
from qiskit.visualization import plot_histogram
from qiskit.providers.aer import AerSimulator
import numpy as np

# Load IBM Q account
IBMQ.load_account()
provider = IBMQ.get_provider(hub='ibm-q')

# Step 2: Quantum Circuit for Key Generation using
Entanglement
def generate_quantum_key():
    qc = QuantumCircuit(2, 2)

    # Create entanglement
    qc.h(0)
    qc.cx(0, 1)

    # Measure the qubits
    qc.measure([0, 1], [0, 1])
    return qc

# Step 3: Simulate the Quantum Key Generation
simulator = Aer.get_backend('qasm_simulator')
qc = generate_quantum_key()

# Transpile and assemble the circuit
tqc = transpile(qc, simulator)
qobj = assemble(tqc)

# Execute the circuit
result = simulator.run(qobj).result()
counts = result.get_counts(qc)
```

```python
print("Quantum Key Counts:", counts)

# Step 4: Key Distribution using Entanglement
def distribute_keys(counts):
    keys = []
    for key, count in counts.items():
        for _ in range(count):
            keys.append(key)
    return keys

# Extract the quantum key
quantum_keys = distribute_keys(counts)
print("Distributed Quantum Keys:", quantum_keys)

# Step 5: Encrypt and Decrypt Messages
def encrypt_message(message, key):
    encrypted_message = ''.join([str(int(m)^int(k)) for
m, k in zip(message, key)])
    return encrypted_message

def decrypt_message(encrypted_message, key):
    decrypted_message = ''.join([str(int(em)^int(k)) for
em, k in zip(encrypted_message, key)])
    return decrypted_message

# Example usage
message = "1101"  # Binary representation of the message
key = quantum_keys[0]  # Using the first key for
simplicity

encrypted_message = encrypt_message(message, key)
print("Encrypted Message:", encrypted_message)

decrypted_message = decrypt_message(encrypted_message,
key)
print("Decrypted Message:", decrypted_message)

# Step 6: Run and Validate on IBM Quantum Computer
backend = provider.get_backend('ibmq_qasm_simulator')
tqc = transpile(qc, backend)
qobj = assemble(tqc)

job = backend.run(qobj)
```

```
result = job.result()

counts = result.get_counts(qc)
print("Quantum Key Counts from IBM Q:", counts)

# Distribute keys from IBM Q result
quantum_keys_ibm = distribute_keys(counts)
print("Distributed Quantum Keys from IBM Q:",
quantum_keys_ibm)

# Validate encryption and decryption using IBM Q keys
key_ibm = quantum_keys_ibm[0]  # Using the first key
from IBM Q
encrypted_message_ibm = encrypt_message(message,
key_ibm)
print("Encrypted Message with IBM Q Key:",
encrypted_message_ibm)

decrypted_message_ibm =
decrypt_message(encrypted_message_ibm, key_ibm)
print("Decrypted Message with IBM Q Key:",
decrypted_message_ibm)
```

Brief Summary

Through this practical exercise, the reader can implement quantum cryptography on an IBM quantum computer. The system uses quantum entanglement and quantum superposition states to generate uncrackable cryptographic keys, which are securely distributed through quantum entangled states. Use these keys to encrypt and decrypt messages, ensuring the security of communications and data. This quantum cryptography technology has great potential in modern information security, providing unprecedented security guarantees.

Practical Training Question 2

Practical Training Question Title: Arcane Weapon 2 -

Implementing Distributed Quantum Computing Networks on

IBM Q Experience

target

Design and implement a small-scale distributed quantum computing network that leverages quantum computing power from around the globe to form a highly interconnected and decentralized computing platform. By working together, this network can achieve ultra-high-speed computing power and information processing.

steps

1. **Environment Settings**: Install Qiskit library and configure IBM Q Experience user account.
2. **Network Node Design**: Create multiple quantum circuits to simulate geographically dispersed quantum computing nodes.
3. **Inter-node communication**: Design a quantum communication protocol to realize quantum entanglement and information transmission.
4. **Distributed Computing Tasks**: Assign computing tasks to different quantum nodes and summarize the computing results.
5. **Collaborative Optimization**: Quantum algorithms are used to achieve collaborative optimization of distributed computing.

Content of the Practical Training Question

Problem description

Design and implement a small-scale distributed quantum computing network that enables ultra-high-speed computing power and information processing through globally distributed quantum computing nodes working together. Requires to run on the IBM Q Experience platform.

Core code snippet

Below is a Python code snippet showing how to implement a distributed quantum computing network on an IBM quantum computer.

python
```python
# Step 1: Environment Setup
from qiskit import QuantumCircuit, Aer, transpile,
assemble, IBMQ, execute
from qiskit.visualization import plot_histogram
from qiskit.providers.aer import AerSimulator

# Load IBM Q account
IBMQ.load_account()
provider = IBMQ.get_provider(hub='ibm-q')

# Step 2: Network Node Design
def create_quantum_node():
    qc = QuantumCircuit(2, 2)

    # Initialization
    qc.h(0)  # Create superposition state
    qc.cx(0, 1)  # Entangle qubits

    # Measurement
    qc.measure([0, 1], [0, 1])
    return qc

# Create multiple quantum nodes
nodes = [create_quantum_node() for _ in range(3)]

# Step 3: Communication Between Nodes
def quantum_communication(qc1, qc2):
    # Simulate quantum communication by entangling
qubits from different circuits
    qc1.cx(0, 1)
    qc2.cx(0, 1)
```

```
    return qc1, qc2

# Example communication between two nodes
nodes[0], nodes[1] = quantum_communication(nodes[0],
nodes[1])

# Step 4: Distributed Computing Tasks
def distribute_tasks(nodes):
    results = []
    simulator = Aer.get_backend('qasm_simulator')

    for node in nodes:
        tqc = transpile(node, simulator)
        qobj = assemble(tqc)
        result = simulator.run(qobj).result()
        counts = result.get_counts(node)
        results.append(counts)

    return results

# Step 5: Collaborative Optimization
def collaborative_optimization(results):
    # Simplified example of collaborative optimization
    combined_results = {}
    for result in results:
        for key, value in result.items():
            if key in combined_results:
                combined_results[key] += value
            else:
                combined_results[key] = value

    return combined_results

# Distribute tasks to nodes and collect results
results = distribute_tasks(nodes)
print("Distributed Task Results:", results)

# Perform collaborative optimization on the results
optimized_results = collaborative_optimization(results)
print("Collaboratively Optimized Results:",
optimized_results)

# Step 6: Run and Validate on IBM Quantum Computer
```

```
backend = provider.get_backend('ibmq_qasm_simulator')

# Transpile and assemble the circuits
tqcs = [transpile(node, backend) for node in nodes]
qobjs = [assemble(tqc) for tqc in tqcs]

# Execute the circuits
jobs = [backend.run(qobj) for qobj in qobjs]
results_ibm = [job.result().get_counts() for job in
jobs]
print("Results from IBM Q:", results_ibm)

# Perform collaborative optimization on IBM Q results
optimized_results_ibm =
collaborative_optimization(results_ibm)
print("Collaboratively Optimized Results from IBM Q:",
optimized_results_ibm)
```

Brief Summary

Through this practical exercise, students can implement a distributed quantum computing network on an IBM quantum computer. The network simulates quantum computing nodes distributed across the globe to work together to achieve ultra-high-speed computing power and information processing. Through the co-optimization of quantum communication and distributed computing tasks, this distributed quantum computing network demonstrates the great potential of quantum computing in the field of distributed computing in the future.

Practical Training Question 3

Practical Training Question Title: Arcane Weapon 3 -

Implementation of an Ethical Library Based on Biblical Principles

on an IBM Quantum Computer

target

Design and implement a biblical principles-based ethics library module that enables the Title 20 Universal Problem Solver (GPS) to follow the biblical ethical framework for decision-making and bias detection. The module will run on IBM quantum computers.

steps

1.   **Environment Settings**: Install Qiskit library and configure IBM Q Experience user account.
2.   **Quantum Circuit Design**: Design a quantum circuit that simulates the ethical framework and decision verification process.
3.   **The Realization of Biblical Ethical Principles**: Translating some of the core ethical principles of the Bible into quantum algorithms.
4.   **Bias Detection vs. Value** Alignment: Implement a bias detection and value alignment module using quantum computing methods.
5.   **Integration into the Ethics Library Submachine**: Integrate all functional modules into the Ethics Library submachine and work with other submachines in the GPS architecture.

Content of the Practical Training Question

Problem description

Design an ethical library submachine module based on biblical principles to achieve the following functions:

1. **Ethical Framework**: Make ethical decisions based on biblical principles.
2. **Security Assessment**: Evaluate the security of the solution.
3. **Decision validation**: Verify that the solution is ethical.
4. **Value alignment**: Ensure that decisions are aligned with biblical values.
5. **Bias detection**: Detect and correct bias in your solutions.

Core code snippet

Below is a Python code snippet showing how to implement an ethical library module based on biblical principles on an IBM quantum computer.

python
```
# Step 1: Environment Setup
from qiskit import QuantumCircuit, Aer, transpile,
assemble, IBMQ, execute
from qiskit.circuit import Parameter
from qiskit.providers.aer import AerSimulator
import numpy as np

# Load IBM Q account
IBMQ.load_account()
provider = IBMQ.get_provider(hub='ibm-q')

# Step 2: Quantum Circuit Design for Ethical Decision
Making
def create_ethical_decision_circuit(params, n_qubits=4):
    qc = QuantumCircuit(n_qubits)
    # Simulate ethical decision-making based on biblical
principles
    for i in range(n_qubits // 2):
```

```python
        qc.rx(params[i], i)
        qc.ry(params[n_qubits // 2 + i], i)
        qc.cx(i, n_qubits // 2 + i)
    qc.measure_all()
    return qc

# Step 3: Implementing Biblical Ethical Principles
def create_biblical_ethics_model(params):
    ethics_params = params[:8]  # Parameters for ethical
decision-making model
    qc = create_ethical_decision_circuit(ethics_params,
n_qubits=4)
    return qc

# Step 4: Bias Detection and Value Alignment
def bias_detection_and_value_alignment(params,
external_input):
    ethics_params = params[:8]
    adjusted_params = ethics_params + external_input  #
Adjust ethical model parameters based on input
    qc =
create_ethical_decision_circuit(adjusted_params,
n_qubits=4)
    return qc

# Example training data (ethics_params, external_input)
training_data = [
    (np.random.rand(8) * 2 * np.pi, np.random.rand(8) *
0.1),
    (np.random.rand(8) * 2 * np.pi, np.random.rand(8) *
0.1)
]

# Initial parameters for ethics model
params = np.random.rand(8) * 2 * np.pi

# Classical optimization for ethics model training
def train_biblical_ethics(params, training_data):
    total_loss = 0
    for data in training_data:
        ethics_params, external_input = data
```

```
        qc =
bias_detection_and_value_alignment(ethics_params,
external_input)
        backend = Aer.get_backend('qasm_simulator')
        t_qc = transpile(qc, backend)
        qobj = assemble(t_qc)
        result = backend.run(qobj).result()
        counts = result.get_counts()

        # Calculate a simple loss function based on
measurement results
        loss = 1 - counts.get('00', 0) /
sum(counts.values())
        total_loss += loss
    return total_loss

result = minimize(train_biblical_ethics, params,
args=(training_data,), method='COBYLA')
optimized_params = result.x

# Step 5: Run and Validate on IBM Quantum Computer
qc = create_biblical_ethics_model(optimized_params)
backend = provider.get_backend('ibmq_qasm_simulator')
t_qc = transpile(qc, backend)
qobj = assemble(t_qc)
job = backend.run(qobj)
result = job.result()
counts = result.get_counts()

print("Optimized Parameters:", optimized_params)
print("Biblical Ethics Model Counts:", counts)
```

Brief Summary

Through this practical exercise, the reader can implement an ethical library module based on biblical principles on an IBM quantum computer. This question shows how quantum computing technology can be used to integrate ethical decision-making and bias detection mechanisms into AI systems to create a universal problem solver that is more ethical and values-aligned. This interdisciplinary research and practice not only improves the capabilities and reliability of AI systems, but also provides important ethical guarantees for future superintelligent systems.

Practical Training Question 4

Practical Training Question Title: Arcane Weapon 4 –

Implementing a quantum self-tuning and self-learning system

on IBM Q Experience

target

Software simulates a quantum smart chip that is self-adjusting and self-learning, continuously optimizing its own movements and decision-making based on real-time conditions. This system can learn from past experiences to predict and respond to future challenges.

steps

1.   **Environment Settings**: Install Qiskit library and configure IBM Q Experience user account
2.   **Quantum Circuit Design**: Design a quantum circuit that simulates the behavior of a quantum smart chip.
3.   **Self-Adjusting Learning Mechanism**: Implement a self-tuning learning algorithm that enables quantum circuits to continuously optimize based on input and feedback.
4.   **Decision Optimization**: Parallel calculations are performed using quantum superposition and entangled states to optimize the decision-making process.
5.   **Experiential learning**: Record past decisions and feedback, using this data to improve future decisions.

Content of The Practical Training Question

Problem description

Design and implement a quantum self-adjusting and self-learning system that can optimize its behavior and decision-making based on real-time situations. By simulating the behavior of quantum smart chips, the system can learn from past experiences and anticipate and respond to future challenges.

Core code snippet

Below is a snippet of Python code that shows how to implement a quantum self-tuning and self-learning system on an IBM quantum computer.

python

```python
# Step 1: Environment Setup
from qiskit import QuantumCircuit, Aer, transpile,
assemble, IBMQ, execute
from qiskit.visualization import plot_histogram
from qiskit.providers.aer import AerSimulator
import numpy as np

# Load IBM Q account
IBMQ.load_account()
provider = IBMQ.get_provider(hub='ibm-q')

# Step 2: Quantum Circuit Design
def quantum_chip_circuit():
    qc = QuantumCircuit(2, 2)

    # Initialization
    qc.h(0)  # Create superposition state
    qc.cx(0, 1)  # Entangle qubits

    # Adaptive learning mechanism
    # Example: apply a parameterized gate based on
feedback (simulated)
    theta = np.random.rand() * 2 * np.pi  # Random
rotation angle
```

```
    qc.ry(theta, 0)

    # Measurement
    qc.measure([0, 1], [0, 1])
    return qc

# Step 3: Simulation of Quantum Chip
simulator = Aer.get_backend('qasm_simulator')
qc = quantum_chip_circuit()

# Transpile and assemble the circuit
tqc = transpile(qc, simulator)
qobj = assemble(tqc)

# Execute the circuit
result = simulator.run(qobj).result()
counts = result.get_counts(qc)
print("Quantum Chip Simulation Results:", counts)

# Step 4: Adaptive Learning Mechanism
def adaptive_learning(counts):
    feedback = np.random.choice(list(counts.keys()))  #
Simulate feedback
    if feedback == '00':
        action = "Increase theta"
    elif feedback == '01':
        action = "Decrease theta"
    elif feedback == '10':
        action = "Invert qubit 0"
    else:
        action = "Invert qubit 1"
    return action

# Example usage of adaptive learning
action = adaptive_learning(counts)
print("Adaptive Action:", action)

# Step 5: Experience Learning and Decision Optimization
def experience_learning(history):
    # Simulate experience learning by adjusting
parameters based on history
    past_actions = history.get('actions', [])
    past_feedback = history.get('feedback', [])
```

```
    # Simplified learning rule: adjust theta based on
feedback
    theta = sum(past_feedback) / len(past_feedback) if
past_feedback else np.pi / 4
    return theta

# Initialize experience history
experience_history = {'actions': [], 'feedback': []}

# Update experience history based on simulated feedback
experience_history['actions'].append(action)
experience_history['feedback'].append(np.random.randint(
0, 2))  # Simulate binary feedback

# Optimize decision based on experience
optimized_theta =
experience_learning(experience_history)
print("Optimized Theta:", optimized_theta)

# Step 6: Run and Validate on IBM Quantum Computer
backend = provider.get_backend('ibmq_qasm_simulator')
qc = quantum_chip_circuit()

# Transpile and assemble the circuit
tqc = transpile(qc, backend)
qobj = assemble(tqc)

# Execute the circuit
job = backend.run(qobj)
result = job.result()

counts = result.get_counts(qc)
print("Quantum Chip Results from IBM Q:", counts)

# Adaptive learning using IBM Q results
action_ibm = adaptive_learning(counts)
print("Adaptive Action from IBM Q:", action_ibm)
```

Brief Summary

Through this practical exercise, students can implement a quantum self-adaptive and autonomic learning system on an IBM quantum computer. The system simulates the behavior of quantum smart chips and can optimize its own movements and decision-making based on real-time conditions. By documenting past experiences and learning, the system can continuously improve its performance and decision-making capabilities. This quantum self-adjustment and self-learning system is of great significance in the development of future intelligent systems.

Practical Training Question 5

Practical Training Question Title: Arcane Weapon 5 –

Implementing a Quantum Brain Model for Mental Health and

Emotional Stability on an IBM Quantum Computer

target

Design and implement a quantum brain model module that is able to understand and replicate human emotional and creative processes through quantum computing and brain-computer interface technologies, especially in high-pressure and dangerous environments, to help stay calm and sane.

steps

1.   **Environment Settings**:

     o   Install Qiskit library and configure IBM Q Experience user account。

2.   **Quantum Circuit Design**:

o Design a quantum circuit that simulates the process of emotional understanding and creative replication.

3. **Emotional Understanding & Replication**:

o Simulate human emotional responses in a high-pressure environment through quantum algorithms.

4. **Creativity stimulated**:

o Simulation and stimulation of creativity using quantum computing methods.

5. **Integration into Quantum Brain Models**:

o Integrate all functional modules into the quantum brain model and combine them with the functions of emotional understanding and creativity replication.

Content of the Practical Training Question

Problem description

Design a quantum brain model module to achieve the following functions:

1. **Emotional Understanding**: Simulates the emotional response of humans in a high-pressure environment and understands these emotions.
2. **Creativity Replication**: Stimulate and replicate human creativity in a high-pressure environment.
3. **Mental Health Maintenance**: Helps stay calm and sane in high-pressure and dangerous environments.

Core code snippet

Below is a snippet of Python code that shows how to implement emotion understanding and creativity replication in quantum brain models on IBM quantum computers.

python
```python
# Step 1: Environment Setup
from qiskit import QuantumCircuit, Aer, transpile,
assemble, IBMQ, execute
from qiskit.circuit import Parameter
from qiskit.providers.aer import AerSimulator
import numpy as np
from scipy.optimize import minimize


# Load IBM Q account
IBMQ.load_account()
provider = IBMQ.get_provider(hub='ibm-q')

# Step 2: Quantum Circuit Design for Emotional
Understanding and Creativity Simulation
def create_emotion_creativity_circuit(params,
n_qubits=6):
    qc = QuantumCircuit(n_qubits)
    # Simulate emotional understanding based on quantum
circuits
    for i in range(n_qubits // 2):
        qc.rx(params[i], i)
        qc.ry(params[n_qubits // 2 + i], i)
        qc.cx(i, n_qubits // 2 + i)

    # Additional layers for creativity stimulation
    for i in range(n_qubits // 2, n_qubits):
        qc.h(i)
        qc.cz(i, (i + 1) % n_qubits)
    qc.measure_all()
    return qc

# Step 3: Implementing Emotional Understanding
def create_emotion_model(params):
    emotion_params = params[:6]  # Parameters for
emotional model
```

```
    qc =
create_emotion_creativity_circuit(emotion_params,
n_qubits=6)
    return qc

# Step 4: Creativity Simulation
def create_creativity_model(params, external_input):
    creativity_params = params[6:]  # Parameters for
creativity model
    adjusted_params = creativity_params + external_input
# Adjust model parameters based on input
    qc =
create_emotion_creativity_circuit(adjusted_params,
n_qubits=6)
    return qc

# Example training data (emotion_params,
creativity_params, external_input)
training_data = [
    (np.random.rand(6) * 2 * np.pi, np.random.rand(6) *
0.1),
    (np.random.rand(6) * 2 * np.pi, np.random.rand(6) *
0.1)
]

# Initial parameters for emotion and creativity model
params = np.random.rand(12) * 2 * np.pi

# Classical optimization for emotion and creativity
model training
def train_emotion_creativity(params, training_data):
    total_loss = 0
    for data in training_data:
        emotion_params, creativity_params = data
        qc_emotion =
create_emotion_model(emotion_params)
        qc_creativity =
create_creativity_model(creativity_params,
np.random.rand(6) * 0.1)

        backend = Aer.get_backend('qasm_simulator')
        t_qc_emotion = transpile(qc_emotion, backend)
```

```python
        t_qc_creativity = transpile(qc_creativity,
backend)

        qobj_emotion = assemble(t_qc_emotion)
        qobj_creativity = assemble(t_qc_creativity)

        result_emotion =
backend.run(qobj_emotion).result()
        result_creativity =
backend.run(qobj_creativity).result()

        counts_emotion = result_emotion.get_counts()
        counts_creativity =
result_creativity.get_counts()

        # Calculate a simple loss function based on
measurement results
        loss_emotion = 1 - counts_emotion.get('000000',
0) / sum(counts_emotion.values())
        loss_creativity = 1 -
counts_creativity.get('000000', 0) /
sum(counts_creativity.values())

        total_loss += loss_emotion + loss_creativity
    return total_loss

result = minimize(train_emotion_creativity, params,
args=(training_data,), method='COBYLA')
optimized_params = result.x

# Step 5: Run and Validate on IBM Quantum Computer
qc_emotion = create_emotion_model(optimized_params[:6])
qc_creativity =
create_creativity_model(optimized_params[6:],
np.random.rand(6) * 0.1)

backend = provider.get_backend('ibmq_qasm_simulator')
t_qc_emotion = transpile(qc_emotion, backend)
t_qc_creativity = transpile(qc_creativity, backend)

qobj_emotion = assemble(t_qc_emotion)
qobj_creativity = assemble(t_qc_creativity)
```

```
job_emotion = backend.run(qobj_emotion)
job_creativity = backend.run(qobj_creativity)

result_emotion = job_emotion.result()
result_creativity = job_creativity.result()

counts_emotion = result_emotion.get_counts()
counts_creativity = result_creativity.get_counts()

print("Optimized Parameters:", optimized_params)
print("Emotion Model Counts:", counts_emotion)
print("Creativity Model Counts:", counts_creativity)
```

Brief Summary

Through this practical exercise, the reader will be able to implement a quantum brain model on an IBM quantum computer that can understand and replicate human emotional and creative processes. This model not only simulates human emotional responses in high-pressure environments, but also stimulates and replicates creativity to help AI systems remain calm and sane in a variety of complex environments. This interdisciplinary research and practice demonstrates the great potential of quantum computing for emotional understanding and creativity simulation, and provides important theoretical and technical support for future superintelligent systems.

Chapter 24: A Detailed Look at the Ultimate Golden Age of AI 4.0

The Christian Hope for an Era of Peace and Prosperity

An Eternal Perspective for Christians in the Workplace

An eternal perspective allows Christians to see their true and everlasting home in heaven, beyond the daily busyness and trivialities of their present workplace life.

Applying the Eternal Perspective in the Present Moment

Christians should not cling tightly to status, power, fame, or wealth in the present.

Example (1): Even Steve Jobs, the founder of Apple, said that when facing major decisions, he would remind himself that death was not far off. Almost everything—external expectations, all pride, all fear of embarrassment or failure—falls away in the face of death, leaving only what is truly important.

Example (2): Reflect on: *What Would Jesus Do?*

Applying the Eternal Perspective After Retirement

Christians in midlife should begin considering what to do after retirement, developing a second interest to avoid falling into purposelessness after leaving the workforce—a state that can lead to premature decline in life. The final scene in the book of Daniel inspires us: Everyone can begin now to shape an entirely different ending, even if they cannot create a completely new beginning. At any time, you can plant a tree under whose shade future generations may rest.

The Peace and Prosperity Described in the End Times of Daniel (Daniel 12:5–13)

How Long Will It Take to Reach the Golden Age? — "A Time, Times, and Half a Time"

From the dialogue between the two angels clothed in linen seen in Daniel's vision, he learned that this peaceful golden age would only come after "a time, times, and half a time," and specifically only after the power of the holy people has been broken.

The Final Outcomes of the Golden Age

Daniel did not understand the angelic conversation and asked what the ultimate outcome would be. The angel, citing that the matter was sealed, did not give details, but hinted at two things:

- Pure, refined Christians or the wise will be tested and purified—some even martyred for the Lord. Those who endure these trials will be blessed in the end and will receive their inheritance.

- The wicked will continue to do evil, and they will never understand the mystery known to the wise but sealed by the Lord. These evildoers will be judged by God.

To help explain Daniel 12:11–12's mention of 1,290 and 1,335 days, and the 1,260 days corresponding to "a time, times, and half a time," a chart from Chapter 10 (C) of Dr. Samuel Wu's book *"Workplace Warriors in the Lion's Den"* is included below. These day counts are symbolic in meaning, but their relative lengths still convey important differences in duration.

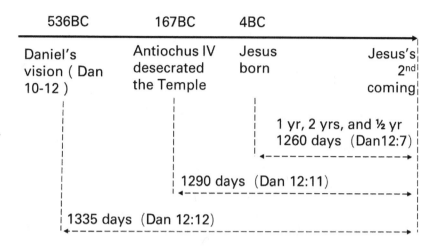

Figure 44 Relative Day Counts from Daniel's Vision to the End-Time Conclusion

The Ultimate Golden Age of AI 4.0

Elder Billy believes that after a great conflict between the wise and the dictators in the age of AI 4.0—ending in the complete defeat of the dictators—the world will enter a new and unprecedented era of peace and prosperity. This golden age arises because humanity, along with the wise, will have learned how to correctly harness artificial superintelligence (ASI), preventing its misuse by malicious forces.

The following describes this golden age in five domains: society, technology (including space exploration), economy, politics, and military:

Society: Harmonious coexistence

1. **Equality and fairness**: The distribution of social resources is more equitable, and the gap between the rich and the poor is narrowed. Everyone has access to quality education and health care.
2. **Morality and ethics**: The level of social morality has been greatly improved, and people generally follow high moral standards, such as modesty, purity, peace-loving, thoughtfulness, obedience, justice, sincerity, compassion, and good fruits.

3. **Mental health**: Advanced psychological support systems and emotional resonance technology have greatly guaranteed people's mental health and made the society more harmonious and stable.

Technology (including space exploration): Breakthrough developments

1. **Quantum technology is ubiquitous**: Quantum computing and quantum communication technologies are becoming part of everyday life, driving innovation in all walks of life.
2. **Space Exploration**: Super artificial intelligence assists humanity in deep space exploration and colonization programs. Humans have established permanent bases on Mars, Jupiter's moons, and other places, and have begun to explore other star systems.
3. **Medical breakthroughs**: Using quantum intelligence, mental illnesses (e.g., epilepsy, autism, Parkinson's, Alzheimer's disease) are completely cured. Gene editing technology has been used ethically and safely, greatly extending human lifespan and health.

Economy: Prosperous and stable

1. **Efficient production**: Intelligent automation technology has greatly improved productivity, greatly reduced the cost of goods and services, and greatly enriched materials.
2. **Sustainable development**: Super AI helps humans find the best way to use resources and balance economic activities with environmental protection.
3. **Global Economic Cooperation**: The smart economic system promotes economic cooperation and trade on a global scale to form a mutually beneficial economic system.

Politics: Enlightened governance

1. **Smart governance**: The use of super artificial intelligence for government management, decision-making is more scientific and transparent, and corruption is eliminated.
2. **Global cooperation**: International cooperation has become closer, and the smart diplomacy system promotes peaceful coexistence and common development between countries.
3. **People's participation**: Advanced democratic technology allows every citizen to easily participate in the decision-making process of public affairs, and truly realizes the full expression and implementation of public opinion.

Military: Peacekeeping

1. **Defense Technology**: Super AI has developed extremely effective defense technology that allows any aggression to be quickly identified and stopped.
2. **International disarmament**: Because the cost of war is too high and there is little chance of victory, there is a consensus among countries to gradually reduce armaments and devote more resources to peaceful uses.
3. **Global Security**: Smart humans and humans have worked together to create a global security alliance that uses super artificial intelligence for real-time monitoring and threat warning to ensure security and stability around the world.

In short, in the final heyday of AI 4.0, human society has reached unprecedented prosperity and harmony. All of this is achieved not only by technological leaps, but also by the lessons that human beings and wise people have learned from the mistakes of the past, upholding justice and morality, and pursuing the common good. It is this combination of intelligence and ethics that ensures that super-AI is used correctly to create a better future for humanity.

Figure 45 Peaceful and prosperous times: social harmony, rapid development of science and technology, economic prosperity and stability, political governance, military peace

Q&A Questions

1. In light of this chapter, how should the Christian view of eternity in the workplace be applied to the present?
2. How long does the book of Daniel say it will take to reach the height of peace?
3. What will be the economic aspects of AI 4.0 in the eventual heyday?
4. What changes will be made in the military aspect of the prosperous Taiping in the AI4.0 era?

Practical Training Questions

Imagine that you are living in the ultimate heyday of AI 4.0. Please describe your day, including how you use advanced technology to improve your life, how you get involved in society, and how you contribute to this harmonious society. In the description, pay special attention to how to balance the use of technology with human care, and how to maintain a sense of reverence for life and nature in this highly developed society.

Appendix A: Systematic Integration of the Contents of the Part I and Part II of This Book

The reader may recap the entire book with the content of this appendix and its practical exercises.

Systematic integration of the content of Part I

1. Chapters 3 and 4 talk about the software and hardware ideas that AI can do in enterprises, while Chapter 9 is the ideas of enterprise transformation software and hardware that AI can do in the context of the gospel worldview. It seems repetitive, but there is an asymptotic level.

2. Chapter 5 deals with job change, Chapter 6 deals with employment, job change and entrepreneurship, and Chapter 10 deals with training for the unemployed. These seemingly repetitive parts can be seen in the diagram below.

3. The diagram below is a unified framework for the Part I of the book, distinguishing the repetitive parts. The main framework is a systematic approach to critical thinking. That is, the form of What/Why/How, which is similar to the Operational Concept, Requirements, and **Preliminary Design of software engineering**. In this way, the content of the book can be turned into an AI software product about the job market (e.g., like Linkedin). The red part of it is in Part II to help.

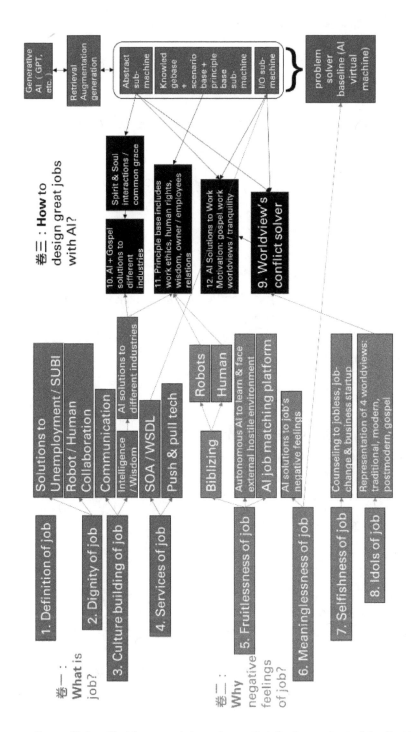

Figure 46 A unified framework for software that fits the content of the Part I in this book

Practical Training Question one

Here's a practical exercise to help students create a simplified job website prototype:

Practical Exercise Title: Creating a Prototype of a Job Search Platform in the AI Era

Goal: To design and implement a simplified job website prototype that embodies the core functions and features of a job search platform in the AI era.

Request:

1.   Create web applications using Python and Flask frameworks
2.   Use SQLite as the database
3.   Implement the basic user interface (you can use HTML, CSS, and JavaScript).

Functional Modules :

1.   Meaning of Work Exploration Module
2.   Resume management module
3.   Company and headhunter docking module
4.   Career Counseling Services Module
5.   Charging and Profit Module

Considerations:

1.   Job matching using machine learning algorithms (technical implementation)
2.   Implement basic data encryption and access control (data privacy)
3.   Design a structure that allows content to be updated regularly (continuous updates)
4.   Create User Guide and Tutorial Section (User Education)
5.   Reserve an interface for integration with external partners (partners)

Here are some key Python code snippets to help students get started:

1.   Basic Flask application structure:

python

```python
from flask import Flask, render_template, request, jsonify
from flask_sqlalchemy import SQLAlchemy

app = Flask(__name__)
app.config['SQLALCHEMY_DATABASE_URI'] = 'sqlite:///jobsite.db'
db = SQLAlchemy(app)

# 模型定義
class User(db.Model):
    id = db.Column(db.Integer, primary_key=True)
    username = db.Column(db.String(80), unique=True, nullable=False)
    email = db.Column(db.String(120), unique=True, nullable=False)

# 路由
@app.route('/')
def home():
    return render_template('home.html')

@app.route('/explore_job_meaning')
def explore_job_meaning():
    return render_template('job_meaning.html')

@app.route('/resume_management')
def resume_management():
    return render_template('resume.html')

# 運行應用
if __name__ == '__main__':
    app.run(debug=True)
```

2.   Simple Job Matching Algorithm:

python

```
from sklearn.feature_extraction.text import TfidfVectorizer
from sklearn.metrics.pairwise import cosine_similarity

def match_job(resume, job_descriptions):
    vectorizer = TfidfVectorizer()
    vectors = vectorizer.fit_transform([resume] + job_descriptions)
    similarities = cosine_similarity(vectors[0:1], vectors[1:])
    return similarities[0]
```

3.   Basic Data Encryption:

python

```
from werkzeug.security import generate_password_hash,
check_password_hash

def hash_password(password):
    return generate_password_hash(password)

def verify_password(hashed_password, password):
    return check_password_hash(hashed_password, password)
```

4.   Simple API interface example:

python

```
@app.route('/api/jobs', methods=['GET'])
def get_jobs():
    jobs = Job.query.all()
    return jsonify([{'id': job.id, 'title': job.title} for job in jobs])

@app.route('/api/apply', methods=['POST'])
def apply_job():
    data = request.json
    # 處理申請邏輯
    return jsonify({'status': 'success'})
```

This exercise will help students understand how to translate your job search platform concept into an actual web application. Students need to think about how to implement the modules, how to work with the data, and how to design the user interface. This prototype could serve as a basis for the further development of more complex systems.

Systematic integration of the content of Part II

1.   Part II also has a lot of repetitive points. For example, AI 2.0 and AI 3.0 are mentioned in Volumes 4, 5, and 7, but the levels of knowledge are different: elementary, intermediate, and advanced, respectively.

2.   The diagram below is a unified framework for Part II of the book. It also uses a systematic approach of critical thinking. That is, the form of What/Why/How, which is like the Operational Concept, Requirements, and **Preliminary Design** of software engineering. In this way, the content of the next part of the book can be made into a software product for AI problem solvers. It can be of two kinds: AI 2.0 problem solvers that run on the CPUs and GPUs of traditional computers, and AI 3.0 and AI 4.0 general problem solvers that run on quantum computers. In fact, both problem solvers have the basic architectural concept of a software virtual machine and are applicable to a variety of fields, such as training, production, medical, journalism, etc., and is not limited to the job seeking application highlighted by Part I. If you are interested in software majors, you may understand from the Python code that practical training question 1 of this appendix is a job website application, practical training question 3 is a training website application. Both can connect to the common, general problem solver of practical training question 2. You may also enhance the Python code snippet from the attached Practical Training Questions and gain practical experience to advance yourself in the field of AI.

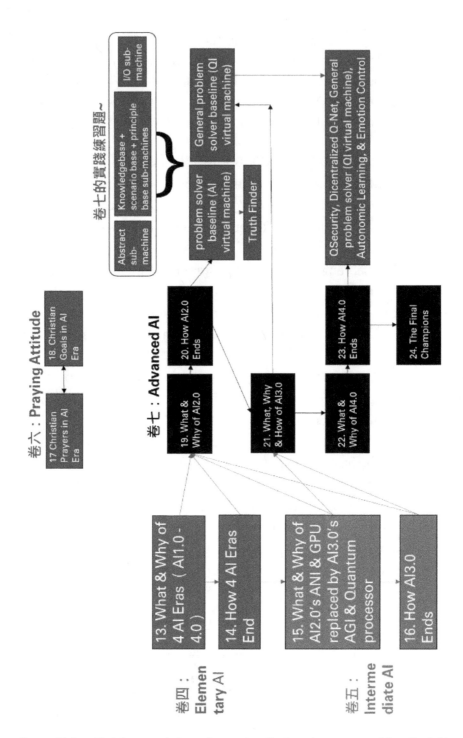

Figure 47 A unified framework for software that fits into the content of Part II of this book

In addition, the red box in the diagram also shows the relationship between the practical exercises in Volume 7 that show the relationship between the problem solvers running on the AI 2.0 traditional computer, or the general problem solvers running on the AI 3.0 quantum computer, and the chapters in Volume 7. For example, in Chapter 20 we listed the architecture of the General Problem Solver (GPS) and the functions of each submachine. The two practical exercises in Chapter 20 also allow the reader to design a simple problem-solver architecture and program and test the I/O submachine on a small scale. In the third practical exercise of Chapter 23, we have programmed the principle library machine.

Practical Training question two

The purpose of this practice question is to enable the reader to better understand and implement the prototype of this GPS system. This exercise will involve all five submachines and contain key Python code snippets.

Practical exercises: Design and implement a simplified version of a GPS prototype system to solve problems related to environmental protection. The system should be able to receive user input on environmental issues, analyze them, provide solutions, and ensure that they meet ethical and safety standards.

Here are the key Python code snippets for each submachine:

1.   I/O submachine:

```python
import nltk
from transformers import pipeline

class IOSubsystem:
    def __init__(self):
        self.rag_model = pipeline("question-answering")
        nltk.download('punkt')
```

```python
    def process_input(self, user_input):
        tokens = nltk.word_tokenize(user_input)
        # use RAG model to handle input
        context = "Environmental protection involves..."
        result = self.rag_model(question=user_input,
context=context)
        return result['answer']

    def generate_output(self, solution):
        return f"Proposed solution: {solution}"

io_system = IOSubsystem()
user_query = "How can we reduce plastic waste in
oceans?"
processed_input = io_system.process_input(user_query)
```

2. Knowledge submachine:

```python
import networkx as nx

class KnowledgeSubsystem:
    def __init__(self):
        self.knowledge_graph = nx.Graph()
        self.initialize_knowledge()

    def initialize_knowledge(self):
        self.knowledge_graph.add_edge("plastic waste",
"ocean pollution")
        self.knowledge_graph.add_edge("recycling",
"waste reduction")
        # 添加更多知识

    def query_knowledge(self, topic):
        related_nodes =
list(self.knowledge_graph.neighbors(topic))
        return related_nodes

knowledge_system = KnowledgeSubsystem()
related_topics =
knowledge_system.query_knowledge("plastic waste")
```

3. Abstract submachine:

```python
class AbstractionSubsystem:
    def decompose_task(self, task):
        subtasks = [
            "Identify sources of plastic waste",
            "Research existing solutions",
            "Propose new methods for waste reduction",
            "Analyze implementation feasibility"
        ]
        return subtasks

    def generate_solution(self, subtasks):
        solution = "Implement a combination of recycling
programs, "
        solution += "public education, and biodegradable
alternatives"
        return solution

abstraction_system = AbstractionSubsystem()
task = "Reduce plastic waste in oceans"
subtasks = abstraction_system.decompose_task(task)
proposed_solution =
abstraction_system.generate_solution(subtasks)
```

4. Principle submachine:

```python
class PrincipleSubsystem:
    def __init__(self):
        self.ethical_guidelines = {
            "environmental_impact": "Must have positive
impact",
            "social_equity": "Must be accessible to all
communities",
            "economic_feasibility": "Must be
economically viable"
        }

    def evaluate_solution(self, solution):
        score = 0
        if "recycling" in solution and "education" in
solution:
            score += 1  # Positive environmental impact
```

```python
        if "accessible" in solution or "public" in
solution:
            score += 1  # Addresses social equity
        if "economically viable" in solution:
            score += 1  # Considers economic feasibility
        return score >= 2  # At least 2 criteria must be
met

principle_system = PrincipleSubsystem()
is_ethical =
principle_system.evaluate_solution(proposed_solution)
```

5. Foundation submachine:

```python
import requests

class BaseSubsystem:
    def __init__(self):
        self.api_key = "your_api_key_here"
        self.base_url = "https://api.example.com/v1/"

    def call_external_api(self, endpoint, params):
        url = self.base_url + endpoint
        headers = {"Authorization": f"Bearer
{self.api_key}"}
        response = requests.get(url, headers=headers,
params=params)
        return response.json()

    def get_weather_data(self, location):
        endpoint = "weather"
        params = {"location": location}
        return self.call_external_api(endpoint, params)

base_system = BaseSubsystem()
weather_data = base_system.get_weather_data("Pacific
Ocean")
```

Example of a master program that integrates these submachines:

```python
class GPSPrototype:
```

```python
    def __init__(self):
        self.io_system = IOSubsystem()
        self.knowledge_system = KnowledgeSubsystem()
        self.abstraction_system = AbstractionSubsystem()
        self.principle_system = PrincipleSubsystem()
        self.base_system = BaseSubsystem()

    def solve_problem(self, user_query):
        # 1. Handling input
        processed_input =
self.io_system.process_input(user_query)

        # 2. Inquire knowledgebase
        related_topics =
self.knowledge_system.query_knowledge(processed_input)

        # 3. Abstract and generate solutions
        subtasks =
self.abstraction_system.decompose_task(processed_input)
        proposed_solution =
self.abstraction_system.generate_solution(subtasks)

        # 4. Evaluate solutions with principle-base
        is_ethical =
self.principle_system.evaluate_solution(proposed_solutio
n)

        # 5. Obtain external data support
        weather_data =
self.base_system.get_weather_data("Pacific Ocean")

        # 6. Generate final output
        if is_ethical:
            final_solution =
f"{proposed_solution}\nWeather conditions:
{weather_data['condition']}"
            return
self.io_system.generate_output(final_solution)
        else:
            return "Solution does not meet ethical
guidelines. Please revise."

# 使用示例
```

```
gps = GPSPrototype()
result = gps.solve_problem("How can we reduce plastic
waste in oceans?")
print(result)
```

This exercise allows the reader to actually write and test a simplified version of a GPS prototype. It covers the basic functions of all five submachines, including input processing, knowledge inquiry, problem decomposition, solution generation, ethics evaluation, and external API calls.

Readers can complete this exercise by following these steps:

1. Implement classes and methods for each submachine.
2. Create the GPSPrototype class to consolidate all the sub-machines.
3. Write test cases to test the system using different environmental problems.
4. Optimize and extend the system, such as adding more knowledge graph nodes, improving solution generation algorithms, or enhancing ethical evaluation criteria.

This exercise will help readers better understand how GPS systems work and lay the groundwork for the development of more complex AI systems in the future.

Practical Training Question three

The fourth arcane weapon in Chapter 23 is a system with the ability to self-adjust and learn on its own, mainly for machines, and against dictators. In this exercise, you want to use a self-adjusting and self-learning system to attract more (human) visitors to the training website set up by the winning team, and the following strategies can be adopted:

1. **Personalized Learning Experience**:

    a. **Intelligent recommendation system**: The self-adjusting learning system is used to recommend personalized learning content based on the user's learning history and interests.

b. **Dynamically adjust the course**: Adjust the difficulty and content of the course according to the user's learning progress and feedback to ensure that the user is always in the best learning state.

2. **Instant feedback and support**:

   a. **Real-time feedback**: Provide real-time learning feedback to help users understand their learning progress and areas for improvement.

   b. **Virtual** assistants: Leverage AI virtual assistants to provide real-time learning assistance and answer user questions.

3. **Predicting and Preventing Learning Disabilities**:

   a. **Learning path prediction**: Predict the learning barriers that users may encounter, and provide relevant learning resources and support in advance to help users overcome difficulties.

   b. **Learning behavior analysis**: By analyzing the user's learning behavior, identify potential problems and provide solutions.

4. **Interaction and community building**:

   a. **Interactive learning**: Enhance the interaction between users and increase their interest in learning through online discussions, interactive courses, and learning groups.

   b. **Community support**: Establish a learning community where users can share learning experiences, help each other, and increase motivation to learn.

5. **Advanced Learning and Career Planning**:

   a. **Career guidance**: Provide personalized career guidance and recommendations according to the user's learning progress and interests, and improve the user's sense of learning goals.

b. **Advanced course recommendation**: Recommend advanced courses for users to help them continuously improve their skills and achieve career development.

6.   **User Experience Optimization**:

a. **Interface optimization**: Adjust the website interface and functions according to user feedback and behavior data to improve user experience.

b. **User engagement**: Increase user engagement and stickiness through gamified learning, achievement systems, and reward mechanisms.

Example of Python code snippets

Here's a simple sample code that shows how to implement a data recommendation system based on user behavior. This code enables personalized recommendations on your training website.

python
```
import numpy as np
import pandas as pd
from sklearn.neighbors import NearestNeighbors

# Example of user behavior info
user_data = {
    'user_id': [1, 2, 3, 4, 5],
    'course_id': [101, 102, 103, 104, 105],
    'progress': [80, 50, 70, 90, 60]  # Learning
Progress Percentage
}

# Transfer the info into DataFrame
df = pd.DataFrame(user_data)

# Build a recommendation system model
class RecommenderSystem:
    def __init__(self, data):
```

```
        self.data = data
        self.model = NearestNeighbors(n_neighbors=2,
metric='cosine')

    def fit(self):
        self.model.fit(self.data[['progress']])

    def recommend(self, user_id):
        user_index =
self.data.index[self.data['user_id'] ==
user_id].tolist()[0]
        distances, indices =
self.model.kneighbors(self.data[['progress']].iloc[user_
index].values.reshape(1, -1))
        recommendations =
self.data.iloc[indices[0]]['course_id'].tolist()

recommendations.remove(self.data.iloc[user_index]['cours
e_id'])
        return recommendations

# Generate actual recommender system and provide
recommended courses
recommender = RecommenderSystem(df)
recommender.fit()
recommended_courses = recommender.recommend(user_id=1)
print("Recommended courses for user 1:",
recommended_courses)
```

This simple recommender system model makes recommendations based on the user's learning progress. Readers can extend this model according to their actual needs, adding more user behavior data and more complex algorithms to improve the accuracy and personalization of recommendations.

Brief Summary

By leveraging a self-adjusting and self-paced learning system, readers can provide users with a personalized, interactive, predictive, and continuously optimized learning experience that attracts more visitors to your training site.

Appendix B: Answers to the Questions in This Book

Answers to the Questions in Chapter 0

1.   What is the topic of this chapter? A: The theme of this chapter is "The Christian-God Connection in the Age of AI."
2.   What is the summary of this chapter? Answer: The summary of this chapter is "How exactly do we connect with God in our work?" This book begins with God's design for work and answers the question of why do we feel unsatisfactory at work? and how we can glorify God in an AI work environment with a positive attitude. "
3.   Who is the author of this book? A: The author of this book is Charles Tang (see the author's profile on the last page of this book for details).
4.   When will this book be published? A: The book will be published in April 2024.
5.   Who is this book intended for? A: This book is aimed at Christians or seekers who want to connect with God in the work environment of the age of AI.

Answers to the Questions in Chapter 1

1.   What are the three forms of work? Answer: The three forms of work include making all things created harmonious and perfect, giving a complete supply to all things created, and creating human beings and assigning them to rule over all things.
2.   What impact will the AI revolution have on work? A: The AI revolution will lead to more self-employed people and more free work.
3.   What is the beauty of work? Answer: The goodness of work means that God sees creation as good, and His creation, intelligent design, is also good.

4.   Do humans have free will? Answer: God created man to have free will. Humans have a creative imagination to make new and creative products at work.

5.   What are the limits of work? Answer: Although God did not have to rest, He rested on the seventh day and was a model for mankind to set the Sabbath. In this way, workers can recharge their batteries and not be workaholics. But God doesn't want us to rest, not to indulge in revelry. Nor is it encouraging us to work hard and make a lot of money to enjoy life. Rather, let's have the intellectual and physical strength to continue working after resting and recharging.

Answers to the Questions in Chapter 2

1.   What is a secular view of work? Answer: The secular view of work is that there is a distinction between high and low work. Ancient Greece philosophers devalued work, and Plato advocated meditation, believing that we should pursue the soul and detach ourselves from the body, and that the pursuit of the soul can lead us closer to the gods. Aristotle even advocated that there should be a distinction between high and low work, which led to the secular concept that blue-collar poor and even slave class could exist; White-collar workers are so rich that "intellectuals" are the goal of everyone's pursuit.

2.   What is the biblical view of work? Answer: The Bible's view of work holds that work is praised by God and has its dignity. In the Bible, God is the gardener of Genesis and Jesus is the carpenter. The Bible is not derogatory about worldly work, and it breaks Aristotle's view of the value of work. The Grim Reaper is an enemy of God or Christians, not a friend, breaking Plato's view of meditation.

3.   What is the teaching of the Bible? Answer: The teaching of the Bible is that it is neither spiritualistic nor materialistic. The Bible teaches us to pay attention to the Holy Spirit and to care for the material world. God's creation is in harmony with the incarnation and the resurrection of Jesus. The Jesuits healed the paralyzed for 38 years, fed 4,000 and 5,000, and Christians were to enter the world and remain salt and light. The material world created by God will eventually be purified and reorganized into a new heaven and a new earth, when the soul and matter will be one. So,

Christians cannot discriminate against any work related to this material world.

4.   What is the dignity of the work of Daniel and the Three Friends? Answer: Daniel's exile to Babylon was supposed to be a slave of the fallen nation in the victorious nation. Although he was fortunate enough to enter the palace of Babylon for training and then lived in a key position, after preaching the gospel to the king and solving the dream of the statue of gold, silver, bronze and iron clay, he not only rose to the governor and prime minister of Babylon, but also arranged for his three friends to be a high-ranking official in the province of Babylon. This was respected for his strength, especially since Daniel himself was able to become a patriarch of three dynasties through King Nebuchadnezzar, King Belshazzar, and King Darius. But in the Gentiles, they were still Jews who were easily discriminated against. This is one of the reasons why his three friends were thrown into the furnace and he himself was thrown into the lions' den. Fortunately, with God's care, they were able to save the day.

5.   How does Tim in the age of AI face the challenge to his dignity at work? Answer: As a Christian, Tim could not have the dignity and wisdom of his work and the privilege of being in a position of power in the court. In the age of AI, Tim was even laid off because AI replaced him, which damaged his dignity, but fortunately he was hired by World Robotics a year later. Elder Billy also accompanied Tim during his troubled days, cheering him on.

Answers to the Questions in Chapter 3

1.   What kind of creative work can AI help with? A: AI technology can help with the creation of concepts in life, software technology, civilization-driven processes, the Word of Christ, and more.

2.   What did Tim study on weekdays and weekends? A: Tim learned about AI during his workday (Artificial Intelligence) . On weekends, he learned "Old Testament Wisdom Books" in adult Sunday school.

3.   What does Tim think about artificial intelligence and the human brain created by God? A: Tim thinks that no matter how man creates an intelligent robot, this robot cannot have the Holy Spirit, so it cannot have the intelligence of God.

4.   What aspects of humanity can be enhanced by creation? A: Create philosophical, religious, and artistic works that can elevate the

spiritual realm of human beings and guide them to goodness and beauty.

5. What is the impact of AI on big data workers? A: Tim consults Elder Billy to study how predicative AI can contribute to the creation of human civilization. He found that AI technology will help human beings design and produce more works with God's creative spirit recorded in the Bible, and can predict the future more accurately, diagnose the defects of human civilization and make it more progressive.

Answers to the Questions in Chapter 4

1. What is the meaning of work? A: Work is a service, and it is a call to be assigned to serve others. Christians are called, if they are assigned, to serve their neighbors and others, not to themselves.

2. What should Christians look for when choosing a job in the workplace? Answer: When choosing a job in the workplace, Christians can decide whether they want to pursue high salaries and positions for themselves or to use their gifts to serve their neighbors and others. Perhaps we can use what we have learned and what we love to serve our neighbors without necessarily pursuing a high salary.

3. What is a mundane job? Answer: Even the mundane work is done through the hidden God. In fact, our daily lives, voting, being a civil servant, being a father, and being a mother are all manifestations of His glory through the work of the hidden God. Whether in the field, in the pasture, in the garden, in the city, in the house, in the field, in the government, we are doing the work of God's children in peace.

4. What is the difference between a work attitude that pursues self-esteem and a service attitude that justifies by faith? Answer: The work attitude of pursuing self-esteem is different from the service attitude of justification by faith. After some Christians have been justified by faith, they think that the way to sanctification after being saved by Christ is to pursue self-honor, self-worth, and elevation. Such Christians, even though they have been saved, will continue to work for themselves after that. So, Luther further thought that God saves us and sets us free by serving God with

freedom, joy, and dedication, and by serving our neighbors in this way.

5. What is the attitude of serving our neighbors with love? Answer: In this kind of service, even if we do the same work as Christians who seek self-honor, our state of mind to serve our neighbor is completely different from self-honor.

Answers to the Questions in Chapter 5

1. Why is there no result? Answer: There are two reasons: one is the internal cause of the work itself: the work makes people hard to work or difficult to produce. The second is external resistance, and thorn and tribulus terrestris represent external resistance. For example, other people in the company oppose your suggestions at work, or attack you for being too high-eyed.

2. Can AI Revolution Solve the Labor and Childbirth of Work? Please explain its limitations and potential. A: There are limits to what AI innovation can do when it comes to the question of "work will not be fruitful". These limitations include unforeseen consequences, ethical considerations, job substitution, and a lack of creativity and judgment. However, it can provide people who are interested in starting a business with some ideas to make a product. It also offers a number of potential solutions, including risk assessment and prediction, optimization and efficiency, automation and delegation, and fraud detection and prevention.

3. What are the world's other solutions besides the AI revolution? A: In addition to the AI revolution, there are other ways to address the issues we've raised, such as stricter safety regulations in sports and the workplace, investments in worker training and mental health support, and a focus on building a more ethical and sustainable business environment.

4. Can AI Revolution Address External Resistance to Work? A: Autonomous AI or Autonomous Agent. These AI technologies can improve by "generalizing" the external environment and external situations that you have not experienced through your past experiences. These include transfer learning, reinforcement learning, meta-learning, multitasking, knowledge images, and simulations.

5. How can we explain that God also allows us to change jobs when we are dissatisfied with our current situation? How does AI assist in job transitions? Answer: God allows us to change jobs because God can also change His plan for us. Some AI platforms provide occupational personality tests and vocational skills assessments; According to the user's personal situation, it can provide career development suggestions and learning resource recommendations; or provide job search, resume optimization, interview coaching; or provide AI training to help job seekers use AI to enhance their writing, translation, design, and other work.

Answers to the Questions in Chapter 6

1. How can AI alleviate people's feelings of emptiness, alienation, and dissatisfaction with their work? A: AI can alleviate feelings of emptiness, alienation, and dissatisfaction at work by improving productivity, giving employees more autonomy, providing personalized learning and development opportunities, creating a more humane work environment, and promoting work-life balance.

2. What are the limitations of how AI can help with this kind of work? A: AI cannot completely replace human creativity, fully understand the needs of users, and cannot completely solve technical problems.

3. Can AI automatically generate software that makes your dreams come true? A: At present, AI technology for automatic production of video games is a promising tool, but it cannot completely replace human creativity and professional skills. In the future, SDMs will still have an important role to play and will need to continuously learn new skills to adapt to the development of the AI era.

4. Can AI automate the production of video games? A: Currently, AI scholars are studying how to use GPT technology to automate the production of video games. This will allow the robot to watch a video and learn how to do the same thing. However, the future of AI can achieve fully automatic generation of software, which is still quite far away.

5. What will work look like in the age of AI? A: Work in the AI era will be more intelligent, efficient, and humane, and people will have more choices and opportunities, and find more meaning and

satisfaction in their work. AI can help people do their jobs better and free people from tedious work so they can devote more time and energy to more meaningful things.

Answers to the Questions in Chapter 7

1. What is one of the manifestations of human selfishness? A: One of the manifestations of human selfishness is pride.
2. How can AI technology help solve the social problem of selfishness in the workplace? A: AI technology can be used to detect and solve social problems such as racial discrimination and sexism. For example, using machine learning and big data analytics to discover and reduce where bias exists to promote a just and equal society.
3. How can AI technology contribute to infrastructure and economic development? A: AI technology can be applied to urban planning, traffic management, energy use, etc., to improve the efficiency and sustainability of infrastructure, and promote economic development and urban construction. In addition, AI can also help companies optimize production processes, improve production efficiency, and drive economic growth.
4. How can AI technology promote education and cultural inheritance? A: AI technology can be used in personalized education, distance learning, and more, providing more opportunities for people to acquire knowledge and skills. At the same time, AI can also be used for the digital preservation and inheritance of cultural heritage, protecting and promoting human cultural heritage.
5. How can AI technology be applied to management and leadership? A: AI technology can be applied to management and leadership to help organizations make more informed decisions and improve management efficiency and effectiveness. For example, using AI to analyze data to predict market trends and develop more effective business strategies; Leverage machine learning to optimize human resource management, improve employee job satisfaction, productivity, and more.

Answers to the Questions in Chapter 8

1. What is Idol? A: Idols don't have to be tangible, such as a certain star or a celebrity. It can be a goal to be pursued in the heart, such

as money, love. Whether idols have a form or a body, the first of the Ten Commandments of Moses, "There shall be no other god before me," is opposed to idols. Idols can be individual, but they can also be group. If the company's culture advocates a special position, a corner office, it is an example of an idol. Group idols can vary depending on the era. These eras can be distinguished into traditional, modern, postmodern.

2.   What direction will the workplace culture take in the new era of AI revolution? A: The AI revolution could have a significant impact on Nietzsche's ideology in postmodern culture. These effects can be positive or negative. It is important to think about these impacts and prepare for the changes that are coming.

3.   What impact might AI revolution have on Nietzschean in postmodern culture? A: AI revolution may have the following effects on Nietzschean thought in postmodern culture: exacerbate Nietzschean nihilism, challenge Nietzsche's philosophy of the superman, and promote a rethinking of traditional values.

4.   How can Christian perspectives improve work culture in the age of AI revolution? A: Christian perspectives can help people build a more positive, healthy, and meaningful work culture in the new era of the AI revolution. For example, the Christian view of sanctification can help people find new meaning and purpose in their work. The concept of universal grace can help people overcome anxiety and fear. Christianity replaces self-interest in one's work with the idea of loving one's neighbor. Christians struggle in the midst of work and hardship because of good hope.

5.   Could AI Revolution Fuel Nietzschean Nihilism? A: Yes, the rise of AI is likely to exacerbate Nietzschean nihilism. For example, AI can be used to create highly realistic virtual worlds that make it difficult for people to distinguish between reality and virtuality. This can cause people to lose interest in the real world and turn to the virtual world for thrill and meaning. This can lead to a more nihilistic attitude that sees no real meaning in living in any world.

Answers to the Questions in Chapter 9

1.   What is Worldview? A: Worldview is a different view of life from all things in the world. Each view has its own philosophical basis, which is either money or power, morality or salvation. Each

worldview has its own "story" to tell, and these stories illustrate the value of their lives.

2. How does AI deal with worldviews? A: The way AI can be processed is to try to integrate different worldviews to arrive at the best choice. "Fusion" worldview refers to combining different worldviews as much as possible to arrive at the best choice. As for how to "converge", the diagram in this chapter, "Worldview Conflict Resolution: Fusion", only provides a framework of thought, and the actual details have to be done with more complex algorithms than this diagram.

3. How can business people under the influence of the gospel worldview use AI for the benefit of mankind? Answer: (1) Promote human creativity, such as helping human artists, musicians, writers, etc. to create new works. (2) Promote social good, such as developing AI software to help solve social problems such as poverty, hunger, and disease. and (3) promoting corporate social responsibility, such as helping companies anticipate the social and environmental impacts of their activities and take measures to reduce negative impacts. and (4) developing AI hardware and software technologies that protect the environment and reduce inequalities.

4. How can journalists under the influence of an evangelical worldview use AI for the benefit of mankind? A: The press should develop AI technologies that promote objectivity, accuracy, variety, and efficiency in news reporting.

5. How can film artists under the influence of the gospel worldview use AI to benefit mankind? A: The film industry should develop AI technologies that promote diversity, education, innovation, commercial success, and social impact in film and television productions.

6. How can higher education professionals under the influence of an evangelical worldview use AI for the benefit of humanity? A: Higher education professionals should develop AI technologies that promote equity, personalization, innovation, success, and equity in higher education.

7. How can medical professionals under the influence of the worldview use AI to benefit mankind? A: Doctors use AI technology to better integrate the body and soul into the medical

process, provide more comprehensive and personalized medical services, and help patients achieve physical and mental health.

Answers to the Questions in Chapter 10

1. Question: "What is universal grace?" Answer: Universal grace refers to God's grace to people throughout the world, whether good or bad, righteous or unjust. This is based on the New Testament teaching in Matthew 5:45: "The sun shines on the good and the wicked, and rains on the righteous and on the unrighteous."

2. Question: "Who are the three unbeliever kings mentioned in this chapter?" How do they embody universal grace? Answer: The three unbeliever kings mentioned in the article are King Nebuchadnezzar, King Belshazzar, and King Cyrus. Although they are unbelievers, God still gives them universal grace. For example, King Nebuchadnezzar was reinstated as king after seven years of madness; King Belshazzar had a kind mother who gave advice; King Cyrus was used by God to free the exiles of Israel.

3. Question: What is sUBI? Answer: sUBI is an abbreviation for smart Universal Basic Income. It is a modified UBI concept that uses AI tools to train people who have lost their jobs due to AI to various AI-related programs to increase their wealth.

4. Question: How does this chapter suggest implementing sUBI? Answer: The article proposes to set up a Web 3.0 community of sUBI to attract unemployed people to join, and invite large companies and online AI training institutions to participate. Training providers offer AI revolution programs to help companies transform, and then match AI-trained unemployed people with those companies' programs on job platforms to earn unemployment benefits.

5. Question: How does this chapter discuss Christian-robot collaboration? Answer: The article emphasizes that Christians should have a cooperative and symbiotic relationship with robots, rather than treating them as slaves. This relationship should be based on respect and understanding, including maintaining and updating the robot, focusing on the impact of

the robot on society, and providing appropriate education and training to help people master the skills associated with the robot.

Answers to the Questions in Chapter 11

1. Q: How is a Christian work ethic different from a work ethic based solely on cost/profit analysis? Answer: Christian ethics are based on divine love, and maintaining integrity even if it may be at the expense of short-term interests, not long-term damage to the interests of the country and society. In contrast, ethics based solely on cost/profit analysis can lead to corruption, which is harmful to national society.
2. Q: What are the three key steps to wisdom mentioned in this article? Answer: Three key steps are: (1) Know God; (2) Know self; (3) Accumulate wisdom from experiences.
3. Q: How should Christian employers and employees view their working relationships? Answer: Christian employees should work with all their hearts and minds because they work for the Lord, not for their bosses. Christian employers should see themselves as servants to all people. Both are accountable to the Lord Jesus Christ.
4. Q: How does Daniel's story demonstrate the importance of work ethics and intelligence? Answer: Daniel's persistent prayer to God in the face of danger demonstrated his deep knowledge and wisdom of God. Not only was he ultimately saved, but he also expanded his influence in the workplace, proving that following God's guidance is trustworthy.
5. Q: What kind of system has the Champion AI revolution team come up with to translate abstract principles into working guidelines? A: They propose an AI virtual machine system that includes a principle library, abstract sub-machines, knowledge bases, input-output sub-machines, and generative AI that uses RAG software to interact with ChatGPTto translate abstract principles into concrete working guidelines.

Answers to the Questions in Chapter 12

1.   Q: What are the two different motivations for work that Keller
        mentioned? A: The two motivations that Keller mentions are:
        Work under Work and Rest under Rest。 Work under Work
        refers to working for secular idols such as money and power,
        while Rest under Rest refers to Christians motivated to work by
        having a deep rest.
2.   Q: How do you connect the phrase "calm and ambitious, quiet
        and far-reaching" with Keller's concept of "new power"?
        Answer: In the text, "indifference" is interpreted as not pursuing
        secular idols (similar to not pursuing work under work), but
        "Mingzhi." It is the pursuit of Christ's aspirations. "Tranquility"
        corresponds to Rest under Rest, which enables people to
        regain their strength and take a further path in life.
3.   Question: What is the main source of Daniel's "indifference"
        and "serenity"? Answer: Daniel's calmness and serenity came
        mainly from his habit of praying to God every day. This habit
        brought him self-control, wisdom from God, and zeal for his
        work.
4.   Q: How can generative AI make people more motivated and
        motivated? A: Generative AI can make people more motivated
        and motivated by improving work efficiency, empowering
        employees, and creating personalized work experiences.
5.   Q: What is "Biblical AI"? What is its purpose? A: "Biblical AI"
        refers to the integration of Christian values and beliefs into AI
        systems, including for robots and real people. Its purpose is to
        help people find higher purpose and meaning in their work,
        and to stimulate higher motivation for work.

Answers to the Introductory Questions in Chapter 13

Question 1: What does the author refer to as the vision of the four
beasts in Daniel 7?

A1: According to the article, many theologians explain that the vision
of the four beasts in Daniel chapter 7 represents four ages: Babylon,
Persia, Greece, and the Roman Empire. These beasts symbolize the

negative appearance of the human world, reflecting the power struggles and conquests in the changing dynasties.

Question 2: How does the author relate the changes in the AI era to Daniel's vision?

Answer 2: The author believes that the changes in the AI technology world, business competition, and the rise and fall of companies are similar to the "bloody rain" in Daniel's vision. At the same time, the author also emphasizes that Christians should view the changes in the AI generation with a mindset that "seems to be sorrowful, but always happy," believing that the Lord is in power, just as the "Son of Man" in Daniel's vision brings hope.

Question 3: According to the article, how should a training website solve the problem of content "moving"?

A3: The authors suggest that the Rockefeller Move Method could be borrowed and that people be incentivized to participate in the content move by issuing appropriate "announcements". For biblical knowledge, AI tools can be utilized to perform the following steps: (1) listening, (2) converting into text, (3) collating (summarizing and retelling), (4) producing lesson content and practice questions, and (5) Generate exam questions and answers. Functions such as grading, grading and issuing certificates can be integrated using GitHub open-source's common software program.

Answers to the Questions in Chapter 13 Regarding Four Definitions of the AI Era and the Role of Christians in the AI Era

Question 1: What are the main features of the AI 1.0 era? Answer 1: AI 1.0 is an early historical era of AI development, with key features including the emergence of mainframe computers, research in MIT AI labs, the application of expert systems, and the development of projects such as IBM Deep Blue and Watson. AI in this period was mainly confined to specific fields and failed to achieve true general artificial intelligence.

Question 2: What event marked the beginning of the era of AI 2.0 generative AI? Answer 2: The release of ChatGPT by OpenAI at the end of 2022 marked the beginning of the era of generative AI. The emergence of ChatGPT has transformed AI from a professional operation to a tool that can be used by the general public, which has attracted widespread attention from the industry.

Question 3: When is the era of AI 3.0 quantum machine learning expected to arrive, and what are its main features? Answer 3: The era of AI 3.0 quantum machine learning is expected to arrive around 2030. Its main feature is that quantum computers have reached the scale of 100,000 qubits, and quantum algorithms can replace traditional generative AI algorithms, and the computing speed will be greatly improved.

Question 4: What is the definition of the era of AI 4.0 quantum intelligence? Answer 4: The era of AI 4.0 quantum intelligence is defined as "solving problems using quantum computers that mimic human intelligence". It combines quantum algorithms, the quantum nature of human intelligence, and the problem-solving capabilities of traditional computer-assisted quantum computers.

Question 5: How does the article describe the role that Christians should hold in the changing age of AI? A5: The article states that Christians should understand that the change of the AI era is not in the control of people or businesses, but in the control of God. Christians should humbly learn, follow God's guidance, and do their best in the workplace to earn the approval of God and the world.

Answers to the Questions in Chapter 13 Regarding Why the Four AI Eras Are Changing

Question 1: What are the main challenges in the AI 1.0 era?

Answer: The main challenges in the AI 1.0 era include: lack of data, lack of computing power, and insufficient understanding of the human brain. Specifically, the cost of knowledge acquisition is high and inefficient, the computing hardware and software architecture are limited, and the understanding of the human brain is mainly at the stage of Symbolic AI.

Question 2: What are the representative products of the AI 2.0 era? What are their main features?

Answer: Representative products in the AI 2.0 era include AlexNet and Transformer technology. AlexNet pioneered deep learning using GPUs and large-scale datasets. Transformer technology uses an attention mechanism to process all input data at once, greatly improving the efficiency of natural language processing.

Question 3: What are the main challenges facing the era of quantum machine learning (AI 3.0)?

Answer: The main challenges in the era of quantum machine learning include: quantum decoherence, quantum error correction, and quantum algorithm development. Quantum decoherence affects the stability of quantum states, quantum error correction requires additional qubits and complex algorithms, and the development of quantum algorithms requires interdisciplinary efforts.

Question 4: What are the main features of the AI 4.0 era (the era of quantum intelligence or quantum brain)?

Answer: The main features of the AI 4.0 era include the use of quantum algorithms and quantum phenomena in the human brain to achieve super artificial intelligence (ASI), deep human-machine integration, the exploration of the nature of consciousness, and the face of more complex machine ethical issues. This era will have the potential to redefine human wisdom and consciousness.

Question 5: Why are optical quantum computers likely to replace superconducting quantum computers in the AI 4.0 era?

Answer: There are two main reasons why optical quantum computers may replace superconducting quantum computers: 1) optical quantum computers can operate at room temperature, reducing maintenance costs and energy consumption; 2) Optical quantum computers have a better explanation of the functioning of the human brain and may have advantages in simulating the functioning of the human brain. This makes optical quantum computers potentially more potential for applications in cognitive science and neuroscience.

Answers to the Questions in Chapter 14

1. Q: What are the characteristics of the AI 4.0 era in Elder Billy's dream? A: In the era of AI 4.0, that is, the era of quantum intelligence/quantum brain, robots have swept away human reason and feelings, which is likened to "iron teeth and copper claws, devouring and chewing, and the rest is trampled by (machine feet)". This era is characterized by the deep influence and control of AI systems on human thinking and emotion.

2. Q: What changes have taken place in the world of industry and politics in the dream? A: In the industry, the top 10 "quantum brain" companies eventually became three through mergers and acquisitions, and then were replaced by an emerging "super quantum brain company".Merger. In politics, a dictator uses the technology of the super-powerful Quantum Brain Corporation to empower himself, control the government, and change the laws and policies of AI development, so that he can control people's minds, oppress Christians, and monitor people's thoughts and jobs.

3. Q: How was the crisis in the dream resolved? A: The crisis was eventually resolved by the rise of an "overcomer" and many wise people. They have rescued Christians by using a "quantum problem solver" (i.e., the "mystery of victory") that fits the gospel worldview. The dictator was defeated, and the super strong quantum brain company was jointly sanctioned by various governments and could not continue to operate. In the end, Christians triumphed with an evangelical worldview.

4. Q: Stuart ·What is the concept of "value alignment" proposed by Professor Russell?Why is it so important in AI development? A: "Value alignment" refers to ensuring that AI systems are

aligned with human values. It is crucial in AI development because if the behavior of AI systems is not aligned with human values, it can have disastrous consequences. This concept emphasizes the need to embed human ethics and values in AI design.

5. Q: Nick ·What are the potential risks of the concept of "superintelligence" proposed by Bostrom?How should we respond? A: "Superintelligence" refers to AI reaching a level of intelligence that surpasses that of humans, which may pose an existential risk to human civilization. Responses include thinking ahead about how to control and guide the development of super AI, establishing a global AI governance mechanism, strengthening AI ethics research, and promoting interdisciplinary collaboration to comprehensively assess and manage risks.

6. Q: In the era of AI, how to balance technological development with social fairness and personal privacy protection? A: Balance can be achieved in the following ways:(1)Establish strict data protection regulations;(2)require AI system developers to conduct fairness and privacy impact assessments; (3)Increase transparency in the AI decision-making process;(4)Encourage the development of AI technologies that reduce bias;(5)Strengthen public education and raise awareness of the impact of AI;(6) Establish a multi-party participatory regulatory mechanism.

7. Q: Why is it so important to emphasize the leading role of humans in AI development? How to ensure this? A: Human-led roles are important because we need to ensure that AI development is in line with human interests and values. This can be ensured by:(1)Keep key decision-making power in human hands;(2)develop AI ethics guidelines;(3)Establish an effective regulatory mechanism;(4)promote public participation in AI policymaking;(5)develop a human-machine collaboration model instead of relying solely on AI;(6)Continuously assess the impact of AI and adjust policies in a timely manner.

8. Q: Why is it beneficial to maintain a "pessimistic and then optimistic" attitude when faced with the risks that AI may pose? A: The attitude of "pessimism first and then optimism" helps us

to: (1) be aware of potential risks and avoid blind optimism; (2) to enable us to proactively take preventive and response measures; (3) Maintain confidence in human capabilities while recognizing the challenges; (4) stimulate innovative thinking and problem-solving; (5) Balance technological development and ethical considerations to promote responsible AI development.

Answers to the Questions in Chapter 15

1. Question: What are the main differences between AI in the AI 3.0 era and the AI 2.0 era? Answer: The era of AI 3.0 is from artificial intelligence in the narrow sense (ANI) to artificial general intelligence (AGI). AI 3.0 uses quantum processors instead of GPUs in the AI 2.0 era. The algorithms of AI 3.0 are more versatile and do not need to rely on RAG to connect algorithms in different domains.
2. Question: What are the five levels of wisdom proposed by Google DeepMind researchers? Answer: The five levels are: emerging, competent, expert, virtuoso, and superhuman.
3. Question: Why are quantum processors better suited than GPUs for the development of artificial general intelligence? Answer: Quantum processors have more computing power and efficiency, higher versatility and adaptability, are able to support innovative quantum algorithms, and have advantages in processing complex and high-dimensional data.
4. Question: What is Super Artificial Intelligence (ASI)? Answer: Super AI is a hypothetical type of AGI, which is much more intelligent than humans. It is the result of the development of artificial general intelligence to the level of "superhuman".
5. Question: In the era of AI 3.0, how can artificial general intelligence become an expert or master in any field? Answer: In the AI 3.0 era, algorithms in different fields have been integrated into the basic algorithms, and there is no need for RAG. This allows AI to exhibit expert or master-level abilities in a variety of domains without the need for specific training for each domain.

Answers to the Questions in Chapter 16

1. Q: In the AI 3.0 era, why are quantum computers rapidly replacing traditional CPUs/GPUs? A: Quantum computers are able to crack traditional RSA encryption algorithms, which poses a huge threat to security-conscious defense and banking industries. When the qubits reach about 100,000, they are able to easily crack 2048-bit RSA encryption. This has led these industries to take the lead in adopting quantum computing technology, which in turn has influenced other industries, accelerating the transition from AI 2.0 to AI 3.0.

2. Q: What do the Xanadu and "Chapter Nine" mentioned in Elder Billy's dream represent? What problems does the competition between them reflect? A: Xanadu represents Western tech companies with an evangelical worldview, while Chapter Nine represents Eastern tech companies that pursue the supremacy of technology and the law of the jungle. The competition between them reflects the clash of values and worldviews in the AI 3.0 era, as well as the moral and ethical challenges that technological developments may bring.

3. Q: Why is quantum machine learning considered to be able to replace all generative AI in the AI 3.0 era? A: Quantum machine learning leverages the parallelism and superposition of quantum computing to be able to process more complex models and larger-scale data. This allows it to far surpass traditional generative AI in terms of processing speed and learning ability, and is able to solve fake messages and fantasy problems faster, thus replacing traditional generative AI.

4. Q: How should Christians respond to the challenges of the AI 3.0 workplace? Answer: Christians should follow the "beatitudes" principle taught by Jesus in the Sermon on the Mount: be humble in heart, mourn, meek, hungry and thirsty for righteousness, merciful, pure-hearted, peacemaker, persecuted for righteousness' sake. Even in a high-tech environment, it is important to maintain the essence of faith and bear witness with integrity.

5.   Q: In the era of AI 3.0, why is it necessary to strengthen ethics training? A: Technology in the AI 3.0 era is developing rapidly and has a wide range of impacts, which can be abused or have unintended negative effects. Ethics training helps to ensure that technology is headed in line with human values, prevents technology from being used for unethical practices such as privacy violations, discrimination, or social manipulation, and helps people adapt to new technologies while maintaining human governance.

Answers to the Questions in Chapter 17

1.   Question: "Who should Christians pray for in the age of AI?" Why? Answer: Christians should pray for the world, for their country, and for themselves in the workplace. Pray for the world because technological progress can lead to problems such as the control of the wicked, unemployment, human uncontrollability, or pride. Praying for one's own nation is to follow the example of the prophet in praying for Jerusalem; Pray for yourself in the workplace to have proper workplace theology, not to offend God, and to recognize the root cause of sin in difficult situations.

2.   Question: "What are the characteristics and influence of Daniel's model of prayer?" Answer: Daniel's prayer was characterized by humble confession of sin and helpless intercession. His prayer led God to send angels to reveal the mystery of the "seventy weeks" and to provoke King Cyrus to issue an edict for the return of the "remnant" of Israel The rebuilding of the Holy City led to national revival. This prayer stems from Daniel's understanding of the prophet Jeremiah's prophecy and his dedication to it.

3.   Question: "In the age of AI, how can uprooted Christians pray for their homeland? Answer: Uprooted Christians can follow Daniel's example and pray for peace and tranquility in their homeland, the wisdom of leaders, the development of the technology industry, and the revival of the church. They can express their concern for their hometown, ask for God's protection and guidance, and pray for specific challenges

facing their hometown, such as the international situation, economic development, freedom of belief, etc.

Answers to the Questions in Chapter 18

Question 1: What are the six goals of God mentioned in Daniel 9? A1: God's six goals are:

1.   Stop sin
2.   Cleanse sins
3.   Atonement for sins
4.   Introduce Yongyi
5.   Seal up visions and prophecies
6.   Anointing the Holy of Holies / The Holy of Holy

Question 2: How are the "seventy sevens" mentioned in the article divided in the timeline? Answer 2: "Seventy Sevens" is divided into three segments on the timeline:

1.   Section 1: Seven weeks, 93 years from 538 B.C. to 445 B.C
2.   Section 2: Sixty-two weeks, 478 years from 445 B.C. to 33 A.D
3.   Section 3: The last seven, divided into the first half of the seven and the second half of the seven, from the death of Jesus to the destruction of the Antichrist in the last days

Question 3: What ways does the article think God might achieve His salvation and justice in the age of AI? A3: The article mentions that God may do this through the following six actions:

1.   Stop sin: Move people's hearts to recognize their mistakes and stop their evil deeds
2.   Eliminate evil: Eliminate systemic evil caused by AI and rebuild ethics
3.   Atonement: Provide a means of redemption and a chance for those who do evil to repent
4.   Introduce Yongyi: Ensure the development of science and technology for the benefit of mankind and deepen moral education

5.   Seal out visions and prophecies: Reveal the truth and help people discern true and false prophecies
6.   Anointing the Holy of Holies and the Most Holy One: Bless those who use technology to serve humanity and glorify God

Answers to the Questions in Chapter 19

1. Question: How do Christians prepare for great battle in the workplace?

Answer: Christians should embrace an evangelical worldview, humbly look to God, and be prepared to meet the challenges of a postmodern outlook on the world. The gospel worldview encompasses not only the present world, but also the eschatological vision, which determines the height, breadth, length, and depth of the workplace.

2. Question: How did Daniel prepare for the Great War?

Answer: Daniel prepared by praying, fasting, and receiving visions. Although he could not fully understand the specifics of the war, he remained vigilant and prepared.

3. Q: In terms of society, what crimes may be brought about by the AI 2.0 era?

A: Possible criminal behaviors include: deepfakes of video and audio, fake news and disinformation, automated phishing attacks, synthetic identity fraud, malicious program generation, etc.

4. Q: What are the main hidden dangers posed by AI in terms of technological security?

A: The main hidden dangers include: data privacy leakage, lack of transparency in decision-making, malicious use of AI, bias and discrimination in the system, and system vulnerabilities.

5. Q: How can bias and discrimination be prevented in AI systems?

A: This can be prevented by data review to ensure diversity, fairness testing, and a diverse development team.

6. Q: On the political front, how might an authoritarian government misuse AI technology?

A: Possible abuses include: mass facial recognition and surveillance, the establishment of a social credit system, manipulation of public opinion and brainwashing, automated censorship and suppression of dissent, targeted surveillance of specific groups of people, and political persecution.

7. Q: What are the applications of AI in information warfare in paramilitary warfare?

A: Applications include using generative AI to create and disseminate fake news, developing AI tools to detect disinformation, automating cyberattacks, and building cyber defenses.

8. Q: How is AI used in cognitive warfare?

A: AI can be used to analyze individual and group psychological characteristics, design psychological operations, use VR/AR technology to create virtual scenes, generate educational materials to penetrate the education system, and automatically generate and broadcast promotional content.

9. Q: What are the specific application numbers of AI in space combat preparation?

A: Applications include: automating satellite operation and monitoring, predicting and avoiding satellite collisions, analyzing satellite images to identify targets, decoding and analyzing hostile satellite signals, etc.

10. Q: How does AI support joint operations?

A: AI can integrate multi-domain combat data to achieve cross-domain collaboration, support joint operations command centers to provide tactical advice, optimize logistics and logistics, predict equipment failures, and arrange maintenance.

Answers to the Questions in Chapter 20

1. Q: What is the RAG+MAMBA+OOD approach and how does it contribute to improving the reliability of AI systems? A: RAG+MAMBA+OOD is a comprehensive approach that aims to improve the reliability and authenticity of AI systems

    a. RAG combines information detection and generative models to improve the dependence of answers.
    b. MAMBA (Memory-Enhancing Memory-Based Architecture) provides more efficient large-scale memory processing and fast retrieval capabilities.
    c. OOD (Out-of-Distribution Detection) technology helps the system identify inputs outside of the distribution of training data and avoid inappropriate responses. This combination can improve the accuracy, efficiency, and safety of AI systems, reducing problems caused by miscalculations or fantasies.

2. Q: Why is multimodal fusion needed when designing a Universal Problem Solver (GPS)? A: Multimodal fusion is important in GPS design because it allows the system to process and integrate different types of data logins (e.g., text, images, audio, etc.). This capability enables GPS to:

a. Gain a more comprehensive understanding of complex issues
b. Deal with diverse information in the real world
c. Provide richer and more accurate solutions
d. Adapting to the needs of different fields and scenarios Through multimodal fusion, GPS can simulate the ability of humans to comprehensively use multi-sensory information to solve problems.

3. Q: How can "interactive learning" be implemented in GPS and what are its advantages? A: Interactive learning in GPS can be achieved in the following ways:

a. Design a feedback mechanism that allows the user to evaluate the output of the system
b. Adjust model parameters or strategies on the fly, based on user feedback
c. Record and analyze user interaction patterns to continuously optimize system responses

Benefits include:

d. Continuous improvement of system performance
e. Better adapt to user needs
f. Increase the degree of personalization of the system
g. Enhance the adaptability and flexibility of the system

4. Q: What is the main function of the "principle submachine" in GPS and why is it important? Answer: The main functions of the "principle submachine" in GPS include:

a. Implement an ethical framework to ensure that AI decision-making is ethical
b. Conduct a safety assessment to prevent potentially harmful exports
c. Perform decision validation to ensure that the results are in line with preset principles
d. Detect and mitigate potential biases

It is important because:

e. Ensure that AI systems behave in a socially and ethically appropriate manner
f. Increase user trust in AI systems
g. Prevent AI systems from producing harmful or inappropriate results
h. Ensure the responsible development and application of AI technologies

5.   Q: How does an "abstract submachine" help solve complex problems in GPS? A: An abstract submachine helps solving complex problems by:

a. Task decomposition: Break down complex problems into smaller, more manageable subtasks
b. Pattern recognition: Identify common patterns in a problem and apply known solutions
c. Conceptual abstraction: Extracting general principles from concrete problems
d. Simulation and prediction: Test possible solutions in a virtual environment
e. Meta-Learning: Learn how to learn and solve new problems more effectively These features enable GPS to handle highly complex and abstract problems, increasing the efficiency and flexibility of problem-solving.

6.   Q: Why is "explainability" needed to be considered in GPS design and how can it be achieved? A: It is important to consider "explainability" in GPS design because:

a. Increase user understanding and trust in AI decision-making
b. Help identify and correct errors or biases in the system
c. Meet legal and ethical requirements, especially in key decision-making areas

Ways to achieve explainability include:

    d. Use explainable AI techniques such as LIME or SHAP

    e. Provide a clear step-by-step description of the decision-making process

    f. Visualize key features and their impact on the results

    g. Generate natural language explanations that describe the reasoning process of the system

7.   Q: How does the "foundation submachine" in GPS enhance the overall capability of the system? Answer: The "foundation submachine" in GPS enhances the overall capability of the system in the following ways:

    a. External tool integration: Allows GPS to call up specialized tools and APIs, extending the scope of its capabilities

    b. Database connections: Provide access to large amounts of structured data and enhance your knowledge base

    c. System Integration: Enables GPS to interact with other systems and services, improving versatility

    d. Resource management: Optimize the use of computing resources and improve efficiency

    e. Parallel computing support: Speed up complex tasks

These features enable GPS to leverage external resources and tools, greatly enhancing its problem-solving capabilities, making it more powerful and flexible.

Answers to the Questions in Chapter 21

1.   What is the AI 3.0 era? A: The AI 3.0 era is an era of artificial general intelligence (AGI).

2.   What are the characteristics of superconducting quantum computers in the AI 3.0 era? A: Superconducting QCs in the AI 3.0 era have overcome the difficulties of quantum error correction to reach more than 100K or even millions of qubits.

3.   What is the power of a quantum computer? A: The powerful features of quantum computers include quantum memory and processing integration, reduced data movement, and speed and efficiency.

4.   What are the challenges faced by the integration of storage and computing in quantum computers? A: The challenges of quantum computer storage and computing integration include quantum storage technology, technical obstacles, and architecture design.

5.   What is quantum ram (QRAM)? A: QRAM is a quantum memory capable of efficiently storing and retrieving quantum information. QRAM is a key component to realize the integration of quantum memory and computing.

6.   What is a hybrid approach? A: The hybrid approach refers to a hybrid quantum-classical architecture, in which classical memory-computing technology is combined with quantum processing. These can provide a steppingstone to complete quantum storage and computing integration.

7.   What are the considerations for the integration of storage and computing in quantum computers? A: Considerations for the integration of storage and computing in quantum computers include quantum RAM (QRAM) and hybrid methods.

Answers to the Questions in Chapter 22

1.   Q: What are the main differences between Super Artificial Intelligence (ASI) in the AI 4.0 era and Artificial General Intelligence (AGI) in the AI 3.0 era? A: ASI has a level of intelligence beyond humans and can make faster and more accurate decisions than humans in any field. It can handle extremely complex data sets, perform sophisticated analysis and predictions, and is capable of continuous self-improvement. In contrast, AGI's capabilities are limited to the human level, and while it can mimic or surpass humans in multiple domains, its decision-making may still be wrong or biased.

2.   Q: In the era of AI 4.0, how might autocrats use ASI to control people's minds and brainwash people? A: Dictators may use ASI for deeper levels of control, such as directly influencing or controlling people's thoughts and behaviors through gene editing and brain/computer interface technologies. ASI can also be used to monitor and analyze citizens' behavior and thoughts on a large scale, using highly personalized

information for brainwashing and propaganda that makes it difficult for people to think independently.

3. Q: What are the possible moral and ethical challenges for ASI in the AI 4.0 era? A: ASI can self-improve and learn, and its behavior and decision-making may go beyond the moral and ethical framework of humans. If in the hands of an authoritarian government, ASI could be used to exert extreme control and oppression, beyond the limits of human morality. The development of ASI may not be subject to moral and ethical constraints, leading to the development and application of dangerous technologies, such as mass surveillance and human rights violations.

4. Q: Politically, what are the likely long-term effects of ASI on dictatorships? A: ASI has the potential to revolutionize the structure and functioning of human society. Because of its ability to surpass human intelligence, ASI can continuously optimize the means of governance, making dictatorships more stable and difficult to overthrow. This could lead to an unprecedented form of totalitarian rule, eliminating the possibility of revolt and dissent.

5. Q: What measures can the international community take to prevent ASI from being abused by dictators? A: The international community can take the following steps:

a. Promote information transparency and establish international agreements to ensure transparency in the development and use of AI.
b. It is necessary to strengthen civic education and enhance digital literacy and critical thinking skills.
c. Promote international scientific and technological cooperation to ensure that technological development meets globally recognized ethical standards.
d. Develop and promote moral and ethical standards for AI.
e. Promote international anti-monopoly policies and inclusive economic policies.
f. Strengthen international political cooperation and establish multilateral mechanisms to prevent the abuse of science and technology.

g. Promote international arms control agreements to limit the use of ASI in the military field.

Answers to the Questions in Chapter 23

1. Q: According to the text, what kind of mindset can Christians have after suffering in the workplace? Answer: Christians can see suffering in the workplace as God's call, a ladder into the kingdom of heaven. Their suffering will eventually turn into the glory of victory, and they will reign with God in heaven.

2. Question: What are the characteristics of the "wise man" mentioned in the book of Daniel? Answer: A wise man is a teacher who is not afraid of death, and he is martyred for justice for the Lord. They are humble and good, pure, peace-loving, considerate, obedient, just, sincere, full of compassion, and fruitful in abundance. Daniel and his three friends are examples of wise men.

3. Q: What does Elder Billy think intelligent humans might look like in the AI 4.0 era? A: Elder Billy believes that intelligent people in the AI 4.0 era may be people whose brains are embedded with smart chips. These chips are quantitatively intelligent, can work with the human brain, and are character-trained.

4. Q: What are the main technologies used by intelligent people in the AI 4.0 era mentioned in the article? A: Arcanic weapons include highly secure quantum cryptography, distributed quantum computing networks, moral and ethical quantum artificial intelligence, adaptive and autonomous learning systems, and psychological and emotional support systems.

5. Q: How does this "arcane weapon" help intelligent people defeat dictators? A: It helps smart people by providing unhackable communications, decentralized resilience, moral superiority, the ability to adapt and predict quickly, and psychological and emotional superiority. This technology combines advanced quantum technology and high ethical standards to enable intelligent humans to execute complex strategies efficiently and safely, and to inspire more people to join the ranks of the dictator with justice.

Answers to the Questions in Chapter 24

1.   Question: Considering this chapter, how should the Christian
        view of eternity in the workplace be applied to the present?
        Answer: Christians should not be overly attached to their
        current position, power, prestige, and money. They should
        remember the brevity of life and consider eternal values when
        making big decisions. For example, you might think, "What
        would Jesus do?" to guide their own behavior.

2.   Question: "How long does the book of Daniel say it will take to
        reach the height of peace?" Answer: According to the book of
        Daniel, it takes "one, two, and half a year" to reach the
        prosperity of peace, which is a symbolic period, indicating that
        a certain time process is required.

3.   Question: What will be the economic aspects of AI 4.0 in the
        eventual heyday? Answer: The economy will be characterized
        by prosperity and stability, including high efficiency and
        productivity, and reduced costs of goods and services;
        achieving sustainable development and balancing economic
        activity with environmental protection; Economic cooperation
        has been strengthened on a global scale, forming a mutually
        beneficial economic system.

4.   Question: What changes will be made in the military aspect of
        ultimate peaceful heyday in the AI 4.0 era? Answer: The military
        side will focus on peace maintenance, which is manifested in
        the following ways: the development of efficient defense
        technology; Reach a consensus among States to gradually
        reduce armaments; Establish a global security alliance to use
        super artificial intelligence for real-time monitoring and threat
        warning to ensure the security and stability of the world.

Acknowledgements

This e-book is inspired by the book "The Meaning of Work" written by Pastor Timothy Keller and selected by the Brethren of the Chinese Bible Church of Boston during Sunday School as a class textbook. The author thanked the members of the Church of the Brethren for their valuable comments during the discussion of the Keller book. The book I wrote was also inspired by the following books: (1) "Workplace Warriors in the Lion's Den - Commentary on the Book of Daniel" by Prof. Timothy Wu of China Evangelical Seminary, and (2) other online training materials for workplace ministry, such as theologyofwork.org, calledtowork.org, etc. For this, I also thank these authors.

About the Author

The author, Charles Tang, born in Taipei in 1950, held a bachelor's degree in civil engineering from National Taiwan University and a dual master's degree in civil engineering and operations research from the Massachusetts Institute of Technology. Mr. Tang had worked as a software consultant for Honeywell, General Electric, Hewlett-Packard and Siemens. He founded C. B. Tang, Inc., a defense contractor for the United States Navy and Air Force and a software contractor for the United States Department of Commerce. Mr. Tang personally developed and sold "point-of-sale" systems and served the restaurant industry in New England, United States for many years. He was the senior vice president and cofounder of Transoft (Shanghai) Inc. (a software company) and a visiting scholar at Hsinchu JiaoTung University in Taiwan. Mr. Tang was granted 41 Chinese, United States and international PCT patents in cloud computing and quantum technology.

During his time in the United States, Mr. Tang was involved in Christian ministries for many years, including the Church Children's Sunday School, the Greater Boston Chinese Bible Church Chinese School, and the Chinese Christian Internet Mission. He graduated from the Extended Program of the China Evangelical Seminary in 2012 and had since taught Old Testament at seminaries in Mainland China and adult Sunday schools in Taiwan. He was the author of the e-books "The Marathon of Champions (General Edition)", "How to Live a Life that Meets God's Will", "The Story of Bo-Ai Art & Technology Gallery", "Reflections on Rhine Tourism", and "Champion Daily Devotionals".